How Governments Borrow

How Governments Borrow

Partisan Politics, Constrained Institutions,
and Sovereign Debt in Emerging Markets

BEN CORMIER

OXFORD
UNIVERSITY PRESS

OXFORD
UNIVERSITY PRESS

Great Clarendon Street, Oxford, OX2 6DP,
United Kingdom

Oxford University Press is a department of the University of Oxford.
It furthers the University's objective of excellence in research, scholarship,
and education by publishing worldwide. Oxford is a registered trade mark of
Oxford University Press in the UK and in certain other countries

Published in the United States of America by Oxford University Press
198 Madison Avenue, New York, NY 10016, United States of America

British Library Cataloguing in Publication Data

Data available

Library of Congress Control Number: 2023948517

ISBN 9780198882732

DOI: 10.1093/oso/9780198882732.001.0001

Printed and bound by
CPI Group (UK) Ltd, Croydon, CR0 4YY

Acknowledgements

This book would have been impossible to complete without the wisdom, kindness, and support of many people in my professional and personal lives.

When I moved to Toronto for my PhD, I knew I wanted to understand how developing countries obtained money from abroad. I would have never progressed from this vague starting point to writing a book without my committee's guidance. Mark Manger's willingness to answer any ridiculous question I have, support me, and work together is something I never take for granted. Antoinette Handley always found time to read everything, have a chat, and share her invaluably clear thoughts. Lou Pauly connected my simple real-world curiosities to political science and IPE. Vincent Arel-Bundock was an incredibly gracious external and has been too kind in offering help at other random points in the years since.

Most of the fieldwork in this book took place during my time at U of T. Thank you to the School of Graduate Studies, the Munk School's Richard Charles Lee Insights Through Asia program, and the Department of Political Science's Michael W. Donnelly political economy fellowship for financial support. Enormous thanks to Paul Cadario, whose support and generosity were essential for planning much of the fieldwork. The fieldwork further depended on the time of many people in Botswana, Peru, South Africa, and Thailand in 2017—thank you to the many interviewees who took time to speak and the support of academics from Thammasat University, University of Pretoria, University of Botswana, Universidad del Pacifico, and Universidad Católica del Perú.

I had the opportunity to turn that work into a book while a postdoc at the LSE. Special thank you to Natalya Naqvi for her collaboration, support, and constant chats. Thank you also to Ken Shadlen for always taking the time to share advice and perspective, and/or head to a football game. Thank you to Mark Copelovitch, Julia Gray, Layna Mosley, Stefano Pagliari, and Natalya – who were all too generous in participating in something as mind-numbing as a virtual book workshop on a too-early draft during lockdown.

I was fortunate to finish this book after joining the University of Strathclyde. Thank you to my colleagues for their support while I got settled in Glasgow and finished this project. Thanks to the reviewers and editors at Oxford University Press for taking this project on. The book links previously published articles at *British Journal of Political Science* (Cormier 2023c) and *Governance* (Cormier 2021), so thank you to the editors for their permission to revisit that work. Thanks also to colleagues at CABRI and more recently at the International Budget Partnership for connecting this research to real-world debt management practices and challenges.

Last but definitely not least, thank you to my New Hampshire friends and family for always keeping me tied to my roots. Thank you to Christina, Lindsay, Jim, and the extended Koen clan for providing me with a whole new home and family to adore in Ontario. Thank you to Brad and to my parents Betsy and Mark for their endless support and love. This book is dedicated to Ashley, who was present for every word, wherever it was written, despite it being very unclear what exactly was happening and where it was all going. You are the best.

Contents

1. Introduction   1
  1.1 EM Sovereign Debt Structure   1
  1.2 South Africa Vignette: Borrowings and Consequences   6
  1.3 The EM Sovereign Financing Landscape   9
    1.3.1 Hard vs. Local Currency Debt   9
    1.3.2 EM External Borrowing Options   10
    1.3.3 The External Borrowing Trade-off   13
  1.4 The International Political Economy of EM Sovereign Debt   19
    1.4.1 Sovereign Debt Models: Creditworthiness, Discipline,
        and Pull Factors   19
    1.4.2 Market Distortions & Push Factors   21
    1.4.3 Official Creditors   22
    1.4.4 Borrower Autonomy   23
  1.5 Partisan Borrowing and Debt Accumulation: The Theory
    in Brief   26
    1.5.1 Class, Partisanship, and Borrowing   26
    1.5.2 Methods   28
  1.6 Implications of Partisan External Sovereign Debt
    Accumulation in EMs   31
    1.6.1 Demand-Side Limits to Market Discipline of
        Government Partisanship in Sovereign Debt   31
    1.6.2 Borrower Autonomy in Models of Market and Official
        Credit Flows   32
    1.6.3 The Politics of Borrower Preferences and EM Sovereign
        Debt Accumulation   33
    1.6.4 The Role and Effect of DMOs   34
    1.6.5 DMO Constraints as a Microcosm of Limits to
        Institutional Effects in the Macroeconomy   35
  1.7 Outline of the Book   36

2. Partisan Politics and Constrained Institutions: A Model of
  Sovereign Debt Accumulation in Emerging Markets   39
  2.1 Introduction   39
  2.2 DMOs: A Primer   41
  2.3 DMOs, Government Partisanship, and EM External Debt:
    A Model and Hypothesis   43
    2.3.1 Debt Accumulation   43
    2.3.2 Borrowing Strategies   45
    2.3.3 Partisan Politics   48
    2.3.4 EM Partisanship and External Borrowings   49

2.4 Implications for Sovereign Debt and Political Economy 52
    2.4.1 Institutions in Sovereign Debt 53
    2.4.2 Institutions in Comparative Political Economy 54
2.5 Conclusion 56

3. Testing the Partisan Model 57
    3.1 Introduction 57
    3.2 Data 57
        3.2.1 Dependent Variable 59
        3.2.2 Independent Variables 65
        3.2.3 Control Variables 66
    3.3 Empirical Strategy 68
        3.3.1 Modelling Strategies 68
        3.3.2 Post-Treatment Bias 69
    3.4 Results 70
        3.4.1 Robustness Tests 74
    3.5 Conclusion 79

4. South Africa and Botswana 80
    4.1 Introduction 80
    4.2 South Africa 81
        4.2.1 ANC Partisanship 81
        4.2.2 The Budget: Setting the Financing Requirement 84
        4.2.3 The ALM: Deciding How to Finance the Budget 86
        4.2.4 State-Owned Enterprises 89
        4.2.5 South Africa Summary 91
    4.3 Botswana 91
        4.3.1 BDP Partisanship 92
        4.3.2 Fiscal Rules Written by the BDP Reinforce Conservatism 96
        4.3.3 Borrowing Process and Choices 97
    4.4 Comparison and Conclusion 100

5. Peru 102
    5.1 Introduction 102
    5.2 Setting the Financing Requirement: Budgets and Politics 104
        5.2.1 The 1999 Fiscal Law 104
        5.2.2 Annual Indebtedness Laws 105
    5.3 Borrowing Process and Politics 106
        5.3.1 Line Ministries and Cabinet 106
        5.3.2 SOEs and Other Guarantees 107
    5.4 Peru Foreign Borrowing from 1990 to 2015 107
        5.4.1 The Late 1980s 108
        5.4.2 Alberto Fujimori (1990–2000) 108
        5.4.3 Alejandro Toledo (2001–2006) 112
        5.4.4 Alan Garcia (2006–2011) 114
        5.4.5 Ollanta Humala (2011–2016) 115
    5.5 Conclusion 117

6. Thailand   119
    6.1 Introduction   119
    6.2 Fiscal and Debt Laws   121
    6.3 Borrowing Process   122
        6.3.1 PDMO Borrowing Options and Criteria   123
        6.3.2 Politics and PDMO Foreign Borrowing Decisions   124
        6.3.3 SOEs   125
    6.4 Thai Foreign Borrowing from 1990 to 2015   126
        6.4.1 Pre-AFC (1990–1996)   126
        6.4.2 The AFC and Post-AFC Democrats (1997–2001)   128
        6.4.3 Thai Rak Thai (2001–2006)   131
        6.4.4 Post-TRT (2006–2015)   134
    6.5 Conclusion   136

7. Conclusion   137
    7.1 Introduction   137
    7.2 Research and Policy Implications   137
        7.2.1 Demand-Side Limits to Market Discipline   138
        7.2.2 Borrower Autonomy, Domestic Politics, and Sovereign
               Debt Structure   139
        7.2.3 The Cyclicality of EM Sovereign Debt Flows   140
        7.2.4 Clearer Theory and Measurement in the IPE of
               Sovereign Debt   141
        7.2.5 DMO Practices and Effects (Transparency and
               Diversification)   142
        7.2.6 Deepening Domestic Public Debt Markets   143
        7.2.7 The Varying Role of Institutions in Different Areas of
               Public Debt and Different Areas of the Economy   144
    7.3 Looking Ahead   145

Appendix: Interviews List   148

References   153
Index   174

1

Introduction

1.1 EM Sovereign Debt Structure

A government's annual borrowing decisions accumulate over time to compose
public—or sovereign—debt structure. Outside of the rich world, the structure of
public debt enhances or limits the capacity of a government to contribute to social
and economic development. Persistently important for most Emerging Markets
(EMs)[1] is the structure of its foreign currency public debt. How much external
debt is owed, the cost of that debt, the maturity of that debt, and the conditions
attached to that debt determine the developmental opportunities, constraints, and
risks associated with an EM government's finances. This book shows how borrower partisanship helps explain the types of external debts that are and are not
added to EM government balance sheets each year—hence how partisan politics
affect the evolution of sovereign debt structure in EMs over time.

EM external public debt structures are dictated by the sources of external
finance that governments prioritize when borrowing each year. Some EMs use
more and come to owe more to private creditors like portfolio investors in bond
markets or commercial banks. Others use more and come to owe more to official multilaterals and bilaterals like the World Bank, the African Development
Bank, or China. Whether an EM uses more market or official finance is important because this determines the composition of its public debt structure and thus
the effect of annual sovereign borrowings on the country's economic and political
circumstances over time. Official creditors offer cheaper finance with longer maturities, but include conditions with short term political and economic consequences
for the borrowing government and citizens. In contrast, market instruments offer
comparatively expensive and shorter-term finance but do not include politically
salient, legally binding conditions that immediately adjust the borrower's political
economy at the time of borrowing.

Given this external borrowing menu and its implications for public debt structure, the broader economy, and domestic politics, how do EM governments

---

[1] EM and Middle Income Country (MIC) are used interchangeably in this book. They refer to a
subset or class of sovereign borrower that has regular access to both official development finance and
sovereign debt markets, giving EMs/MICs a unique external borrowing menu. High income, middle income, and low income country categorizations at the World Bank largely map on to developed,
emerging, and frontier market country distinctions made by sovereign bond indexes. This is discussed
in detail later in this chapter.

How Governments Borrow. Ben Cormier, Oxford University Press. © Ben Cormier (2024).
DOI: 10.1093/oso/9780198882732.003.0001

borrow? How do EM sovereigns make external borrowing decisions and why would they make different annual decisions, leading to different debt structures across EMs over time? Much of the sovereign debt literature leaves these questions unanswered because it typically emphasizes the supply side of capital flows, focusing on the reasons creditors do or do not allocate capital to governments. This leads to the expectation that a sovereign's borrowings are largely determined by supply-side assessments of an EM's creditworthiness based on a potential borrower's economic and political features.

In international and development economics, this 'market discipline' principle is typically theorized as necessary for the sovereign debt market to function at all. This stems from limitations in sovereign debt contract enforcement: creditors must analyze 'country characteristics' to assess the sovereign's ability and willingness to repay, then determine if, how much, and at what price to lend (Eaton and Gersovitz 1981, 290). Disciplinary logic typically underpins theories of both initial debt flows and subsequent borrower repayments of those debts, with forward-looking reputational concerns incentivizing sovereigns to service debts in order to borrow more in the future (Eaton, Gersovitz, and Stiglitz 1986; Tomz 2007).

Currently, much International Political Economy (IPE) research on sovereign debt seeks to add political variables to our understanding of how markets assess developing country risk and allocate capital. This includes policy choices (Brooks, Cunha, and Mosley 2022; Kaplan 2013; Mosley 2003) and institutional factors like democracy and transparency (Beaulieu, Cox, and Saiegh 2012; Biglaiser and Staats 2012; Cormier 2023b; Schultz and Weingast 2003). Informational shortcuts (Brooks, Cunha, and Mosley 2015), international political affiliations (Gray 2013), global liquidity (Ballard-Rosa, Mosley, and Wellhausen 2021; Bauerle Danzman, Winecoff, and Oatley 2017; Zeitz 2022), and market structure (Cormier and Naqvi 2023) may nuance or condition lending based on true fundamentals, but disciplinary capital allocation based on supply-side scrutiny of sovereign risk remains central to theorizing capital flows to developing country sovereigns. Similarly if for different reasons, IPE largely expects that capital allocation by official creditors is also a function of supply-side factors, be it strategic bilateral interests (Dreher, Nunnenkamp, and Thiele 2011; Dreher et al. 2018) or political and institutional constraints at multilaterals (Hawkins et al. 2006; Weaver 2008; Clark and Dolan 2021; Winter et al. 2022).

But as summarized below and detailed in Chapter 3 figures, the variation in external borrowings observed across EMs in the twenty-five years following the Cold War does not strictly match these expectations. Both within-country and cross-country borrowings in the EM class of sovereigns indicate more variation in debt accumulation than supply-side models of market and official flows can explain. Neither annual borrowings nor ensuing public debt structures simply reflect disciplinary theories of capital allocation. This implies the demand side of sovereign debt—the political economy of how governments borrow—should be incorporated if we are to better understand the types of debt that do and do not end up on EM government balance sheets.

This book unpacks the demand side of EM sovereign debt. It argues that through the annual fiscal policymaking process, domestic partisan politics significantly affect how EM governments borrow abroad each year and accumulate external debt over time. Specifically, *EM governments with working classes as core political constituencies, and thus left-leaning policy preferences, borrow proportionally more from markets.* This partisan effect on the instruments used to meet annual external financing requirements occurs independent of the national economic fundamentals, institutional features, and structural factors traditionally expected to pull or push capital in supply-side models of sovereign debt flows. Partisan politics is a significant demand-side determinant of the types of capital flowing or not flowing into EM sovereigns, and thus a significant demand-side determinant of the debt structures EM governments build over time. Beyond adding to a growing literature on the politics of the demand side of sovereign debt outside of the rich world (Bunte 2019; Zeitz 2022; Ballard-Rosa, Mosley, and Wellhausen 2022), this argument has two main implications for political economy.

First, it puts limits on assumptions that left-leaning EM governments should have relatively poor sovereign debt market access, and thus use markets less than other governments (Mosley 2003, chap. 4; Kaplan 2013). This is not the case. Left-leaning EM governments use sovereign debt markets relatively *more* than other EMs, and they do this despite any disciplinary price reactions to their partisan policy preferences (see Vaaler, Schrage, and Block 2006; Breen and McMenamin 2013; Barta and Johnston 2018; Cotoc, Johri, and Sosa-Padilla 2021; Brooks, Cunha, and Mosley 2022) and the availability of cheaper financing alternatives. In other words: even if markets charge risk premiums in order to discipline left-leaning parties in EM sovereign debt contracts, this will not keep left-leaning EMs from taking on those costs because domestic politics incentivize them to use market instruments to meet their external financing needs. Partisan constraints on how governments borrow give rise to significant demand-side limits to theories of disciplinary capital allocation to EM sovereigns based on government partisanship.

In the following chapters, nearly one hundred interviews in four cases across three continents and a variety of econometric models provide evidence that this pattern of EM sovereign debt accumulation can be explained once sovereign debt markets are seen as sources of relative policy autonomy for EM sovereigns when borrowing. Left-leaning EM governments use sovereign debt markets more than other EM governments because, in comparison to alternative external financing options, debt markets provide autonomy rather than discipline, at least at the time of borrowing and in the short run. Perhaps counterintuitive to expectations, then, markets are the preferred external financing source for left-leaning EM governments due to their *lack* of discipline at the time of making annual borrowing decisions, particularly compared to official sources. The long term implications of using more volatile and expensive market flows are important—but do not inform annual borrowing decisions as much as the immediate interest in avoiding conditionality to maintain policy autonomy at the time of borrowing. This leads market instruments to constitute more of a left-leaning government's annual borrowings and subsequent debt structures than other EMs.

This reframes the relationship between global financial markets and developing country policy autonomy in ways that more closely match the composition of sovereign debt observed in real-world data. Insofar as strictly supply-side capital allocation models of sovereign debt cannot fully explain what sources of finance do and do not land on EM balance sheets, the book's partisan argument identifies significant political demand-side factors to account for in sovereign debt research and practice. That left-leaning EM governments have political incentives to use relatively expensive but condition-free markets as an exit option from cheaper but conditional official credit, and that this affects annual sovereign borrowings and the evolution of EM external debt structure over time, also gives rise to questions about the true nature of political-economic constraints on and discipline of EM sovereign borrowing.

Second, the book advances our understanding of the role of institutions in sovereign debt, adding to comparative political economy research on the role of institutions in the macroeconomy more generally. In the public debt context, development practitioners (Currie, Dethier, and Togo 2003; World Bank 2015b) and recent political economy studies (Sadeh and Porath 2020; Sadeh and Rubinson 2018) submit that Debt Management Offices (DMOs) can have autonomous or politically independent effects on public debt structure. Others argue that financialization of the state has made sovereign debt accumulation and management an essentially technical exercise largely unaffected by political interests and control (Fastenrath, Schwan, and Trampusch 2017; Trampusch and Gross 2021; Schwan, Trampusch, and Fastenrath 2021). But this book illustrates how EM DMOs face significant partisan political constraints in managing annual external borrowings and thus the subsequent evolution of their country's external sovereign debt structure. EM DMOs cannot borrow from sources that partisan leaders will not approve or ratify as part of the annual fiscal policymaking process. Because EM DMOs face major political constraints in doing their work, models of institutional independence and financialization are less applicable to EM external debt accumulation than this book's partisan model.

This has implications for sovereign debt literature as well as more general political economy research on the relationship between political interests, bureaucratic state institutions, and economic policy outcomes. For sovereign debt, a partisan model of borrowing, with particular focus on the external areas of EM balance sheets, adds to our understanding of the ways in which DMOs and politics interact to determine annual borrowings and ensuing public debt structures. Moreover, by specifying the constraints DMOs face in managing public debt due to their relatively reactive role in the annual fiscal policymaking process, the model is also relevant for practitioners. It articulates a framework that developing country DMOs can and must work within to enhance public debt sustainability each year and over time, indicating practices that may be more implementable than others (such as transparency; see for example Cormier 2023b; International Monetary Fund and World Bank 2018b).

Beyond external debt, how this book's partisan model of constraints on DMOs contrasts with other models of these institutions (such as those emphasizing independence) signals why theories of the relationship between institutions, political interests, and public debt structure should vary on specific dimensions. Three such dimensions identified in this book are the policymaking processes in which these interests and institutions interact, the specific outcomes or 'dependent variables' they are being theorized to affect, and national income level insofar as it reflects different positions in the global financial system and different degrees of access to markets and international organizations. For example, the maturity structure of a sovereign's bonds may be more subject to DMO control than external borrowing decisions (compare this book with Sadeh and Porath 2020), and this may vary by income level (compare this book with Trampusch and Gross 2021). Making distinctions along such dimensions can provide clearer insight into the effect DMOs may and may not have in managing various aspects of sovereign debt.

More generally the book illustrates how and why models of the relationship between political interests and ministerial institutions in one economic policy area should not be assumed as readily applicable to other economic policy areas (Wren-Lewis 2013). In this sense, the book is an example of the gains to be made by using qualitative research to trace and compare the varied policymaking processes economic ministries are part of as they work to manage various parts of national macroeconomies, perhaps particularly in developing countries (Bertelli et al. 2020; Williams 2020).

This chapter further introduces these themes, arguments, and implications. The next section provides a brief vignette of South African external borrowing since the end of Apartheid, summarizing the book's central arguments. The third section details the EM borrowing menu, presenting a stylized decision tree DMOs follow when fulfilling annual government financing requirements and setting the scope of where on the balance sheet this book's partisan theory affects sovereign debt accumulation. The fourth section then critiques how the vast sovereign debt literature cannot adequately explain the different ways in which EMs use that borrowing menu each year and the ensuing variation observed in EM sovereign debt structures over time. The fifth section presents the partisan theory of EM external borrowing in brief and previews the multiple methods used throughout the book to test the theory. The sixth section discusses implications for various literatures and practitioners. The final section outlines and previews the book's chapters.

1.2 South Africa Vignette: Borrowings and Consequences

To give a flavor of the book's arguments, this section provides a vignette of external sovereign borrowing in post-Apartheid South Africa. From 1994 through the 2010s, the South African government, with working classes as core political constituencies, almost strictly used bond markets rather than official creditors when borrowing externally. This occurred despite macroeconomic characteristics that would lead many to expect South Africa to have borrowed differently in these years.

The story also signals the consequences of such a borrowing strategy over time, as building a burdensome public debt structure by the early 2020s led to limited fiscal space and corresponding difficulty responding to the Covid-19 pandemic (Nedbank 2020). Indeed, in early 2020, as the economic impact of Covid-19 became clear, Moody's downgraded South Africa's sovereign credit rating to junk. The pandemic meant every country faced reduced economic activity and subsequent debt repayment challenges. But rating agencies downgraded only 20% of sovereigns in early 2020 (Standard & Poor's 2020). So Moody's decision was not simply a function of Covid-19's economic effects. Why was South Africa, one of the largest EM economies, in this position while many other countries were not?

Among many reasons was years of expensive government borrowing, including on external bond markets.[2] Rates on foreign-denominated South African sovereign bonds increased from 2.4% to nearly 6% in the ten years after the global financial crisis.[3] Repeated issuances despite worsening terms put the country's public debt obligations on an 'inexorable rise', making 'rising financing costs' central to the Moody's downgrade (Moody's 2020). And this had been coming for some time (Nedbank 2020). S&P and Fitch had already downgraded South African debt to junk in 2017 due, in part, to concerns about public debt (Wigglesworth and Megaw 2017; Cotterill 2017).

South Africa did not need to cover its external financing needs on bond markets at these prices. The government could have diversified its external debt with cheaper credit at longer maturities from official multilateral and bilateral lenders. For example, one 2010 World Bank loan to a South African state-owned company was priced at below market interest rates with a nearly three-decade maturity (World Bank 2010b).[4] Cheaper and longer-term finance than what the South

---

[2] As detailed in Chapter 4, local bond markets are also important in South Africa.

[3] The 2.4% figure is for a 2009 USD bond from historical data provided by interviewees. Among many examples indicating such rising interest rates over the following ten years, see 2018 USD bond ISIN US836205AY00.

[4] LIBOR-plus rates are variable so change slightly over time. But to signal the large cost difference from what the government was paying on markets, in April 2021 the spread on this type of loan for South Africa's country group was 1.22% (IBRD Flexible Loan Group B, see World Bank 2021b; 2021c).

African government was obtaining on markets was available. But South Africa did not use such options. From strictly a cost and maturity perspective, avoiding cheaper and longer-term official credit could be called irrational, particularly since it contributed to such increased risk that South African bonds were rated as junk by the late 2010s.

Existing work on capital allocation, market discipline, and borrower preferences cannot explain South Africa's annual borrowings. Some might expect South Africa to have been priced out of markets by scrutinous investors and pushed to official creditors as economic fundamentals, credit ratings, and borrowing costs deteriorated (Mosley 2003, chap. 4). Some market discipline theories would expect South Africa's fiscal policy to have tightened, leading to smaller deficits, less borrowing, and so less debt accumulation as well as lower borrowing costs (Kaplan and Thomsson 2017). Others expect governments representing labor, like South Africa's dominant African National Congress (ANC) party, to avoid markets and use official creditors in the first place (Bunte 2019). But South Africa continued to use markets despite poor credit ratings, large deficits, and a government representing labor.[5]

Instead, South Africa used expensive bond markets to meet external borrowing needs because the alternative—official credit—would include conditions unpalatable to the left-leaning ANC government. The conditions would force adjustment on core ANC constituencies such as labor, the public sector, and the poor in a variety of ways, making the political transaction costs of using cheaper official credit too high. In this sense, sovereign debt markets provided the ANC government a politically 'silent' financing option compared to cheaper-but-conditional official credit. The ANC's partisan politics are therefore central to explaining why South Africa relied on relatively expensive bond markets for external finance. Over time, these annual borrowings led to an external debt structure mostly comprising relatively expensive repayment obligations. Without partisan politics, South Africa's borrowings could have been otherwise.

This framing shows South Africa's annual foreign borrowings were not irrational, despite prices and maturities. The political incentive for this borrowing strategy was policy autonomy for the governing party. The ANC was able to support its left-leaning constituencies without the threat of official creditors curtailing, adjusting, eliminating, or generally undermining the party's political and economic aims with various project or program loan conditions. Using bond markets for external financing needs allowed relative policy autonomy at the time of borrowing and in the short term. Yet meanwhile, these annual borrowing decisions were gradually aggregating to constitute a sovereign debt structure that was increasingly unsustainable, negatively affecting South Africa's sovereign credit

---

[5] Chapter 4 traces the South Africa case in detail.

ratings and increasing the risk of a debt crisis-related reduction in policy autonomy in the long term.

The tension between ANC interest in maintaining policy autonomy and concern about borrowing costs remained evident as the Covid-19 pandemic intensified. From 2020 into 2021, ANC constituent resistance to official creditors persisted even as Covid-19 created a multi-year economic crisis. In the words of ANC and union leaders: '[we are] very concerned by the suggestions . . . that [we] approach the IMF or the World Bank for "assistance" . . . [We] need to safeguard South Africa's . . . sovereignty [and] our independence—which are non-negotiable, even in the midst of a crisis' (Makinana 2020). Labor leaders also feared China would take advantage of the pandemic to pressure the country into 'extortionate' conditional loan agreements with significant negative implications for South African working classes and consumers (Mail & Guardian 2020). The government accordingly continued to cover its foreign borrowing needs with comparatively pricier bonds through the early 2020s, ensuring ANC policies promoting spending and a large role for an interventionist state in the economy persisted as they had throughout the ANC's post-Apartheid leadership (Nedbank 2020; The Economist 2021).

This occurred despite the more negative consequences of using costly market instruments over the years becoming manifest. The state's ability to minimize the social and economic impact of Covid-19 was greatly constrained by the fact that over 20% of government spending in 2020–2021 was allocated to repaying sovereign debt (The Economist 2020). By mid-2021, the pandemic's unaddressed economic strains combined with long-standing state inefficiency and corruption issues to spark the most violent civil unrest in the country since Apartheid (Cotterill 2021). While these events were not a direct function of public debt, public debt structure had come to limit the fiscal space government had to address social and economic inequalities before and in response to Covid-19. If conditional official credit had been used, foreign debts would have been cheaper and longer term, easing debt repayment obligations in exchange for production and policy adjustments. However, while adjusting the economy in order to meet various official creditor conditions and use their cheaper finance may have eased pressure on South Africa's sovereign debt structure, the ANC would have faced significant political consequences for doing so.

This political and economic trade-off between sovereign borrowing costs and policy autonomy underpins why annual EM external borrowings are not simply a function of supply-side allocation decisions. Most EMs have external financing options most of the time, which provides them autonomy when turning abroad to borrow. The next section details the EM borrowing menu and its implications, before presenting the book's theory that partisanship informs how EMs approach their borrowing menu each year.

1.3 The EM Sovereign Financing Landscape

This section describes the financing options EM sovereigns have, and the implications of using those options. This sets the scope for where a partisan effect on EM sovereign borrowings, summarized in the story above, does and does not affect EM sovereign debt accumulation. The first section discusses external and domestic debts, with a focus on hard and local currency distinctions. It highlights that while stylized policy advice is to maximize local currency resources, EMs do not meet all, and often do not meet most, of their financing needs by using local currency instruments. This is why external debts have long been and remain central to EM annual borrowings and sovereign debt structures. It is at the point of making external borrowings that this book's partisan theory of debt accumulation is at work, helping determine which external sources of finance EM governments do and do not prioritize when meeting their annual external borrowing needs. The remainder of the section details these external options, the distinctions between them, and why the effects they have on different groups in a borrower incentivize EM sovereigns to use more or less of each type of financing when borrowing externally.

1.3.1 Hard vs. Local Currency Debt

Governments can pay for expenditures with taxes, reserves, or borrowed funds. When borrowing, EMs can do so in foreign or local currency. Holders of any currency denomination can be foreign or domestic residents, with implications for capital accumulation as well as the legal framework of any future restructurings. But this book focuses on the currency dimension because external currency debts are central to sovereign debt structure and thus debt sustainability across EMs (Panizza 2010). While access to local currency debt has risen significantly for some EMs in the 2000s (Ballard-Rosa, Mosley, and Wellhausen 2022), this is concentrated in a few large economies. In 2019, for example, China alone made up 47% of the EM local currency bond market and outside of Asia EM governments issued between two and five times as much foreign as domestic debt on average (Dehn 2020, fig. 3). Outside of a few large exceptions (see Aizenman et al. 2021; Dehn 2020, fig. 5), most EMs have long relied on and continue to rely on external debt as an essential financial resource (Hausmann and Panizza 2003; Eichengreen, Hausmann, and Panizza 2007, 124; Eichengreen, Hausmann, and Panizza 2023). In addition, official credit is typically in hard currency,[6] which as discussed throughout this book also remains an important financing option for EMs.

---

[6] Some major multilaterals have developed currency swap mechanisms for a few large EM borrowers. But this is a relatively new strategy with minimal reach, and initial transactions remain in hard currencies (see World Bank 2020).

The currency denomination of EM sovereign debt informs the types of financial benefits and risks accrued on a government's balance sheet. More local currency debt implies less repayment risk based on exchange rate volatility, and governments can theoretically inflate away repayment obligations (Panizza and Taddei 2020). But risks with local currency debts include such inflation, and partly for this reason, local currency debts are typically more expensive and shorter term than hard currency debts as investors charge risk premiums (Gadanecz, Miyajima, and Shu 2014, 10; Panizza 2010, 91). Local currency debt may also incentivize financial repression to reduce public debt, with significant implications for the rest of the economy (see Jafarov, Maino, and Pani 2020, 6).

In contrast, external currency debts in EMs incur the 'original sin' (Eichengreen and Hausmann 1999), exposing the borrowing government to currency mismatch in their public debt structure. If the borrower's currency depreciates or the currency owed appreciates, repayment obligations can rapidly become more expensive and difficult to meet. Yet the benefits of foreign currency borrowings are essential to development. In terms of capital accumulation and debt, foreign debt provides access to financial resources that cannot be generated domestically or in local currency, and typically provides lower rates and longer maturities than local currency debt (Fatás et al. 2019). In terms of broader economic development, hard currency remains essential for the import of capital goods and other expensive foreign inputs on which growth depends (Thirlwall 2011).

Taking the benefits and risks of local and external debts into account, the ability to avoid original sin is a major boon to public debt structure and the sustainability of EM sovereign debt (Panizza 2010, 92) because foreign debt obligations are more likely to lead to crises (Bordo, Meissner, and Stuckler 2010). This has led to a trend where IFI advice (World Bank 2015b; IMF 2021b; Hardie and Rethel 2019) is to encourage EM DMOs to maximize their local currency borrowings before turning abroad (Panizza 2010, 98). But as detailed above, in most EMs external debts have long been and remain central to how EM governments finance themselves.

1.3.2 EM External Borrowing Options

Once an EM DMO identifies the amount they need to borrow externally each year, they have a set of options with which they can fulfill this financing requirement. EMs have a unique set of financing options when borrowing externally. They are both poor enough to access official multilateral or bilateral creditors and creditworthy enough to access markets. This gives EMs different borrowing options than Low Income Countries (LICs), which means they should be analyzed separately rather than as developing countries writ-large (IMF 2021a, n. 1). LICs face more significant constraints than EMs when using capital markets (Hostland 2009).

LICs also use grant or extra-concessional windows that EMs typically cannot access, making official loans significantly cheaper with different conditionalities and implications for LICs than loans to EMs (Loser 2004; World Bank 2012, paras 8, 20, 21; 2017, 9). The effect of these different menus is that LIC and EM sovereign borrowers are not easily comparable, theoretically or empirically. This also gives EMs a different borrowing menu than developed High Income Countries (HICs), which cannot regularly access development banks outside of crises. High, middle, and low income country groupings largely coincide with terminology used by banks and bond index providers which distinguish between developed, emerging, and frontier markets.

Figure 1.1 captures the effect of these different borrowing options on borrowing outcomes in developing countries. It plots the average percentage of new external debt from market rather than official sources for countries in each income group each year. The further up the y-axis, the more new debt comes from markets for that subset of developing countries. LICs use official credit with minimal market use. EMs cover more of their external financing needs with market instruments.

Indeed, for EMs, these financing options are statistical and practical substitutes at the time of borrowing. Statistically, there is a negative correlation between official credit flows and market flows (Galindo and Panizza 2018, 120). In practice, markets and official creditors are substitutes because they carry different implications for sovereign debt structure, repayment obligations, and thus domestic economics and politics. These different practical implications are why debt managers organize national balance sheets around how much they borrow from and thus owe to 'official [versus] commercial creditors' (Wheeler 2004, 18; see also World Bank 2015b, 14; 40–41). As detailed below, official creditors' lower interest rates and longer maturities ease pressure on national accounts but limit policy autonomy. Markets have a more burdensome effect on repayment obligations but allow for policy autonomy because they do not impose overt conditions at the time of borrowing. Which substitute a borrower prioritizes matters in the long run: beyond clear cost and maturity structure implications, whether an EM owes more to official creditors or markets also determines the cyclicality of subsequent capital flows, with major implications for social and economic development and the probability of crises (Galindo and Panizza 2018; see also Rey 2015; Reinhart and Rogoff 2009).

There are two points to make when framing market and official instruments as substitutes. First, differences between specific multilaterals or bilaterals (Humphrey and Michaelowa 2013; Prizzon, Greenhill, and Mustapha 2017; Bunte 2019; Cormier 2023a) or specific banks and markets (Mosley and Rosendorff 2023; Hardie 2006) are of course also politically and economically significant. Disaggregating financial instruments at such granular levels is both academically and practically important.

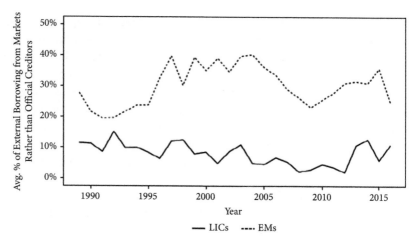

Figure 1.1 Average External Borrowing Mixture, EMs vs. LICs
Source: World Development Indicators and author's calculations

In this book, however, they exist within the contours of a sovereign's initial decision to prioritize markets or official creditors—and their respective implications—when borrowing externally each year. The market-official distinction is an important level of flow aggregation because it has policy relevance with clear political and economic implications. Focusing on the market-official distinction does not deny the importance of the political economy of other groupings of flows. The aim is to better understand the politics that shape one of many essential aspects of sovereign debt composition with which technocrats and policymakers are concerned for both economic and political reasons.

Second, this stylized depiction of official and private sources as substitutes may lose some traction coming out of crises. Under these conditions IMF lending may have a catalytic effect on markets, making official and market flows more complementary than substitutional. However, it is notable that this is not always the case. IMF programs are sometimes a seal of approval for private flows, but at other times are a sign of trouble, drive down private flows, and remain a substitute rather than a complement (Chapman et al. 2015; Vadlamannati 2020).

Regardless, even if under specific conditions official creditors and markets are not perfect substitutes, it remains true that some percentage of a country's external borrowings will come from markets and the rest will come from official creditors. And this ratio will vary. So even if these two sources of credit are complementary under some crisis conditions, and jointly drive total external borrowings up at such times, the sources prioritized when doing so will still determine the major political and economic implications that stem from new borrowings. An IMF program may coincide with minimal market flows, large market flows, or no market flows. And as this book highlights, there is reason to suspect a borrower's partisan preferences help determine which is the case.

1.3.3 The External Borrowing Trade-off

Given this scope, the starting point for considering the economic and political trade-off EMs face when borrowing externally is that official credit carries cost and debt management benefits. Official creditors offer lower interest rates and longer maturities than markets. This is true of major multilaterals (Humphrey 2014), regional development banks (Griffith-Jones, Griffith-Jones, and Hertova 2008; Humphrey and Michaelowa 2013), and Western, Chinese, or other emerging bilateral sources (Morris, Parks, and Gardner 2020; Prizzon, Greenhill, and Mustapha 2017). Figures 1.2 and 1.3 compare the average interest rate and maturity on EM borrowings from official creditors and markets. Notably, the Figures confirm that differences between these borrowing options persist through the period of historically low global interest rates following the 2008 financial crisis. This is intentional. Official creditors tie their interest rates to LIBOR or other benchmarks to ensure a gap between themselves and market prices persist as global rates change (see for example World Bank 2021b; 2021c).

But to obtain these price benefits from official creditors, borrowers must be willing to accept loan conditions. Of course official loan conditions are not identical, as detailed in a moment. But the very presence of numerous overt and legally codified conditions means official loans are fundamentally different propositions for borrowers than market instruments, which operate with a different profit motive, pricing approach, and risk management rationale than official creditors (Tomz

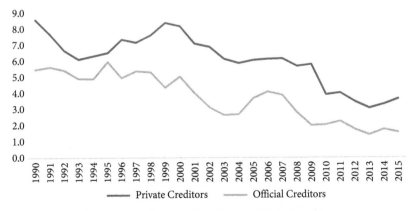

Figure 1.2 Average Interest Rate on New External Debt in EMs

Source: World Development Indicators and author's calculations

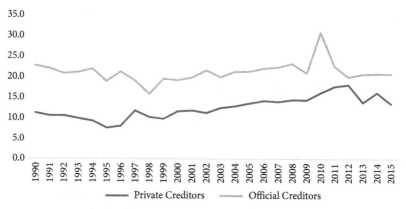

Figure 1.3 Average Maturity for New External Debt in EMs

Source: World Development Indicators and author's calculations

2007, 23–26; see also Reinhart and Rogoff 2009; Loser 2004; Thompson and Runciman 2006).

Official creditors include loan conditions that legally and overtly adjust or constrain a borrower's policy *at the time of borrowing*. Of particular importance here is that they typically adjust the position of the working classes more than other economic groups in the borrower. Again, as detailed below, official lenders and their conditionalities are certainly not identical. But they do share this core trait that distinguish them from bond markets and commercial banks: *they disproportionately adjust the position of working classes in the borrower more than other economic groups*. This is important to emphasize, as it is central to the book's partisan theory of annual external EM borrowing and subsequent sovereign debt accumulation (though detailed at length below, for other discussions to this point see for example Babb 2013; Chwieroth 2009; Roos 2019; Stiglitz 2002; Winter et al. 2022; Woods 2006).

The remainder of this section outlines the effects of official creditors' project and program conditions on borrowers, setting up space for a domestic political economy theory of when an EM government is likely to prefer borrowing more from official creditors or markets when they turn abroad for finance.

1.3.3.1 Project Conditions

Multilaterals and bilaterals condition project loans on some set of adjustments by the borrower. Project conditions may:

(1) adjust or upgrade what is produced in the country by offering to fund only certain projects in certain sectors, which can lead to significant changes in labor's status-quo access to work and political power (Doner and Schneider

2016; Prizzon, Greenhill, and Mustapha 2017; Sun et al. 2015; Taglioni and Winkler 2016);

(2) adjust labor markets in ways that that reduce or limit wages, weaken unions, introduce new employment competition in the sector receiving the loan, adjust labor standards in ways that either increase production costs and drive investment elsewhere, or reduce status-quo protections (Vreeland 2002; Anner and Caraway 2010; Caraway, Rickard, and Anner 2012, 33; Blanton, Blanton, and Peksen 2015; Isaksson and Kotsadam 2018b; Reinsberg et al. 2019);

(3) adjust trade and investment policies, alter supply chains, limit subsidies, or increase privatization to promote bilateral, regional, or global economic integration and efficiency at the expense of those who depend on interventionist protections and status-quo production (Kikeri and Kolo 2005; Griffith-Jones, Griffith-Jones, and Hertova 2008; Kentikelenis, Stubbs, and King 2016a; OECD 2011; Raman 2009; Alonso 2016; Reinsberg et al. 2020; Kaplan 2021).

All Western and non-Western official creditors condition project loans on some set of these adjustments. This means different official lenders tend to create similar political-economic winners and losers within borrowers. These groups are distinguishable by class, as those most subject to adjustment through these arrangements tend to be the working class. This is key to the book's theory and worth reiterating. Even while taking seriously important differences in the exact form and purpose of various official creditor conditions,[7] many aspects of most official creditor projects negatively affect labor more than capital in the borrower. These effects have corresponding political consequences for governments that use them. The political salience of these conditions' effects can, depending on the governing party's partisan leanings, constrain DMO bureaucrats fulfilling borrowing requirements each year.

For example, Western bilaterals condition loans on foreign firm entry, limiting control over industrial policies that could be used to benefit local labor (Bunte 2019, 39). In a similar fashion, Chinese finance is also conditional on market access for its firms and integration into their supply chains (Bräutigam and Gallagher 2014, 351; Dreher et al. 2018, n. 9; Kaplan 2021, chap. 3). Moreover, Chinese loans are often formally conditional on use of Chinese labor and also attract further Chinese labor migration into the borrowing country (Cervellati et al. 2022; Huang, Xu, and Mao 2018, 33, 242–243, 251; Mattlin and Nojonen 2015). These effects make domestic labor and unions worse off in areas receiving these Chinese funds (Isaksson and Kotsadam 2018b) with benefits accruing to elites that support

---

[7] See, for example, differences between Chinese and Western official lenders' loan contracts (Gelpern et al. 2021), including transparency (Cormier 2023a).

Chinese firm entry (Isaksson and Kotsadam 2018a). Indeed, these 'elite kickback' schemes reduce the gains local working classes obtain from Chinese loans and related projects (Kern and Reinsberg 2021).

This is why 'China has [been] met with difficulty in cultivating a positive image among publics—as opposed to among governing elites' in developing country borrowers (Thornton 2020, 4). For example, Chinese dismissal and abuse of local labor has long been a politically salient issue among Zimbabwe's working classes (Smith 2012; Nyathi 2021). Evictions of local laborers and privileges for Chinese firms underpin resistance to Chinese finance in Cambodia (The Economist 2017). South African unions lobby their government to limit Chinese finance conditional on 'selling the country' (Mail & Guardian 2020) despite strong political and economic ties in other areas of their relations such as trade and diplomacy (Burke, Naidu, and Nepgen 2008, 16–21).

That different official creditors' conditions have similar effects on borrower's political-economic constituencies helps explain why different official creditors do not crowd out one another and are often complementary. This is true of both Western and Chinese flows, as well as multilateral and bilateral flows.

On the former, Western and Chinese credit flows are actually correlated (Humphrey and Michaelowa 2019). If different creditors had different effects on economic production and policy in borrowers, we would likely not see such complementary flows. Nor does Chinese lending undermine the 'effectiveness' of Western lending (Dreher et al. 2017) or undercut Western prices (Morris, Parks, and Gardner 2020), signaling important points of complementarity between them. In fact the World Bank tends to emulate what China does when both lend to a borrower rather than diversify (Zeitz 2021). And while the World Bank may include fewer conditions if China is present (Hernandez 2017), there is no evidence that this changes the content of World Bank conditionality (Cormier and Manger 2022; Winter et al. 2022).

On the latter, broad complementarity of official creditors also explains the prevalence of co-financing arrangements between multilaterals and bilaterals. Co-financing occurs when official creditors lend not only to the same country but for the same project. For Western lenders, co-financing is explicit and strategic, designed to increase efficiency and impact (for example, see Kotchen and Negi 2019). 'Multi-bi' aid is an increasingly common form of this, where a flagship lender like the World Bank will lead a project but coordinate co-financing with a number of bilateral and smaller multilateral lenders (Reinsberg 2017; Cormier, Heinzel and Reinsberg 2022). Leaving aside questions about the effectiveness of such arrangements (Heinzel, Cormier, and Reinsberg 2023), for this book's purposes the key is that co-financing makes it unlikely that borrowers avoid significant conditionalities as these modalities gain prevalence. This is because conditions must meet the standards of the most stringent co-financer, which typically is a major multilateral (Babb 2013, 289; Humphrey and Michaelowa 2013). That co-financing is so common and Western creditor conditions have such similar political implications for borrowers may explain why developing country citizens perceive little difference between Western multilaterals and bilaterals (Findley, Milner, and Nielson 2017).

Moreover, co-financing between Western and Chinese-led official creditors like the Asian Infrastructure Investment Bank is increasingly common (Asian Infrastructure Investment Bank 2016; Pacheco Pardo and Rana 2018; Reuters 2018). Chinese bilaterals are an exception: at the time of writing, the World Bank co-finances with Chinese-led multilaterals but does not with Chinese bilaterals (Interview 103). But again, even if not tied to the same specific project, Chinese bilateral flows still correlate to Western flows rather than crowd them out (Humphrey and Michaelowa 2019). This is why many recent analyses based on improved data push back on claims that Chinese finance is a source of significant change in development lending (Liang 2019; Beeson and Xu 2019; Ray 2021). For developing countries making borrowing decisions, Chinese project lending 'is not special' at the time of borrowing compared to Western lenders (Fuchs and Rudyak 2019, 394) despite differences in transparency (Cormier 2023a) and implications of default down the line (Behuria 2018; Kaplan 2021; Gelpern et al. 2021).

In sum, Western and non-Western project loans share important similarities from the perspective of a borrower at the time they are devising annual external borrowing strategies. Official creditors are a group of below-market-cost but conditional lenders that adjust borrowers' production profiles and threaten to negatively affect the material position of working classes more than other economic groups. This is key to the book's theory so worth reiterating. Despite differences in the exact form and purpose of some official creditors' conditionality (including Chinese and Western official creditors), official creditor project loans negatively affect labor more than capital in a borrower, with accordant political consequences for governments that use them.

1.3.3.2 Policy Conditions

Largely used by Western creditors (see Kaplan 2021), policy conditions in official loans which adjust the borrower's economic policies have changed slightly over time. The Washington Consensus informed 1990s conditionality, prioritizing trade and investment liberalization, limited expenditure, broadened tax bases, and other integration-friendly policies (Williamson 1990). This paradigm expanded after the 1990s to include second generation conditions focused on good governance alongside first generation structural conditions (Rodrik 2006). However, this does not mean policy conditions no longer force adjustment on borrowers with the aim of global market integration that ultimately adjusts the position of working classes more than other domestic groups. New forms of policy conditions expand on and add layers to traditionally core aims of policy conditionality—they do not eliminate or constitute a break from them (Güven 2018; Kaya and Reay 2019). This evidence supports views that any changes at these lenders are cautious rather than significant wholesale behavioral shifts (Babb 2013; Best 2014, 203), reflecting a combination of institutional constraints and ideational limitations (Barnett and Finnemore 2004; Weaver 2008; Fine 2009; Roos 2019).

Indeed, through the 2000s, World Bank and IMF loans continued to include a combination of liberalization, privatization, fiscal consolidation, tax-base expansion, and expenditure as well as debt reduction conditions alongside governance and social spending conditions (Cormier and Manger 2022; Kentikelenis, Stubbs, and King 2016). By some measures, fiscal and financial reforms remained particularly common compared to second-generation governance conditions throughout the twenty-first century (Güven 2018). This helps explain why, throughout this ostensibly post–Washington Consensus period, the IMF and World Bank continued to treat conservative governments that shared their policy preferences more leniently (Nelson 2017; Winter et al. 2022). This also helps explain persistent findings that relationships between major Western official creditors and their borrowers depends on shared economic policy paradigms (Woods 2006; Heinzel et al. 2021).

In this sense, second generation conditions promoting good governance should not be seen to reflect some anti-integration paradigm shift in policy conditions. They are a layer on top of still central first generation structural conditions (Kaya and Reay 2019, 386; Güven 2018), leading some to see governance conditions as simply pushing market-friendly policies through different means (Babb and Carruthers 2008; Navia and Velasco 2003). Many explain the persistence of economic liberalism in conditions by highlighting rigid organizational structures (Barnett and Finnemore 2004; Weaver 2008) or lack of a clear alternative approach to developmental economic policy (Babb 2013; Best 2014).

In sum, despite some changes over time, policy conditions remain politically salient points of contestation that are likely to hurt labor, the poor, and other groups of working-class citizens more than other groups in a borrower. For the purposes of this book, the key point is that borrowing countries do *not* have to adopt such overt adjustments when using market instruments. Instead, markets provide a comparatively condition-free financial option for EM sovereigns, at least in the short term. The long term effects of using more volatile and expensive market flows are important. But as theorized in this book, for left-leaning governments interested in avoiding official creditor conditions that would infringe on their policy autonomy and carry immediate political consequences, these longer-term considerations do not inform borrowing preferences as much as the immediate interest in avoiding conditionality.

1.4 The International Political Economy of EM Sovereign Debt

The above section illustrates the character and implications of the menu EMs must navigate once they identify an amount to borrow externally each year. The observation that there are borrowing options implies that how borrowers approach that menu—how governments borrow—is central to sovereign debt outcomes. Why would EMs prefer to prioritize cheap but conditional official credit, and why would EMs prefer to prioritize expensive but condition-free markets?

The sovereign debt literature, from international economics to political economy to development studies, sheds relatively little light on questions about which external financing options ultimately do and do not end up on EM government balance sheets given some degree of borrower autonomy. There is of course much on supply-side constraints EMs face when borrowing on sovereign debt markets, and extensive work on supply-side determinants of multilateral and bilateral lending. But there is less on how borrowing governments navigate these market and official external financing options when both are available, which is the case for most EMs most of the time. There is also much on the politics of repayment and default (Tomz 2007; Roos 2019; Ballard-Rosa 2020), but less on how borrowing governments select financial instruments each year and build public debt structure over time.

This section reviews how the literatures on EM sovereign debt markets and official creditors emphasize the supply side of flows. It then turns focus to the demand side of sovereign debt, driven by the observation that the presence of these external financing options implies EMs have a degree of autonomy when making external borrowing decisions. EM use of this autonomy is an understudied but important component of annual EM sovereign debt accumulation and thus the composition of EM sovereign debt structures.

1.4.1 Sovereign Debt Models: Creditworthiness, Discipline, and Pull Factors

Sovereign debt contracts create a credible commitment problem, particularly outside of the rich world (Eaton and Gersovitz 1981; Eaton, Gersovitz, and Stiglitz 1986; Bulow and Rogoff 1989; Stasavage 2003, 1). Lenders are wary of political incentives to defer repayment or to default when sovereign debt repayment obligations come due. Because EM sovereign external debt contracts are made under conditions of anarchy (i.e., are not subject to entities enforcing repayment), models of sovereign debt typically give primacy to supply-side interests and information. Investors in developing economies scrutinize a more expansive set of borrower political-economic characteristics than they do in rich countries (Mosley 2003, chap. 4), update their perceptions about the creditworthiness of that potential borrower, then 'condition lending decisions' on that information (Tomz 2007, 10).

If a potential borrower's characteristics indicate low default probability, lenders should be willing to hold more of that creditworthy country's debt, at lower interest rates and longer maturities. If a potential borrower's characteristics indicate high default probability, lenders should be willing to hold less of that country's debt, at higher interest rates and shorter maturities. This 'market discipline' principle underpins the essence of capital allocation in any financial market, sovereign or otherwise (Eaton and Gersovitz 1981; Eaton, Gersovitz, and Stiglitz 1986, 1–34; more broadly, see Knight 2003; Stiglitz and Weiss 1981). This is why a number of national political and economic characteristics are expected to attract or 'pull' external finance toward creditworthy sovereigns, and away from riskier sovereigns (Fernandez-Arias 1996; Hausmann and Panizza 2003). Disciplinary pull pressures are often seen as particularly likely in external rather than domestic sovereign debt markets (Rommerskirchen 2020). Country features typically expected to determine sovereign risk and thus whether a sovereign pulls capital include macroeconomic, institutional, and political or policy characteristics.

Important economic fundamentals include GDP growth, public debt levels, public debt structures, credit ratings, and balance of payments positions (Hernández, Mellado, and Valdés 2001; Mosley 2003, 126; Koepke 2019, 533–534). Higher growth, lower public debt levels, longer-term debt structures, lower risk according to credit rating agencies, and manageable current or capital account deficits should attract capital to EMs. These intuitive relationships reflect how stronger fundamentals make an EM more able, and likely more willing, to repay debts and thus more creditworthy.

Domestic institutional characteristics also inform creditworthiness (Gelos, Sahay, and Sandleris 2011). Extensive literature argues that democracies are more creditworthy because accountability to citizens and other parts of the state incentivizes governments to honor their repayment obligations (Schultz and Weingast 2003; Stasavage 2003; Beaulieu, Cox, and Saiegh 2012). Refined versions of the democratic advantage thesis argue that strong rule of law and respect for property rights, features of democratic regimes, are particularly responsible for reducing risk (Biglaiser and Staats 2012). Others show that central bank independence (CBI) enhances EM creditworthiness because institutional independence from political intervention increases the credibility of inflation-targeting monetary policy (Bodea and Hicks 2015a). Predictably, corruption decreases creditworthiness while transparency enhances it (Connolly 2007; Glennerster and Shin 2008; Bastida, Guillamón, and Benito 2017; Cormier 2023b).

Political policy choices are also said to affect EM sovereign debt market access (Claessens, Klingebiel, and Schmukler 2007). Tight fiscal policy, low inflation, and privatization policies attract capital to EMs (Grabel 1996) while exchange rate pegs and consumption-driven fiscal policies or subsidies can negatively affect creditworthiness (Mosley 2003, 126). These relationships reflect expectations that globalized financial markets incentivize developing countries to pursue market-friendly policies that prioritize repayment among or above other uses of capital and other macroeconomic policy priorities (Kaplan 2013; Kaplan and Thomsson 2017; Wibbels 2006; Rommerskirchen 2020).

Variation in government policy preferences underpins evidence that government partisanship affects a variety of financial markets (outside of sovereign debt markets, see for example Sattler 2013; Bechtel 2009; Jensen and Schmith 2005; Bernhard and Leblang 2002). In rich world sovereign debt markets, left governments have been shown to receive lower credit ratings despite broad convergence on actual policy outcomes, possibly reflecting an attempt to preemptively discipline implementation of left-leaning policies (Barta and Johnston 2018).

In EM sovereign debt markets, however, there is mixed evidence about whether and how partisanship determines market access. This book clarifies this potential dissonance by emphasizing the distinction between risk (measured by interest rates or credit ratings, for example) and actual borrowings (the volume of new debt taken on and added to national accounts each year, regardless of creditworthiness). In this framing, studies that find a partisan effect on EM risk (Vaaler, Schrage, and Block 2006; Cho 2014) and studies that find no partisan effect on EM capital flows (Frot and Santiso 2013, 42–44), then, do not necessarily conflict with one another. As argued throughout the book, even if markets discipline left-leaning governments with premium prices, borrowers can still borrow in the volumes they need to meet their financing requirements.

1.4.2 Market Distortions & Push Factors

An EM government's ability to attract or 'pull' finance in debt markets is determined by national economic and political features. But financial flows to EM sovereigns are not simply a function of one sovereign's risk relative to other sovereigns. They are also a function of investor behaviors and exogenous events. Much recent work highlights the role of such market imperfections and structural 'push' factors on the cost and flow of capital to EMs.

Investors, particularly in developing country contexts, face informational limitations and often rely on heuristic cognitive shortcuts to assess a sovereign's creditworthiness. These include country categorizations (Brooks, Cunha, and Mosley 2015) and institutional membership (Gray 2013). At the same time, investor assessments of sovereign risk are subject to pro-cyclical biases, further limiting the degree to which flows are a function of pull rather than push factors (Naqvi 2019). Others suggest that there is disagreement about the appropriateness and effect of certain policies, leading even informed investors to make different capital allocation decisions (Mosley, Paniagua, and Wibbels 2020).

In addition to informational imperfections, market structure also curtails the disciplinary role of pull factors. For example, the expansion of index investment practices limit the disciplinary character of EM sovereign debt markets, as index investing creates a high floor of 'natural demand' for EMs included in indexes regardless of national fundamentals (Cormier and Naqvi 2023; Pandolfi and Williams 2019). Meanwhile, US monetary policy shapes the total amount of capital available to EMs as an asset class. When US interest rates are low, yield-seeking investors make more capital available to EMs. Higher US interest rates provoke a flight to quality leading EMs to find financing relatively scarce and expensive (Bauerle Danzman, Winecoff, and Oatley 2017; Milesi-Ferretti and Tille 2011; Rey 2015). EM sovereign debt markets may be more or less disciplinary based on these rich world monetary cycles (Campello 2015; Ballard-Rosa, Mosley, and Wellhausen 2021).

Both pull and push groups of research give primacy to the supply side of sovereign debt flows. In doing so they hold the demand side constant. 'Pull' research argues EM borrowings are disciplined by investor assessments of national economic fundamentals and political features, reducing sovereigns to reactionary actors that either struggle to borrow or change policies in response to disciplinary investor preferences. 'Push' research identifies important limitations to this model but still holds constant many borrower features, reducing actors on the demand side to mere price-takers.

But these are significant scoping limitations that leave the demand side of sovereign debt in a 'black box'. Whether and how EM governments use markets is an important question because they have financing options other than debt markets. In principle, EMs do not have to use markets for all (or any) of their foreign financing needs. In the context of external borrowing, the major alternative is official credit. But as discussed next, the literature on official creditor flows shares an emphasis on supply-side rather than demand-side factors.

1.4.3 Official Creditors

EMs can also access official creditors when turning abroad for finance. Official loans are cheaper than debt markets or commercial banks but require the acceptance of conditions that force adjustment on specific economic and political groups in the borrowing EM. This makes use of official loans politically salient and controversial within the borrower, providing a different set of financial and political implications than market-based instruments. The particulars of loan conditionality, as well as the price and maturity differences between official credit and markets, were detailed in this chapter's previous section. Here, the aim is to make the general point that the literature on official lending is as focused on the supply side as the literature on sovereign debt markets.

Prominent work on multilateral and bilateral lending emphasizes strategic interests. In multilaterals, US and other major donor countries have a significant effect on which countries receive more and larger loans, the number of conditions in loans, and the nature of those conditions. This is true of the World Bank (Clark and Dolan 2021; Fleck and Kilby 2006; Hawkins et al. 2006; Kilby 2009), the IMF (Stone 2011; Dreher, Sturm, and Vreeland 2015; Nelson 2017), and regional development banks like the Asian Development Bank (Kilby 2006; 2011; Lim and Vreeland 2013). Strategic interests also inform bilateral lending, including or particularly as the number of bilateral lending agencies proliferates (Dreher, Nunnenkamp, and Thiele 2011; Dreher et al. 2018; 2022; Cormier 2023a).

Studies considering the internal dynamics of multilaterals also focus on how these institutional characteristics inform the supply side of official credit flows. Bureaucratic structures (Weaver 2008; Winter et al. 2022), changes in internal governance (Best 2014), inertia of dominant economic ideas (Wade 2002; Babb 2013), or shifts in policy priorities (Rodrik 2006; Güven 2018; Kaya and Reay 2019; Cormier and Manger 2022) combine to determine allocation of capital by official creditors. These studies highlight how the supply of official credit and lending decisions may change, but not the extent to which the supply side is the primary driver of official flows. The emphasis on lender interests and preferences in explaining official flows is reminiscent of the emphasis on the supply side of sovereign debt markets in explaining capital flows.

1.4.4 Borrower Autonomy

These literatures imply a simple but important observation: EMs have external financing options. Within constraints that shape the supply of each option, how do EM governments decide how much market finance and how much official finance to use to meet their annual external borrowing needs?

Development studies have begun to recognize the importance of this question for understanding variation in the evolution of public debt structures across EMs over time. For example, the 'age of choice' has been used to refer to the fact that the expansion of bond markets has increased EM sovereign debt market access and the proliferation of official lenders simultaneously provides more concessional options (Prizzon, Greenhill, and Mustapha 2017). As EMs 'shop' among these options each year, questions emerge about how and why annual foreign borrowings vary (Humphrey and Michaelowa 2013).

And there is variation to explain. Figure 1.1 above showed aggregate mixing of official and market financing in EMs. Figure 1.4 plots the annual foreign borrowings of four EMs from 1988 to 2016. Thailand, South Africa, Botswana, and Peru are representative of the variation in EM annual external borrowings observed across the EM asset class, presented here because they are the subject of this book's

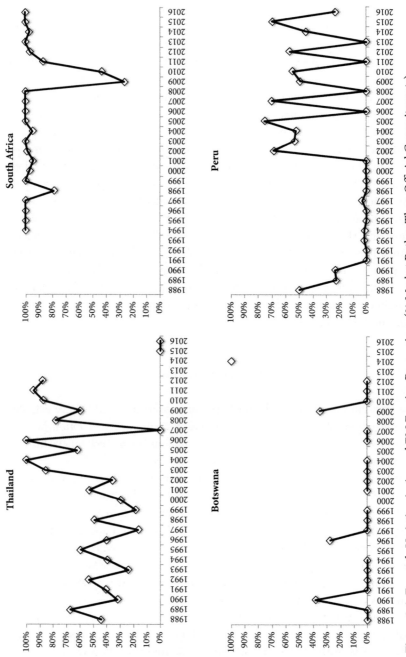

Figure 1.4 Example Variation in Annual EM Foreign Borrowings (% Market Rather Than Official Commitments)

Source: World Development Indicators and author's calculations

comparative case study chapters. Figures 3.1, 3.2, and 3.3 in Chapter 3 further detail variation in annual and over-time borrowing strategies within and between EMs across regions when setting up quantitative empirical tests.

As detailed throughout the book, this variation cannot be simply explained by sovereign risk, institutional characteristics such as governance quality or institutional capacity, regime type, default or crisis histories, structural factors like US interest rates, or relationships with major official creditors. To the extent that these supply side factors that are so central to IPE models of sovereign debt do not fully explain observed borrowings, the variation in the debt instruments that actually do and do not end up on government balance sheets implies significant variation in borrowing preferences among agents on the demand side of sovereign debt. In short, the data signals EM sovereigns have some significant degree of autonomy when borrowing externally. Just as Tomz (2007, 12–17) argues domestic politics inform heterogenous sovereign debt repayment preferences, it is likely that domestic politics inform variation in how EMs use their autonomy when making annual borrowings in the first place.

Most work on borrower autonomy exists in the IMF literature. Well-known studies argue that ideological alignment between the IMF and a government increases the likelihood that a government will borrow from the IMF. Seminal work on two-level games in international relations includes a discussion of how 'conservative' borrowers will use the IMF as both a scapegoat and enforcement mechanism for implementing economic policies that may otherwise be politically difficult to implement (Putnam 1988, 457). This argument has been extended in empirical work on the IMF (Vreeland 2003; Nelson 2017), both the IMF and World Bank (Woods 2006), and Western official creditors as a whole (Bunte 2019). Others highlight the importance of borrower preferences regarding transparency and subsequent effects on official credit flows (Cormier 2023a; Mosley and Rosendorff 2023).

While contributing importantly to our understanding, this strand of research typically has a narrow focus, analyzing the relationship between a potential borrower and official lenders. The role of and implications for other options available to EMs seeking external finance, particularly market-based financing options, is scoped out from the analysis. There are two notable exceptions. One suggests that governments backed by labor-based coalitions also prefer to avoid market finance (Bunte 2019), but this implies that different right and left-leaning coalitions ultimately share some of the same preferences. Another highlights the importance of global interest rates in borrowing decisions (Zeitz 2022), making crucial points about structural factors, so leaving the parsing of domestic political factors aside. Together, IPE can say more about when countries are likely to use proportionally more market-based finance vis-à-vis official options to meet their external borrowing needs.

1.5 Partisan Borrowing and Debt Accumulation: The Theory in Brief

This book theorizes why and illustrates how partisan politics in a borrower inform the demand side of sovereign debt. It does this by building a model of how EM borrowing decisions are made as part of the annual fiscal policymaking process, then identifying how partisan politics significantly affect external borrowings through that process. Procedurally, partisan politics are inherent in EM borrowing processes and decisions because annual budgetary financing plans must be ratified by partisan political leaders. Politically, the partisan effect is that EM governing parties with working classes as core constituencies, and associated left-leaning policy preferences, prefer market finance as a relatively 'quiet' exit option from controversial official creditor conditionalities.

This section summarizes the importance of class politics in EMs, the relationship between class constituencies and a party's economic policy preferences, and why these politics inform a governing party's external borrowing preferences. It then discusses the multiple empirical methods used in the book to test the argument. The full model and theory of partisan external public debt accumulation in EMs is elucidated in Chapter 2 then quantitatively and qualitatively tested in Chapters 3-6.

1.5.1 Class, Partisanship, and Borrowing

Class-based political cleavages are particularly salient in EMs. As poor countries grow enough to have diverse economies, 'the class content of politics also grows, as both capital becomes more powerful and an emerging working class is likely to assert its rights' (Kohli 2004, 416). In recent decades the salience of class cleavages in EM politics have only been reified by intensifying inequality, stemming in part from hollowing out of sectors that would be the sources of broad-based and inclusive growth and employment (Rodrik 2016). This helps explain why one effect of decades of globalizing, integrative economic policies has been that developing country politics are organized around class interests: '[developing country citizens] mobilize along income/social class lines [because the effects of the] globalization shock takes the form mainly of trade, finance, and foreign investment' (Rodrik 2017, 2). Put differently, 'the political battles [stemming from] globalization will be primarily perceived as distributional and fought as . . . battles between those elites well-situated to compete and thrive in the global economy versus those "common folk" losing ground and left behind' (Franzese 2019, 15).[8] The intensity

---

[8] This quote is used to theorize about trade policy preferences. So while not specifically about sovereign borrowing, it helps capture the salience of distributional class-based politics and that these cleavages underpin foreign economic policy preferences around the world and across policy areas.

of these class-based political cleavages, and further fragmentation within them, help explain the lack of broad political coalitions that would be necessary for EMs to upgrade their economies and escape the 'Middle Income Trap' (Doner and Schneider 2016).

Where class politics are so salient, it follows that the class constituencies of a governing party inform a government's policy preferences. For governing parties to be responsive to the material interests of their core class constituencies, they pursue 'partisan' policies that provide distributional benefits for those classes (Garrett 1998; Franzese 2002). The link between class and party policy preferences is typically shorthanded by distinctions between left-leaning and right-leaning parties. While a left–right spectrum cannot fully capture the complexities of a party's policy platform (Rudra and Tobin 2017, 296) the class constituents of a party underpin essential differences in economic policy preferences and ideologies. These partisan distinctions help explain not only various aspects of sovereign debt (Ballard-Rosa, Mosley, and Wellhausen 2022; Beazer and Woo 2016; Barta and Johnston 2018), but also foreign and domestic policy in other areas of the economy outside of the rich world (Bodea, Bagashka, and Han 2019; Pinto 2013; Murillo 2002). Generally applied across such various economic policy areas, left parties represent groups dependent on wage labor, unions, government spending, and state intervention in various markets for protection from adjustments and promotion of economic equality. Right parties represent capital-owning groups who prefer that policy prioritize economic efficiency and stability over other possible priorities, with reducing the role of state intervention in the economy a key component of such policy preferences.

A central argument of this book is that EM external borrowing preferences are informed by these class interests and corresponding economic policy preferences. Left-leaning governing parties with working classes as core constituencies should be likely to avoid official lenders whose conditions expose working classes to negative adjustments in practice and in reputation. Official loans conditional on fiscal discipline, debt reduction, labor market flexibility and competition, privatization, or integration with various global or lender markets and firms all expose working classes to more negative economic adjustment than capital-owning classes. Accordingly, left-leaning governments representing these groups should be likely to use proportionally more market-based finance because it is comparatively condition free. In this sense, markets provide an exit option or 'silent' borrowing option compared to official creditors whose immediate and legally binding conditions would force overt adjustment on the governing party's core constituencies and likely produce a political backlash on governing policymakers. In the anticipation that official creditor conditions will limit policy autonomy and adjust policy from core preferences, left governments reflexively prioritize markets as a means of avoiding these political risks.

In contrast, right-leaning governments are not as likely to resist official creditors that condition loans on such adjustments. These are policies that wealthier classes and right-leaning governments prefer in the first place. And, insofar as capital values public debt sustainability, official creditors also serve that objective with lower interest rates and longer maturities than market-based financial sources. For these governments, because they anticipate official creditor conditions will not significantly adjust policies from what they would otherwise be, they do not reflexively avoid official creditors when making annual borrowings as much as left-leaning governments.

This does not mean discipline never exists in EM sovereign debt markets. If highly indebted around elections, borrowers may interpret investor preferences as conditions and change behavior (Kaplan 2013; Kaplan and Thomsson 2017). But this would be an exception that proves the more general rule. While investors monitor a few macroeconomic indicators in developing countries (Mosley 2003, chap. 4), these generally shape prices rather than the very availability of finance. This is an important distinction, as higher prices do not mean a country cannot or will not borrow (Beaulieu, Cox, and Saiegh 2012, 710). Outside of crises, moral hazard and the search for yield ensure markets are often all too willing to invest even when imprudent (Jeanne and Zettelmeyer 2001; Reinhart and Rogoff 2009; Rey 2015; Naqvi 2019). This book's partisan model of public debt accumulation highlights how and why even disciplinary bond prices or risky credit ratings will not necessarily keep EMs from using to bonds to finance their government, should partisan politics incentivize such borrowing decisions.

1.5.2 Methods

The book details this partisan external EM borrowing thesis in Chapter 2, then uses multiple methods to test the argument. Econometric hypothesis testing in Chapter 3 tests the generalizability of the thesis across EMs. Chapters 4–6 use four comparative case studies to trace how EM DMOs are constrained, through annual fiscal policymaking processes, by partisan politics.

The model of public debt accumulation in Chapter 2 provides observable implications for quantitative hypothesis testing in Chapter 3. If government partisanship affects annual external borrowings in the theorized way, we should see greater shares of external borrowings coming from market sources than official creditors in years where left-leaning governing parties with working-class core constituencies are in power. Chapter 3 uses shares of annual external borrowings from market and official creditors as the dependent variable, then models these as functions of governing party class constituencies using the Varieties of Parties dataset (Lührmann et al. 2020) and governing party ideology using the Database of Political Institutions (Beck et al. 2001). Across a variety of models and specifications controlling for national economic fundamentals, borrower institutional features, and structural factors, the more important working classes are to an EM's governing party the more the EM uses markets to fulfill its external borrowing needs each year. In contrast, the more important elite economic constituencies are to an EM's governing party the more they use official credit to fulfill their annual external borrowing needs.

Chapters 4–6 then qualitatively test the model through four case studies. The cases trace the causal process by which a partisan effect on external borrowing takes place, emphasizing the importance of seeing borrowings as part and parcel of the annual fiscal policymaking process. The chapters illustrate how and why EM DMOs, the ministerial institutions ostensibly responsible for sovereign borrowing, can only borrow from the external sources that partisan politicians will approve. It is through the annual fiscal policymaking process that EM DMOs are significantly constrained by partisan politics, leading to partisan effects on EM external debt accumulation each year and the composition of sovereign debt structure over time.

The four cases are Botswana, Peru, South Africa, and Thailand, selected for a variety of reasons. First, they exhibit variation on the dependent variable (see Figure 1.4). Second, they do so in ways that counter expectations given other characteristics. For example, as discussed in Chapter 4, South Africa was seen as much less creditworthy than Botswana in the decades following the end of Apartheid. Yet South Africa almost strictly used market instruments while Botswana almost strictly used official creditors. In other words, the annual and over time public debt accumulation patterns observed in these countries in recent decades do not simply reflect the economic characteristics that inform sovereign risk assessments. Instead, their sovereign external borrowings were primarily a function of differences in government partisanship.

Other cases then investigate instances of within-unit changes in government partisanship. In Chapters 5 and 6, the Peru and Thailand cases show that external borrowings shift as government partisanship shifts. In addition, these cases vary on the dimension of regime type, providing evidence that the partisan political economy of borrowing applies across democratic regimes, unprogrammatic or one-party regimes, and post-coup military regimes. Accounting for a variety of other factors, external borrowing preferences in EMs are shown to be significantly determined by the need for the government to borrow in ways that have material benefits for, or at least do not give rise to new constraints and adjustments on, the core partisan constituencies of the governing party. EM DMOs are significantly constrained by these politics when they borrow each year.

The case studies are informed by around one hundred interviews, most of which took place during fieldwork in 2017. Most of the time in-country was spent interviewing debt managers, other finance ministry officials, central bankers, politicians, multilateral and bilateral bank staff, as well as foreign and domestic bankers and asset managers. Fieldwork also allowed for the collection of primary documents, like debt management strategies or minutes of meetings, which often are not available online or in digital format.

Interviewees were recruited over the course of three months in each region. I first contacted each DMO directly. I was able to speak with the entire current DMO staff in each country and many former DMO staffers. I then contacted World Bank, IMF, and regional development bank staff that research each country and manage each institution's financial relationship with each country. I was able to speak with current staff and former staff across these institutions in each case. On the DMO and official creditor side, then, the interview sample is representative of the relevant actors. I then asked for introductions to bankers and asset managers that hold each country's sovereign debt (as well as reaching out directly once learning of the primary dealers and other banks central to the country's sovereign debt market). This sample may be less complete because the size of the finance industry varies across countries and has extensive external linkages— but I was able to speak with primary dealers, domestic bankers, and international bankers that hold each country's bond debt. Interviews concentrated on identifying their institution's relationship with a given country's DMO, their view of the government's annual sovereign borrowing decisions and debt structure trajectory, their view of the DMO's debt management strategy given the accumulated debt structure, their views on the creditworthiness of the borrower and the extent to which this informed capital allocation decisions, and the effect of political parties on these themes over time.

Interviews were primarily semi-structured. I entered each session with six to eight open-ended questions designed to get interviewees talking about these main themes (Harvey 2011, 434; Aberbach and Rockman 2002), then listened for whether and why political factors (partisan and otherwise) did and did not explain the history of sovereign debt accumulation in the country. In instances where interviewees could not meet in person or talk on the phone, fully structured email questionnaires with a list of specific issues were used. In this book's case study chapters, core arguments rely on pieces of information corroborated by multiple interviewees. Illustrative quotes are used where they are particularly helpful for capturing widely corroborated views and arguments. Where there is disagreement or an inability to widely corroborate key events, these are used in supplementary discussions and not used as central pieces of information in favor of any arguments. This avoids biased use of evidence that can seep into interview-based research.

Taken together, this sampling and interview strategy meets standards advocated for in methodological texts on interview-based political science research (Mosley 2013). Given the interest in tracing the *process* by which a generalizable and quantitatively-tested argument takes place, the nonrandom selection of 'elite' subjects for in-depth interviews is a feature rather than a bug of these qualitative chapters (George and Bennett 2004; Tansey 2007). The interview table in the appendix is a truncated version of recommendations for transparent interview tracking and reporting (Bleich and Pekkanen 2013). A full interview table, including interviewees who turned down interviews, is available from the author on request.

1.6 Implications of Partisan External Sovereign Debt Accumulation in EMs

A partisan model of external EM sovereign debt accumulation has several implications. For the IPE of sovereign debt these include: (1) highlighting limits to models of capital flows to EM sovereigns strictly based on market discipline of a borrowing government's political constituencies and policy preferences; (2) reframing how countries outside of the rich world perceive and pursue policy autonomy when navigating globalized sovereign debt markets and official creditor options; and (3) helping explain variation in EM sovereign debt structures by illustrating the role of borrower partisanship. A partisan model of EM public debt also has implications for public administration and the comparative political economy of development by: (4) specifying how the role and effect of DMOs likely varies on particular dimensions and in different areas of the national balance sheet; and (5) exemplifying how models of the role and effect of institutions and ministries in one area of a country's macroeconomy are not easily comparable to the role and effect of institutions and ministries responsible for governing other areas of the macroeconomy. This last implication stems from identifying how different state institutions hold different positions in their respective policymaking processes, meaning they face different political and economic constraints in executing their technocratic mandates. These implications provide suggestions for future research not only on EM sovereign debt but on the relationship between political interests, institutions, and macroeconomic policy outcomes more broadly. These points are discussed in turn before outlining the plan for the book.

1.6.1 Demand-Side Limits to Market Discipline of Government Partisanship in Sovereign Debt

The first implication is that annual external borrowings, namely the degree to which EMs use and thus bring more or less market and official external finance onto national balance sheets, are not strictly determined by creditworthiness or supply-side factors. Creditor constraints on capital flows to developing country governments are of course important, but cannot fully explain variation in the composition of external debts that are and are not ultimately added to government balance sheets each year. The demand side of sovereign debt is also a significant factor. This is because partisan politics, through annual fiscal policymaking processes, affect the financing options governments prioritize when meeting their annual foreign borrowing needs. These options, in turn, shape the cost and policy benefits, constraints, and risks governments accrue through their borrowings over time. The point that annual financial flows to EM governments, and subsequent variation in sovereign debt structure across EMs over time, cannot be separated from the borrower's domestic politics highlights that borrower autonomy—the demand side—is essential to account for in models of sovereign debt.

The partisan argument leads to the related point that there are limits to the role of disciplinary capital allocation in sovereign debt markets based on government policy preferences. All else equal, 'conservative' governments do not use proportionally more market finance and 'left-leaning' governments do not use markets less. Even if markets increase prices for policies they dislike, EM sovereigns will still borrow at that higher price if domestic partisan politics incentivize them to do so. Left-leaning governing parties are thus likely to accumulate comparatively more market-based finance than other EMs, which disciplinary economic models of globalized sovereign debt cannot easily explain.

1.6.2 Borrower Autonomy in Models of Market and Official Credit Flows

Second and relatedly, how EMs use their autonomy when borrowing externally has implications for the international political economy of finance. A core trade-off EMs face when borrowing abroad is between optimizing costs and prioritizing policy autonomy. Perhaps paradoxically, since some EM governments prefer markets as an exit option from cheaper-but-conditional official creditors, this means markets provide relative autonomy in contrast to financial arrangements with various multilateral or powerful bilateral creditors. This reframes foundational IPE questions about the conditions under which developing countries obtain, or the ways in which developing countries attempt to obtain, autonomy in an open and integrated financial system.

Traditionally, debt markets are seen to imply a loss of policy autonomy and lead to political backlash by those losing out from the policy response to market incentives (for a thorough review of this in the sovereign debt context, applicable across rich and developing settings, see Mosley 2003, chap. 1). But as this book illustrates, EM sovereign debt markets provide borrowing governments relative autonomy at the time of borrowing and in the short term, even if at a comparatively higher material cost. In this sense, the characteristics of modern sovereign debt markets implicitly reify how international financial institutions and powerful bilateral lenders continue to represent controversial infringements on autonomy outside of the rich world (Krasner 1985). EM governments will sometimes prefer to make forms of payment (in the external borrowing context, accepting higher costs and taking on shorter maturities when borrowing externally) to avoid the policy adjustments and political implications associated with the official international financial architecture. This reframing provides clearer insight into the political opportunities and costs contemporary financial markets and international financial organizations present to citizens and governments in countries with regular access to both.

Highlighting that developing country governments have a degree of autonomy when borrowing, and the importance of the politics that inform behavior given that space, also has implications for research on official credit. Outside of crises, official credit flows are not strictly a function of a sovereign's inability to access markets. Yet studies often use this premise to model official lending. This book provides further evidence (Bunte 2019; Humphrey and Michaelowa 2013; Zeitz 2022) that research on official credit cannot study official flows in isolation from markets, nor assume official credit flows are merely an inverse function of a country's creditworthiness (particularly outside of IMF lender-of-last-resort loans). IPE can account for these points by consistently incorporating borrower politics and preferences in theoretical and empirical models, and accounting for the availability of market instrument substitutes in models of official lending.

1.6.3 The Politics of Borrower Preferences and EM Sovereign Debt Accumulation

The third implication is to explain how and why partisan politics have a significant effect on sovereign debt accumulation and the composition of external debt structures outside of the rich world. In this sense the book adds to a growing literature on sovereign borrower preferences. A main contribution in this context is to provide an alternative view on the relationship between left-leaning governments and sovereign debt markets (Bunte 2019).[9]

Bunte's well-received book and this study share the long-standing view that capital-oriented governments prefer many forms of official credit (see also Putnam 1988; Vreeland 2003; Woods 2006; Nelson 2017). Theoretical differences emerge, however, where that book argues labor prefers to avoid bond markets and private creditors. Reasoning that because 'workers disapprove of [repaying debts],' labor resists market finance that repays investors (Bunte 2019, 51). In contrast, this book argues that labor prefers market instruments due to the comparatively condition-free character of those instruments at the time of borrowing.

---

[9] And reason to question claims that left-leaning EM governments face such a significant and generalizable increased degree of difficulty tapping markets when implementing their preferred fiscal policies that they spend less (Kaplan and Thomsson 2017).

One reason the books have different theories of labor's borrowing preferences is different causal mechanisms. This book theorizes that partisan borrowing preferences emerge through the fiscal policymaking process. When fulfilling borrowing requirements under left-leaning governing parties, debt management bureaucrats are constrained by the government's macroeconomic policy preferences, fiscal and otherwise. DMOs must borrow from sources that will not infringe on the policy space required to use these policies to serve left-leaning constituents like labor, the poor, and the public sector. This roots this book in theories of class politics and economic policy preferences, shown to affect borrowing outcomes through a fiscal policymaking mechanism.

In contrast, that book employs a set of informed theoretical assumptions to identify coalitions' distributional interests and derive borrowing preferences. As noted, the assumptions yield some of the same theoretical expectations as this book, but also some different propositions. For example, varied assumptions about sensitivity to debt repayment implications over the short and long terms yield different claims about the left. For Bunte, workers disapprove of using private creditors because they resist the long term implications of repaying them. In contrast, industry is theorized to prefer market instruments because government benchmarking makes private credit cheaper. Taken together, labor's preferences are derived from long-term borrowing costs though other preferences are derived from short-term borrowing benefits, with a note that deriving labor's preferences is 'challenging' (Bunte 2019, 49–51). For future researchers, the point is that different causal mechanisms lead this book to propose different borrowing preferences than other recent studies. This and other differences (including, for example, different approaches to dependent variable construction) provide fertile ground on which further studies can improve our understanding of developing country sovereign borrowing decisions and patterns of sovereign debt accumulation.

1.6.4 The Role and Effect of DMOs

A fourth implication is that the book's model illustrates how and why EM DMOs face partisan constraints in their efforts to manage annual external borrowings and thus the composition of accumulated external sovereign debt over time. EM DMOs have limited ability to significantly alter key aspects of external public debt trajectories from politicians' preferences (compare with Sadeh and Porath 2020; Fastenrath, Schwan, and Trampusch 2017). This means that DMOs are likely more constrained in some areas of public debt management and less so in others. Models of DMO institutional effects on public debt likely depend, at least in part, on the area of sovereign debt being considered (i.e. the component of the national debt structure in question) and national income level (see Chapter 2 for discussion).

1.6.5 DMO Constraints as a Microcosm of Limits to Institutional Effects in the Macroeconomy

Finally, a related but broader fifth implication is to not only improve our understanding of the role that institutions do and do not have in managing public debt, but to signal paths for policy-relevant research on the relationship between macroeconomic institutions and domestic politics in developing countries. With respect to public debt management, the book's partisan model is relevant to international organizations, technocrats, and observers interested in how DMOs and related institutions may or may not affect public debt sustainability (Currie, Dethier, and Togo 2003; Wheeler 2004; von Hagen 2009; Kopits 2013; World Bank 2015b; International Monetary Fund and World Bank 2018a). By highlighting significant partisan constraints on external debt accumulation that inevitably emerge through the fiscal policymaking process, the book provides a framework for identifying EM public debt management best practices (such as transparency) that may be more politically feasible (Cormier 2023b).

Such policy-relevant implications depend on clear theorization of the relationship between political interests, bureaucratic institutions, and policy outcomes. Here, the book is an example of why models of the relationship between political interests and bureaucratic institutions in one policy area should not be assumed to be readily applicable to other policy areas (Wren-Lewis 2013). An obvious area of contrast is monetary policy. With nuances and caveats, it is widely held that central banks with institutional independence are delegated responsibility for monetary policy and thus achieve lower inflation levels than what politicians would pursue on their own (Bodea and Hicks 2015b; Cukierman 2008). Some have applied the same logic to public debt management. Delegating 'authority to individuals who are committed to . . . repaying debt' (Stasavage 2003, 2), such as a 'truly non-partisan and independent DMO' (Bertelsmann 2013, 90–91), can increase the borrowing government's credibility (Sadeh and Porath 2020) and significantly enhance public debt sustainability from what politicians would yield on their own (see also von Hagen 2013, 32–36; World Bank 2015b, 6–8, 13–14). Arriving at a similar view that debt management can be largely apolitical are those arguing that financialization of the state has made DMOs technical bureaucracies whose work is largely removed from political calculations and influence (Fastenrath, Schwan, and Trampusch 2017).

But this book shows that, because of the inevitable political constraints EM DMOs face given their position in the annual fiscal policymaking process, institutional models of independence and financialization are unlikely to capture the degree to which EM DMOs can apolitically manage important components of sovereign debt structure. This not only gives rise to questions about the role of institutions in enhancing public debt sustainability and what it means to 'govern' public debt, but also gives reason for new comparative research on the relationship between political interests and macroeconomic institutions in different areas of the macroeconomy. Chapter 7 further discusses these and other implications (see also Cormier 2021).

1.7 Outline of the Book

The rest of the book develops a partisan theory of external public debt accumulation by EM governments and tests its validity using multiple methods. Chapter 2 details the partisan theory of public debt accumulation in EMs, based on a novel model of how politics inevitably inserts itself into external borrowing decisions through the annual fiscal policymaking process. The chapter contrasts the partisan model with other models of the relationship between DMOs, political interests, and public debt outcomes. The discussion also considers the implications for wider political economy and public administration research on the relationship between bureaucracies, politics, and policy outcomes.

Chapter 3 presents statistical tests of the observable implications of Chapter 2's partisan model of EM sovereign external borrowing. The hypothesis is that the more left-leaning an EM government, the more they borrow from markets. The tests use the Varieties of Party dataset (Lührmann et al. 2020) as its main resource for coding government partisanship, capturing the importance of working classes to a governing party's constituency. The tests also use the Database of Political Institutions (Beck et al. 2001) dataset for government policy preferences. Models show that, controlling for supply-side push factors as well as the borrower's national political-economic features traditionally thought to pull more or less finance, government partisanship is a significant determinant of annual external borrowings by EM sovereigns. This chapter expands on findings in previous research (Cormier 2023c).

Chapter 4 compares annual fiscal policymaking processes and borrowing outcomes in South Africa and Botswana. These countries are helpful initial comparative tests of the book's theory because they have borrowed in ways that defy disciplinary expectations. Despite junk credit ratings, rising interest rates, and left-leaning governments, South Africa has almost strictly used bond markets rather than official creditors when meeting annual external borrowing needs. In contrast, despite investment grade credit ratings, repeated encouragement by investors to issue bonds, and a conservative government, Botswana has almost strictly used official credit when borrowing each year. The chapter illustrates how these annual borrowings and subsequently different public debt structures can only be explained by government partisanship. South Africa's left-leaning ANC uses markets to avoid conditional official loans that would constrain their policies and yield political backlash from constituents, despite markets being more expensive than official creditors. Meanwhile, Botswana's conservative government implements policies that official creditors prefer in the first place, so Botswana does not seek to avoid conditionality and is able to use official creditors' cheaper credit without risk of political backlash for loss of policy autonomy.

Chapter 5 presents the case of Peru, a valuable third case for two reasons. First, government partisanship changed multiple times over the timeframe of the study. This allows for a within-case comparison of partisanship's effects on foreign borrowings, adding to the between-case South Africa and Botswana comparison in Chapter 3. Second, the country's DMO is a unit within a notoriously independent and powerful bureaucratic 'island of efficiency' often credited for maintaining 'neoliberal' policies in many areas of Peru's economy despite the election of increasingly left-leaning governments since the early 2000s (Crabtree and Durand 2017, chap. 4). If this book's model of public debt accumulation is credible, the effect of government partisanship on external borrowing should persist despite these partisan shifts and an ostensibly influential and ideological DMO. The chapter shows this is the case. As Peru elected more left-leaning governments in recent decades, Peru's DMO was forced to use more market finance to meet its external borrowing needs despite its preference for official credit.

Chapter 6 presents the case of Thailand, a country with further within-unit change on many political and economic dimensions important to this study. For example, while government partisanship in Peru generally trended from right to left from 1990–2015, Thailand's governments oscillated between conservative and left-leaning populist parties. Moreover, some of these changes occurred not through democratic elections but through military coups, providing variation on regime type not only in comparison to the other cases but also over time within the same case. In addition, Thailand's central role in the Asian Financial Crisis makes it an important test for assessing whether and how major economic crises affect this book's partisan model of public borrowing. Finally, Thailand developed its domestic public bond market over this period, providing a financial resource for the state that could affect foreign borrowing strategies. Despite all of these points of variation, Chapter 6 shows how and why Thailand's annual external borrowings remained primarily informed by government partisanship.

The concluding chapter details more implications for research and policy, including: (1) setting demand-side limits to discipline of left-leaning governments in sovereign debt markets; (2) showing the politics of borrower autonomy—how governments use markets and official creditors—are at least as important to public debt accumulation and ensuing variation in public debt structures as supply-side factors; (3) suggesting the demand side helps contribute to the cyclicality of EM financial flows; (4) highlighting ways to clarify theorization and measurement in the IPE of sovereign debt; (5) advancing questions about (and suggestions for) politically feasible DMO effects on public debt structure and sustainability (such as transparency and diversification); (6) emphasizing the academic and practical importance of further research on deepening domestic public bond markets; (7) identifying how and why the role and effect of bureaucratic institutions like DMOs vary not only across different aspects of sovereign debt structure, but across different areas of macroeconomies.

2

Partisan Politics and Constrained Institutions

A Model of Sovereign Debt Accumulation in Emerging Markets

2.1 Introduction

This chapter presents a partisan model of sovereign debt accumulation in EMs, focused on external borrowings. It describes Debt Management Offices (DMOs) and identifies their role in annual fiscal policymaking processes. It theorizes about the partisan political constraints they face through this process when borrowing externally each year, then specifies observable implications to set up multi-method tests of partisan external borrowing in subsequent chapters. The chapter concludes by discussing how a partisan model contrasts with other models of the role of DMOs in public debt accumulation and management, with implications for literature on sovereign debt as well as comparative political economy more generally. These points and arguments are made in two sections.

The first half of the chapter provides the book's partisan model of EM borrowing and debt accumulation. It introduces DMOs by outlining their typical operations and mandates, the latter of which includes optimizing borrowing costs. It then positions DMO borrowing decisions within a government's broader annual fiscal policymaking process, which gives rise to partisan constraints on external borrowing decisions each year. Partisan constraints emerge through both initial budgetary decisions (setting what is in the budget) and veto control over final borrowing strategies (ratifying financing plans for each budget). The end of the section summarizes the model's observable implications for multi-method tests of its validity in Chapters 3–6.

The second half of the chapter locates this partisan model in literature on the relationship between DMOs, political interests, and sovereign debt structure. It argues that because DMOs have a relatively reactive role in the annual fiscal process—insofar as they must respond to and fund whatever expenditures and borrowing requirements emerge from politicians' budgets—political economy models of DMOs focused on institutional independence (Sadeh and Porath 2020; Sadeh and Rubinson 2018) or financialization of the state (Fastenrath, Schwan,

How Governments Borrow. Ben Cormier, Oxford University Press. © Ben Cormier (2024).
DOI: 10.1093/oso/9780198882732.003.0002

and Trampusch 2017; Trampusch 2019) are less applicable to EM external borrowings and debt composition than a partisan model.

On independence, for an institution to have politically independent effects on policy, the institution must be delegated enough control over that policy to make it different from what political principals prefer. In public debt, this would mean DMOs must have autonomy and 'institutional independence in designing the parameters of debt issuance' (Sadeh and Porath 2020, 745). But EM DMOs cannot obtain such independence when making external borrowing decisions. Procedurally, they are recipients of financing requirements and must borrow from sources that do not threaten those expenditures or otherwise limit the governing party's space to implement its preferred policies.

On financialization, for a DMO to be financialized it must shift away from 'financing decisions based on short-term expediency' toward portfolio management techniques organized around 'predominantly marketable debt instruments' (Fastenrath, Schwan, and Trampusch 2017, 4, Table 1). EM external debt does not necessarily reflect these characteristics. On the former, as detailed below, EM DMOs face partisan constraints on external borrowing choices. This means an EM DMO's external borrowings do not reflect a 'decline' in the 'political determination of credit' (Fastenrath, Schwan, and Trampusch 2017, 14). Instead, EM DMO external borrowing choices remain in the first instance largely a function of political expediency rather than other possible debt management priorities. On the latter, as detailed throughout the book, not all EM external borrowings are marketable instruments. First, EMs still use non-market instruments from official creditors. Second, not all EM foreign currency bonds are marketable with liquid secondary markets. A liquid secondary market for a country's debt is a key condition for truly financialized public debt management because secondary markets underpin most financial management techniques (Fastenrath, Schwan, and Trampusch 2017, 7). This leaves EM DMOs less 'financialized' than in the rich world, and thus the composition of external sovereign debt less 'financialized' than other areas of a government's debt structure.

In EM external public debt, a partisan model of accumulation captures the relationship between DMOs, politics, and borrowings better than models based on institutional independence or financialized states. This has implications for sovereign debt and broader political economy debates about the relationship between political interests, ministerial institutions, and economic policy outcomes. For sovereign debt, a partisan model of debt accumulation in the external areas of EM balance sheets adds to our understanding of the ways in which DMOs and politics interact to determine annual borrowings and ensuing public debt structures, highlighting how this varies by the component of debt structure or area of the national balance sheet under consideration.

Extrapolating out to broader political economy, how a partisan model contrasts with other models of DMOs exemplifies important dimensions on which the relationship between politics and bureaucracies varies across different policymaking contexts. Honing in on such dimensions can sharpen theorization of the relationship between bureaucratic institutions, political interests, and economic policy outcomes. This chapter gives two examples of this. First, the relationship between politics and institutions varies by the specific policymaking process in which they are interacting, and thus the specific outcome they are being theorized to affect. This may be true within policy areas (i.e. external rather than other components of sovereign debt structure) as well as across policy areas (i.e. the role of DMOs in debt management is not easily comparable to the role of central banks in monetary policy). Second, the relationship between politics and bureaucracies varies by national income level insofar as this reflects different positions in the global financial system and different degrees of access to various markets and international organizations. These implications are detailed in the chapter's concluding pages.

2.2 DMOs: A Primer

DMOs are the ministerial institutions responsible for planning and executing annual sovereign borrowings. They negotiate with various creditors each year then manage the effect of those accumulated debts over time. DMOs are typically located in finance ministries. In some developing countries, debt management functions may be spread across the finance ministry and the central bank. But even if scattered, debt managers have the same tasks (Ülgentürk 2017, n. 1). Most DMOs are organized according to these tasks. The front office is the DMO's portfolio management group, maintaining relationships with creditors. The middle office devises medium- and long-term strategies to manage debt risk over time. The back office serves an accounting role. Even if not formally cohered in such a structure in a country, the bureaucrats performing these functions are the state's debt managers (Wheeler 2004, 69–72; Williams 2013, 668).

A, if not the, primary DMO objective is 'to finance the government's borrowing needs . . . and to ensure that the government's debt-servicing obligations are met' (Wheeler 2004, 13). An essential link between annual borrowings and ability to service those debts when they come due is borrowing at the lowest possible cost at the time of borrowing, enhancing debt sustainability. Longer-term maturities also enhance sustainability, insofar as they minimize the rollover risks associated with high ratios of short-term repayment obligations. While other sovereign debt management priorities[1] mean DMOs may not solely focus on obtaining the lowest costs and longest maturities when borrowing, optimization of cost and maturity are unavoidably important for countries that rely on foreign currency borrowing: 'for many emerging market borrowers, the main debt management objective is to

---

[1] These may include prioritizing liquidity at certain points on the yield curve, issuing new debt instruments to reinforce monetary policy or encourage local currency bond market deepening (Wheeler 2004, 13), or in wealthy countries, actively managing the state's debt in an effort to generate profits (Wheeler 2004, 96; Trampusch 2019, 14).

obtain financing at a reasonable cost' (Wheeler 2004, 16). And even where other debt management priorities are present, DMOs are responsible for 'minimizing debt service costs' (Fastenrath, Schwan, and Trampusch 2017, 6) in terms of not only the lowest possible price (Hodula and Melecký 2020, 254) but also managing and often extending maturities (Sadeh and Porath 2020, 743–744). At its core, a DMO's 'job is to get capital at the lowest cost,' broadly defined (Gulati and Weidemaier n.d.).

The main reason DMOs get capital, or borrow, each year is to fund the annual borrowing requirement that emerges from annual budgets. At a minimum, this is the fiscal deficit, the annual difference between revenues and expenditures. Whatever budgetary expenditures cannot be covered by taxes, or alternative resources such as reserves, must be covered by new borrowings. While cash management, refinancing, benchmarking in a new market, or other DMO operations may bring debts on to national balance sheets that are not a direct function of fiscal policy, these are the exceptional operations that highlight how EM sovereigns mainly borrow to finance budgetary expenditures (World Bank 2015b, 10; Fatás et al. 2019).

This makes fiscal politics a necessary starting point for conceiving of not only public debt accumulation generally, but a DMO's role in and effect on public debt accumulation specifically. Annual financing needs are a function of budgets. The gap between revenues and expenditures, and the items on which government is spending money, cannot be easily affected by DMOs. Sequentially this makes DMOs recipients of, rather than shapers of, borrowing requirements. This implies the amount that needs to be borrowed each year, and the expenditures that need to be paid for with financing, are not easily affected by DMOs. DMOs must fund whatever borrowing requirement emerges from politicians' budgets. This makes both the annual increase in total debt a 'political decision' (World Bank 2015b, 8) and the level of outstanding debt over time a 'consequence of . . . fiscal policies . . . not under the control of debt managers' (Das et al. 2011, 365). DMOs may advise during budget deliberations, and projecting how budgets will affect public debt sustainability may alter fiscal policymakers' choices (Wheeler 2004, 31). But the degree to which providing such information and advisory input does or does not affect final budgets and financing requirements is at least partly a function of political will, which DMOs cannot force onto policymakers.

In the main, then, budgetary outcomes are logically prior to borrowings. This positions DMOs as largely reactive to the budgets produced by whatever fiscal politics characterize a country. To be sure, the politics of fiscal policy are complex (Alesina and Perotti 1995), depending on competing partisan interests and the political institutions in which these interests interact (Brender and Drazen 2005; Hallerberg, Scartascini, and Stein 2009). But eventually, regardless of the specific interests, institutions, and executive–legislative relations that combine to determine national budgetary outcomes, all fiscal policymaking processes yield some borrowing requirement, no matter how large or small and no matter what the expenditures are. Once governments get down to an amount that will be borrowed, this is where the decision of *how* to borrow, and the role of DMOs in the broader fiscal policymaking process, takes center stage.

2.3 DMOs, Government Partisanship, and EM External Debt: A Model and Hypothesis

Given this position in the fiscal process, EM DMOs face significant constraints when borrowing. Some constraints stem from the fact that DMOs cannot force fiscal policymakers to adjust budgets in the name of borrowing for different purposes or taking on less debt with smaller financing requirements. In this sense, the purpose and amount of sovereign debt accumulated annually is a political constraint on DMO management of debt structure each year and over time. Other constraints stem from the fact that DMOs must borrow from sources that do not adjust or threaten the items in those budgets, nor the policy preferences of the policymakers that made those budgets. In this sense, the borrowing strategies EM DMOs pursue each year, particularly when it comes to external borrowing as discussed below, are constrained by the political preferences of partisan policymakers.

A minimum set of political and economic constraints on EM DMOs are summarized in Figure 2.1 below. Two of these constraints are partisan and the emphasis of this book, because they constrain an EM DMO's annual external borrowing strategy. But these are not the only constraints DMOs face in managing annual public debt accumulation. This section discusses all constraints in Figure 2.1 in turn.

2.3.1 Debt Accumulation

Three constraints limit an EM DMO's ability to apolitically manage annual public debt accumulation—how much debt, and for what purposes, a sovereign borrows each year. DMOs cannot control the amount of debt government accumulates each year nor the expenditure items that need to be paid for with new borrowings. This passive role in debt accumulation is compounded by minimal or flexible fiscal and debt laws which often have little if any constraining effect on budgets. In addition, explicit and implicit guarantees can bring other obligations that a DMO did not coordinate or negotiate onto the government's balance sheet.

First, as discussed earlier, DMOs are recipients of, rather than shapers of, financing requirements given their role in the fiscal process. What is being borrowed for is not under the control of a DMO. For example, while a debt manager may hope that borrowing is only used to fund capital investment expenditures that promise to increase growth and thus pay for themselves over the long term,

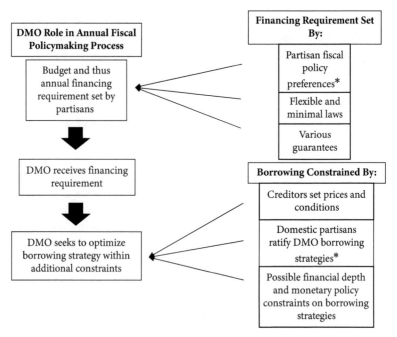

Figure 2.1 Model of Annual Sovereign Debt Accumulation and Borrowing in Emerging Markets

Note: * indicates the focus of this study

'real political agendas' mean 'the allocation of resources across spending programs is a political decision' and borrowing requirements 'are not wholly in line with [such] principles' in either rich or developing country contexts (Diamond and Potter 1999, 23–24).

Second, the direct relationship between fiscal politics and debt accumulation is often reinforced by the flexible nature of fiscal and debt laws in developing countries. It is possible that laws minimize the latitude politicians have when making budgets, placing a check on fiscal policy in the name of debt sustainability. This could indirectly reflect the interests of a DMO and implicitly constrain fiscal policy on its behalf. But in many developing countries fiscal and debt laws are either nonexistent, constantly altered, unenforceable, or otherwise 'poorly-designed' (Kopits 2001; Lledó and Poplawski-Ribeiro 2013; Eyraud et al. 2018), leading studies to find they have a procyclical rather than constraining effect on fiscal policy (Bova, Carcenac, and Guergil 2014). Flexible laws ultimately reinforce rather than limit the partisan political effects on debt accumulation over time.

Relatedly, while DMOs may set internal benchmarks for sustainable debt, many DMOs do not do so, many benchmarks are imprecise, and they are not enforceable. DMOs cannot point to technocratic benchmarks with any surety that they will alter politicians' fiscal preferences (Cabral 2015, 25). DMOs can hope benchmarks encourage policymakers to take debt risks into consideration during budget deliberations, but again, whether or not DMO benchmarks alter fiscal policy and debt accumulation remains up to the preexisting political will of policymakers themselves. Moreover, revenue challenges that emerge independent of expenditure decisions can undermine even sincere governing party efforts to adhere to sustainable fiscal policy principals, particularly in developing economies (Besley and Persson 2014).

Third, guarantees granted by politicians to public or private sectors put further pressure on public debt that DMOs cannot easily control. At best, guarantees are explicit and increase debt with the DMO's knowledge. But often guarantees are implicit and DMOs may not be informed of them until after the debt is incurred. Even where guarantee processes are formal and transparent, it is difficult for a DMO to do more than rely on politicians' accountability in keeping use of guarantees minimal (see Ülgentürk 2017). While the effects of guarantees on debt accumulation is not necessarily a function of partisanship, they are important for painting a full picture of the political constraints DMOs face.

2.3.2 Borrowing Strategies

Three additional constraints limit a DMO's ability to apolitically manage the composition of sovereign debt structure. These constraints emerge at the point of making annual borrowing decisions. Given a financing requirement once the budget is set, DMOs are tasked with devising a borrowing strategy to fund that financing requirement. But DMOs cannot design borrowing strategies independent of political constraints. Without preexisting political will, developing country DMOs cannot simply borrow from the sources it sees as most cost-effective or risk-optimal. This is true in both external and domestic borrowing, in various ways.

First, with all the important limitations and caveats noted in Chapter 1, global financial markets constrain developing country market access to some extent (Mosley 2003, chap. 4) while international political relationships affect developing country access to official multilateral (Clark and Dolan 2021; Dreher, Sturm, and Vreeland 2015; Lim and Vreeland 2013) and bilateral (Dreher, Nunnenkamp, and Thiele 2011) creditors. These supply-side forces mean that, aside from ensuring technical operations are sound, EM DMOs may have little effect on the price, volume, or conditions of the external finance that markets and official creditors do or do not make available to EMs.

The second constraint emerges when an EM DMO is deciding whether and how to mix the external financing options that are available. This book argues that partisan politics significantly constrain how DMOs prioritize these two options when meeting annual external financing requirements. These partisan constraints on borrowing strategies materialize through two parts of the annual fiscal process.

Initially, DMOs are constrained by the fact that they must use financial options that do not alter, limit, undermine, or somehow threaten the items that fiscal policymakers included in their budget before handing the financing requirement to the DMO. More generally, they cannot borrow from financial sources that would limit the government's space to implement policies that serve their core constituencies. This is particularly likely to limit a DMO's ability to use official creditors that include project and program conditions in their loans. The more budget items that official creditors would scrutinize, adjust, negotiate limits to, or simply not fund, the more DMOs must use markets to finance the budget. The more official project and program loan conditions would more generally threaten the government's ability to materially support their core partisan constituencies with their preferred policies beyond fiscal policy, the more DMOs must avoid those sources of finance and use comparatively condition-free market instruments. In turn, the more agreeable to official creditors a budget is, and the more agreeable official creditor project and program conditions are to a borrowing government across policy areas, the more a DMO is able to use official creditors without incurring political transaction costs.

Politics may also affect use of market finance in other, not necessarily partisan, ways. For example, politicians may only ratify borrowing at long-term maturities to avoid repayment, which markets may demand be floating rather than fixed rate and thus suboptimal for ensuring sustainable repayment plans (Wheeler 2004, 149, 173). Another example is that politicians may force DMOs to use a certain currency, affecting the nature of risks that emerge from foreign borrowing strategies over time (World Bank 2015b, 13–14). But in terms of the first-order decision to use either more official or more market finance to meet annual financing requirements, partisanship is a major constraint on EM DMO external borrowing strategies.

Later in the process, after borrowing strategies are devised, ministers and legislators retain ratification power (Melecky 2007, 3; World Bank 2015b, 7). DMOs are not left to independently execute borrowing strategies once they receive the annual financing requirement. Approval of borrowing strategies, often a component of agreements ratifying the overall budget and concluding the annual fiscal policymaking process, ensures political constraints on DMO borrowing strategies are formal as well as informal (as they may be earlier in the process).

These procedural constraints on DMOs are central to understanding where and how partisan politics consistently affect annual borrowings. The book's theory is based on the premise that governing policymakers have an interest in avoiding conditions that would constrain the policy space they have to serve their core political supporters. In other words, citizens (in democracies or other regimes) may or may not be aware of or have strong opinions about specific creditors and their implications (heuristic or otherwise). Bureaucrats and policymakers, however, are aware—particularly debt managers making borrowings, and governing party officials who must ensure they maintain the policy space necessary for serving their political base. By constraining policymaking through these ministerial and partisan actors, this partisan theory of borrowing does not depend on wide salience of borrowing options and trade-offs across citizens.[2] This is evident throughout the cases and interviews, and is why the theory prioritizes the fiscal policymaking process rather than direct pressure from citizens. This is also why the theory applies across regime types. Partisan borrowing constraints do not necessarily depend on direct electoral pressure that emerges from popular salience of these financial alternatives and implications (though, where present, this adds to the strength of the constraints). Instead, partisan borrowing constraints do necessarily depend on the constraints and opportunities that the different financing options present for ministerial bureaucrats and policymakers, which are effectual across democratic, competitive-hybrid, or authoritarian regimes (see Levitsky and Way 2010).

Third, borrowing may be constrained by the operations of other state institutions that do not prioritize debt sustainability. For example, central banks prioritizing monetary stability may advocate for issuing more foreign-denominated debt or more variable-rate debt because bearing this repayment risk would signal that the government is committed to low inflation (Aguiar et al. 2013, 9). DMOs would typically prefer to avoid this borrowing strategy (Blommestein and Turner 2012, 21–22). Such competing priorities between economic ministries became increasingly relevant as monetary policy tools reached their limits following the global financial crisis and the Covid-19 pandemic. While this is not necessarily a partisan issue and not the focus of this study, it is important to note this additional constraint on DMO control over borrowing operations.

Figure 2.1 summarizes these constraints in a model of annual EM sovereign debt accumulation. It is a stylized procedural depiction of the many ways in which DMOs, the ministerial institutions responsible for managing public debt, face significant and inevitable political constraints as borrowing decisions are made each year. These annual constraints ultimately constrain DMO control over the composition of (particularly external) sovereign debts accumulated over time. While not the only constraint, partisan politics are hypothesized to have a significant constraining effect in multiple parts of Figure 2.1. The next section defines partisanship and theorizes about this partisan effect on EM external borrowings in greater depth.

---

[2] Though, of course, where external borrowing politics are widely salient among the population, this only reinforces the partisan political constraints on borrowing identified in this book (see, for example, the popular salience of borrowing politics in the South Africa and Thailand cases in later chapters).

2.3.3 Partisan Politics

A governing party's policy preferences underpin variation in economic policy outcomes, even within domestic institutional and global economic constraints. These policy preferences are informed by the incentive to use office to serve constituents: 'competing parties cultivate strong ties to different groups . . . and nurture reputations for policy making that favors those groups and accords with their ideologies. Parties . . . value these partisan reputations and ties, so incumbents conduct recognizably distinct partisan policies, yielding appreciably distinct economic outcomes' (Franzese 2002, 391).

Central to partisan politics are the *class constituencies* of a political party and their economic policy preferences. Parties representing labor, the poor, and other working-class groups that depend on a role for the state in the economy such as the public sector, are associated with policies including expansive government spending, industrial policies, various market interventions in any number of policy areas, large public sectors, and union or other labor protections. Parties with capital-owners as core constituents are associated with policies that pursue economic efficiency and stability over other possible priorities, with reducing the role of state intervention in the economy a key vehicle for such policy aims.

As short-hand, these parties and constituencies are typically distinguished on a left-right spectrum (Garrett 1998; Franzese 2002). While this cannot fully capture the complexities of a party's policy platform (Rudra and Tobin 2017, 296) the class constituents of a party underpin essential differences in economic policy preferences. Class politics have been shown to explain not only various aspects of sovereign debt (Ballard-Rosa, Mosley, and Wellhausen 2022; Beazer and Woo 2016; Barta and Johnston 2018; Vreeland 2003) but policy variation throughout developing country economic policies. This includes partisan effects on labor market regulations (Murillo 2005), union protections (Murillo and Schrank 2005), privatization of state-owned enterprises (Murillo 2002), monetary policy (Way 2000; Bearce 2003), and openness to foreign direct investment (Pinto 2013). In turn, where they can, core constituencies will punish governing parties should they not implement their preferred economic policies (Bodea, Bagashka, and Han 2019; see also Lupu 2016). Insofar as governing parties must 'adopt . . . policies with concentrated effects on traditional supporters to keep their backing' (Murillo 2005, 441), partisanship identifies the policies that allow a party to serve and maintain its core class constituencies.

This link between class and economic policy is why government partisanship varies across regime types.[3] Left and right authoritarian governments

---

[3] Though of course certain aspects of partisan policymaking may be primarily applicable in democratic regimes (electoral cycles, for example).

promote the interests of different classes.[4] Influential research on 'competitive authoritarianism,' for example, highlights how competitive political pressures 'between autocrats and their opponents' implies the need for autocrats to serve core constituencies to remain in power (Levitsky and Way 2010, 54). In addition to coercion, party politics and control over economic policy are essential tools for autocrats that successfully stay in power (Levitsky and Way 2010, 61–68). Even the most authoritarian regimes 'generate cooperation . . . by making policy concessions' (Gandhi and Przeworski 2006, 2) because if the winning coalition in a country is small, policy concessions of some significance are necessary for serving those core constituents and surviving in office (Bueno de Mesquita et al. 2005, 10). In the end, leaders in democracies, nondemocracies, one-party democracies, or countries with unprogrammatic party politics must generate benefits for and cooperation from core class constituencies be they working classes or economic elites.

In EMs, class-based politics are particularly salient and partisanship sets key political cleavages. As poor countries grow enough to have diverse economies, 'the class content of politics also grows, as both capital becomes more powerful and an emerging working class is likely to assert its rights' (Kohli 2004, 416). In recent decades, the salience of material class distinctions in EM politics has only been reified by intensifying inequality, stemming in part from hollowing out of the sectors that would underpin broad-based and inclusive growth and employment (Rodrik 2016). This helps explain why one effect of decades of globalizing, integrative economic policies has been that developing country politics are organized around class interests: '[developing country citizens] mobilize along income/social class lines [because] the [effects of the] globalization shock takes the form mainly of trade, finance, and foreign investment' policies (Rodrik 2017, 2). Put differently, 'the political battles [stemming from] globalization will be primarily perceived as distributional and fought as . . . battles between those elites well-situated to compete and thrive in the global economy versus those "common folk" losing ground and left behind' in the economy (Franzese 2019, 15).

2.3.4 EM Partisanship and External Borrowings

Given the prominence of partisanship in EM politics, this book argues that partisanship significantly affects EM annual external borrowings. This is because external borrowings have different implications for different classes. The theory

---

[4] For example, the Database of Political Institutions ideology variable (Beck et al. 2001) identifies both left-leaning and right-leaning economic ideologies among EMs coded as nondemocracies in Polity. Left-leaning authoritarians include years in Algeria, China, Congo, Laos, Namibia, Turkmenistan, Tunisia, Uzbekistan, and Vietnam. Right-leaning authoritarians include years in Croatia, Kyrgyzstan, Lebanon, Nigeria, Peru, Paraguay, Russia, Senegal, and South Africa. Such lists are available from the author on request.

is as follows: left-leaning governing parties will prefer markets because they allow government to avoid official creditors whose project and program loan conditions would disproportionately adjust the position of their core working-class constituents. Right-leaning governing parties will not resist official creditors that condition loans on such adjustments, allowing them to take advantage of official creditors' below-market prices and longer maturities. DMOs, due to the partisan constraints that emerge through the annual fiscal policymaking process as depicted in Figure 2.1, will prioritize the external borrowing options preferred by the country's governing party when meeting annual external borrowing needs.

As detailed in the introductory chapter's borrowing menu section, each year EM governments identify an amount of finance they need to obtain from external sources. EMs can meet these external financing needs by using market sources (bond markets or commercial banks) or official sources (multilateral and bilateral lenders). Markets provide comparatively expensive but condition-free finance, while official creditors provide cheaper and longer-term but conditional finance (see Figures 1.2 and 1.3 and surrounding discussion). This means official and market financing options present different cost and policy implications, which affect working classes and economic elites in different ways. The politics of these borrowing decisions constrain EM DMOs because partisan policymakers, through multiple parts of the annual fiscal policymaking process illustrated in Figure 2.1, both informally incentivize and formally ensure that EM DMOs prioritize the external borrowing options that reflect the interests of their core partisan constituencies.

Left-leaning governing parties with working classes as core constituents should prefer to avoid official project and policy loan conditions that in practice and reputation expose working classes to negative adjustments. Project loans conditional on the borrower deregulating labor markets and weakening unions (Anner and Caraway 2010; Blanton, Blanton, and Peksen 2015; Isaksson and Kotsadam 2018b), introducing tied labor (Cervellati et al. 2022; Huang, Xu, and Mao 2018, 33, 242–243, 251; Mattlin and Nojonen 2015), privileging foreign firms (Kaplan 2021; Bunte 2019, 39), modifying to integrate with global and lender value chains (Sun et al. 2015; Prizzon, Greenhill, and Mustapha 2017; Dreher et al. 2018, n. 9), or implementing other production and employment changes in the domestic economy expose working classes to more negative adjustment than capital. Similarly, policy loans conditional on austerity and fiscal discipline, tax base expansion, debt reduction, privatization, labor market flexibility, and other macroeconomic adjustments that favor economic efficiency over other priorities also expose working classes in the borrower to more negative adjustment than economic elites (Cormier and Manger 2022; Kentikelenis, Stubbs, and King 2016b; Caraway, Rickard, and Anner 2012; Rodrik 2006; Babb 2013).[5]

---

[5] To minimize repetitive discussion, please see Chapter 1 for a detailed analysis of project and policy conditionality across different official multilateral and bilateral lenders.

Accordingly, left-leaning governments representing working classes should be likely to use proportionally more market-based finance because it is comparatively condition free. In this sense, markets provide an exit option from, or 'silent' borrowing option compared to, official creditors whose immediate and legally binding conditions would force adjustment on the governing party's core constituencies and produce negative political repercussions for policymakers. In contrast, right-leaning governments should be unlikely to resist official creditors that condition loans on such adjustments. Wealthier classes and right-leaning governments prefer these policies in the first place and, insofar as capital values debt sustainability, official creditors serve that objective with lower interest rates and longer maturities than markets.

This theory provides observable implications: the more important working classes are to an EM governing party's core political constituency, the more government should use market instruments rather than official creditors to fulfil their annual external borrowing needs. This leads to the following testable hypothesis, evidence of which would suggest the partisan model of EM sovereign borrowing and debt accumulation is applicable across EMs:

H1: All else equal, EM governments with working classes as core constituencies and left-leaning economic policy preferences use a greater proportion of market-based finance to meet annual external borrowing needs.

The following chapters present a multi-method test of *H1*. Chapter 3 uses econometric hypothesis testing to probe the generalizability of the thesis across EMs. It uses the Varieties of Party dataset (Lührmann et al. 2020) as the primary government partisanship variable, capturing the importance of the working classes to a governing party. It also uses the Database of Political Institutions (Beck et al. 2001) to code government policy preferences. Hypothesis tests yield robust evidence in favor of *H1*, controlling for supply-side factors as well as borrower economic and political features traditionally thought to pull or push more or less finance to EM sovereigns.

Chapters 4–6 use comparative case studies to trace the process through which partisanship affects external borrowing in EMs. These provide qualitative evidence of the applicability of the model presented above, and the causal mechanism by which we can understand the statistical relationships identified in Chapter 3.

Chapter 4 compares South Africa and Botswana, neighboring EMs that have historically borrowed in ways that defy typical expectations. Despite junk credit ratings, high interest rates, and left-leaning governments, South Africa almost strictly used bond markets rather than official creditors when meeting annual foreign borrowing needs from the 1990s through the mid-2010s. In contrast, despite investment grade credit ratings, repeated encouragement by investors to issue bonds, and a conservative government, Botswana almost strictly used official credit when borrowing abroad in this period. These annual borrowings and sub-sequently different external sovereign debt structures can only be explained by government partisanship. South Africa's left-leaning ANC used markets to avoid conditional official loans that would constrain their policies, despite markets being more expensive than official creditors. Meanwhile, Botswana's conservative gov-ernment implemented policies that official creditors prefer in the first place, so Botswana did not avoid conditionality and used cheaper and longer-term official credit without risk of political repercussions for loss of policy autonomy.

Chapter 5 covers Peru, an important third case for two reasons. First, govern-ment partisanship changed multiple times in the timeframe of this study, allowing a within-case comparison of partisanship's effects on foreign borrowings that expands beyond Chapter 4's between-case comparison of Botswana and South Africa. Second, the country's DMO is a unit within a finance ministry notorious for being a powerful 'island of efficiency' that promotes 'neoliberal' policies in many areas of Peru's economy despite the election of increasingly left-leaning govern-ments since the early 2000s (Crabtree and Durand 2017, chap. 4). Illustrating the generalizability of this book's partisan model of sovereign debt accumulation, the effect of government partisanship on external borrowing persisted in Peru despite an ideological and otherwise influential ministry.

Chapter 6 covers Thailand, another case of within-unit change on many impor-tant dimensions. While government partisanship in Peru trended from right to left from 1989 to 2015, Thailand's governments switched between left and right parties through democratic elections as well as military coups. Thailand's role in the Asian Financial Crisis also makes it an important case for considering the effect of major crises on external borrowing decisions and public debt accumu-lation. Thailand also developed its domestic public bond market in this period, providing a financial resource for the state that could alter the partisan effect on external borrowing strategies. Chapter 6 shows Thailand's annual foreign borrow-ings remained informed by government partisanship despite these regime type, domestic financial depth, and crisis factors.

2.4 Implications for Sovereign Debt and Political Economy

Insofar as this partisan model and hypothesis withstand multi-method tests in sub-sequent chapters, it has implications for interdisciplinary sovereign debt research as well as political economy research on the relationship between political inter-ests, state institutions, and economic policy outcomes.

With respect to sovereign debt, one implication is to highlight the extent to which EMs have autonomy when borrowing externally and to specify that use of this autonomy depends on government partisanship. This sets limits to disciplinary assumptions and arguments in the sovereign debt literature. While supply-side factors constrain capital flows to developing country governments, these cannot fully explain variation in the composition of external debts that are and are not ultimately added to government balance sheets each year. The demand side of sovereign debt, namely variation in preferences across borrowing governments, is also a significant a factor. In relation to other work emphasizing the demand side of sovereign debt and effects on debt structure, a partisan theory of EM external borrowing preferences counters arguments that developing country governments representing labor avoid markets when they borrow (Bunte 2019) while controlling for the extent to which global liquidity can affect the decision to use official or market finance (Zeitz 2022). It also adds to work on how partisanship affects the currency composition of public debt (Ballard-Rosa, Mosley, and Wellhausen 2022).

With respect to comparative political economy more generally, the model has implications for literature on the role and effect of ministerial institutions (such as DMOs) on economic policy. In the narrow context of sovereign debt and questions about the effect of DMOs on sovereign debt structure, the implication is that DMOs are unlikely to have similar effects across all areas of public debt. In the context of broader literature on the relationship between political interests, ministerial institutions, and economic policy outcomes, the implication is to suggest specific dimensions on which the relationship between interests, institutions, and policy outcomes may be expected to vary. These two implications for political economy theory and research on the role of institutions are discussed in turn here.

2.4.1 Institutions in Sovereign Debt

Because DMOs have a relatively reactive role in the fiscal policymaking process as summarized in Figure 2.1, political economy models of DMOs emphasizing institutional independence (Sadeh and Porath 2020; Sadeh and Rubinson 2018) or financialization of the state (Fastenrath, Schwan, and Trampusch 2017; Trampusch 2019) are less applicable to EM external borrowings and debt structure than this chapter's partisan model.

On independence, for institutions to have politically independent effects on policy, the institutions must be delegated enough control over that policy to make it different from what political principals prefer. Applied to public debt, a DMO with 'institutional independence in designing the parameters of debt issuance' would be 'less focused on the short term compared to politicians' so borrow differently than politicians would prefer (Sadeh and Porath 2020, 745). Such apolitical borrowing may mean democracies with autonomous DMOs have better credit ratings because 'DMO autonomy increases credibility' (Sadeh and Rubinson 2018, 42). Other studies do not consider variation in DMO autonomy but note DMO autonomy is international policy advice that has gained traction across most developing country government debt managers and institutions (Ballard-Rosa, Mosley, and Wellhausen 2022, 36).

But EM DMOs cannot obtain such stark political independence, at least in the context of making annual external borrowing decisions. Procedurally, they are recipients of financing requirements and must borrow from sources that will not adjust or threaten policymaker preferences. Identifying procedurally determined constraints on DMOs can help sharpen theorization and subsequent studies of the role of institutions in sovereign debt accumulation and management. Perhaps, for example, DMOs have more control over some aspects of debt accumulation (currency composition and maturities, as suggested in the above literature) than others (annual financing requirements and external borrowing decisions, as theorized in this chapter).

On financialization, for a DMO to be financialized it must shift away from 'financing decisions based on short-term expediency' and manage 'predominantly marketable debt instruments' (Fastenrath, Schwan, and Trampusch 2017, 4, Table 1). But EM external debt does not reflect these characteristics. On the former, the partisan constraints on EM DMO external borrowing strategies mean these external borrowings do not represent a 'decline' in the 'political determination of credit' (Fastenrath, Schwan, and Trampusch 2017, 14) but are largely a function of DMOs working within first-order political constraints. On the latter, many EM borrowings are not market-based instruments because they have access to official creditors. Moreover, not all bonds issued by EMs are marketable instruments with liquid secondary markets (Fastenrath, Schwan, and Trampusch 2017, 7). This suggests that, in addition to varied DMO effects on different components of debt accumulation, it is also likely that the effect of DMOs on public debt varies by national income level, as this reflects a sovereign's position in global financial markets and access to international organizations.

2.4.2 Institutions in Comparative Political Economy

Extrapolating out from the narrow DMO and sovereign debt relationship, this discussion has implications for broader comparative political economy theory and research on the relationship between political interests, ministerial institutions, and economic policy outcomes. One implication is that the interaction between interests and institutions is not easily comparable across economic policy areas, despite a tendency to apply similar models across different contexts. For example, while 'authors have used the apparent success of independent central banks to argue a similar idea can be applied to fiscal policy' (Wren-Lewis 2013, 54), this book's argument illustrates the ways in which such efforts may lead to mis-identifying or mistakenly positing institutional effects in areas of the macroeconomy other than monetary policy. This section details this point.

Theories of the relationship between interests and institutions are central to political economy research. Interest-based political economy models have been used to explain various economic policy outcomes by emphasizing production factors, sectors, classes, coalitions, electoral cycles, and political survival (Rogowski 2009; Frieden 1991; Walter 2008; Pinto 2013; Franzese and Jusko 2009). In this view, policy outcomes largely depend on the preferences of the most powerful economic interest groups in a national polity. Others emphasize the intervening effect institutions may have in altering the link between interests and policy outcomes, using rational and historical frameworks (Hallerberg and Yläoutinen 2010; Brooks and Kurtz 2012; Mosley 2010). A strand of this research considers institutional independence or autonomy. Rooted in principal–agent theory, this work uncovers how independent state ministries might intervene in policymaking processes in ways that lead to different policy outcomes than political interests would lead to on their own.

In political economy, this framing is most common in studies of central banks and monetary policy. Many argue that independent central banks (ICBs) have a moderating effect on the interest politicians have in pursuing inflationary policy at the expense of long-term stability (Rogoff 1985). Despite complexities and limitations (Bodea and Hicks 2015b), common wisdom holds that ICBs, all else equal, have more credibility and are expected to lower inflation over time (see discussion in Fernández-Albertos 2015). Even if ostensibly independent monetary authorities are simply captured by the financial sector or economists, the same policy outcome emerges because those capturing the central bank use the institution to pursue monetary stability over other priorities (Carré and Gauvin 2018).

This framework has been applied to sovereign debt and DMOs. Such application is an example of how independent central banks have been seen as effective, and in turn used as a departure point for theorizing about the role of institutions in other areas of the economy, including public debt and fiscal policy (Wren-Lewis 2013). In a public administration sense, this move may be seen as an example of broader efforts to depoliticize fiscal policy with 'greater reliance on independent fiscal agencies' (Fernández-Albertos 2015, 231).

But this chapter's model of public debt accumulation provides an example of ways in which emphasis on institutional independence may mis-identify institutional effects in areas of the macroeconomy other than monetary policy. As argued above, the concept of institutional independence is less-relevant to EM DMOs, and EM external debt accumulation in particular, than it is to other institutions in other areas of economic policymaking. While central banks may plausibly be granted independent control over monetary policy and achieve lower inflation than what political principals would otherwise pursue, EM DMOs cannot plausibly be granted independent control over external borrowing decisions. Their role as passive recipients of annual financing requirements subjects DMOs to formal and informal constraints on borrowing decisions.

It follows that the role of institutions in sovereign debt is different than the role of institutions in monetary policy. Tracing and explicitly considering policymaking processes in the manner of this chapter can illuminate the different ways in which political interests and institutions interact to set policy in different parts of the economy. Emphasis on process tracing can sharpen political economy research on variation in economic policy outcomes by more-explicitly grounding studies in real world policymaking practices. This, in turn, could increase the policy relevance of comparative political economy research.

2.5   Conclusion

This chapter presented a model of EM public debt accumulation where DMOs are significantly constrained, particularly by partisan politics when borrowing externally. This model provides observable implications, allowing for a multi-method test of partisan constraints on EM external borrowings in subsequent chapters.

The argument has implications for several literatures. For sovereign debt, it means that sovereign external borrowings are significantly determined by partisan politics. For comparative political economy, it signals that the role and effect of institutions in sovereign debt (1) varies across different areas of debt structure and (2) cannot be easily compared with the role and effect of institutions in other areas of macroeconomic policy.

But such implications, at least based of this book's model of sovereign debt accumulation, depend on evidence that an EM DMO's annual external borrowing decisions are significantly constrained by partisan politics as theorized above. The following chapters test this argument, beginning with a variety of econometric hypothesis tests in Chapter 3.

3

Testing the Partisan Model

3.1 Introduction

This chapter presents econometric tests of the argument that domestic partisan politics significantly affect annual external borrowings by EM sovereigns. The hypothesis, derived from the model of EM sovereign debt accumulation in Chapter 2, is:

> H1: All else equal, EM governments with working classes as core constituencies and left-leaning economic policy preferences use a greater proportion of market-based finance to meet annual external borrowing needs.

The next section outlines the data used in the study. It defines EMs, discusses selection bias considerations given that definition, and lists the countries included in various samples. It then constructs the dependent variable, plots observed variation in that dependent variable, constructs multiple explanatory variables, and identifies control variables. The third section discusses the data generation process, specifies the main model, plans a series of estimation strategies, and discusses post-treatment bias concerns given the included control variables. The fourth section presents results and a variety of robustness tests. The conclusion notes that the causal mechanism by which we can understand these statistical relationships can only be identified through qualitative process-tracing studies, setting up the case studies in the next three chapters.

3.2 Data

The study uses a panel dataset of years in which countries were EMs from 1989-2016. To define the universe of EMs, the sample includes country-year observations in which the country was categorized as a Middle Income Country (MIC) by the World Bank. As discussed in Chapter 1, EMs/MICs are countries with regular access to both markets and official creditors when borrowing abroad each year, meaning they have the borrowing menu theorized about in this book. High Income Country (HIC), MIC, and Low Income Country (LIC) categories correspond to developed, emerging, and frontier market country groupings used by index providers to distinguish different degrees of market access across sovereigns.

How Governments Borrow. Ben Cormier, Oxford University Press. © Ben Cormier (2024).
DOI: 10.1093/oso/9780198882732.003.0003

Initial correlations modelling borrowing without any control variables include 1,153 observations across sixty-nine MICs. Fully specified models with all controls include forty-five MICs, due to standard data missingness issues when using quantitative analysis in studies of developing countries. The countries included in various samples are listed in Table 3.1.

Table 3.1 Countries in Sample

Albania*	Lesotho*
Algeria	Mauritania
Angola*	Mauritius*
Argentina	Mexico*
Armenia*	Moldova*
Azerbaijan*	Mongolia*
Bangladesh	Morocco*
Bolivia*	Myanmar
Bosnia and Herzegovina*	Nicaragua*
Botswana*	Nigeria
Brazil*	North Macedonia*
Bulgaria*	Pakistan
Cameroon*	Paraguay*
China	Peru*
Colombia*	Philippines*
Congo, Rep.*	Romania
Costa Rica*	Russian Federation*
Dominican Republic*	Senegal
Ecuador	Serbia
Egypt*	South Africa*
El Salvador*	Sri Lanka*
Gabon*	Sudan
Georgia*	Tajikistan
Ghana*	Thailand*
Guatemala*	Timor-Leste
Honduras*	Tunisia*
India*	Turkey*
Indonesia*	Turkmenistan
Iran	Ukraine*
Jamaica*	Uzbekistan
Kazakhstan*	Venezuela
Kenya	Yemen, Rep.
Kyrgyz Republic*	Zambia
Lao PDR	Zimbabwe
Lebanon*	

Notes: Only countries with over 1 million population included
* = 45 countries included in sample when all controls included in models (Table 3.5, Models 2–5)
See replication data for specific country-years included in a given sample for a specific model

MIC categorization is an exogenous threshold determined by national GDP-per-capita (Knack, Xu, and Zou 2014). This means that, in the majority of cases, countries cannot select into being a MIC. They are either in the MIC income range or they are not. At times, there are exceptions at the low and high ends of the income range. For example, the World Bank may allow a country 'graduating' to high income status a few extra years of access on MIC terms before forcing them to strictly use markets (as is expected of HICs). Similarly, if graduating from LIC to MIC, a country may maintain access to grants and thus not face the same borrowing options theorized about in this study. To ensure that such self-selection into certain borrowing strategies around the ends of the MIC range do not bias the main estimations, robustness checks below (1) drop all IDA recipients, accounting for countries on the low end of the MIC income range that might select into maintaining access to extra-concessional grant windows at official creditors and (2) drop countries that would ultimately graduate in the next two years to HIC status, ensuring countries that may have been negotiating selection into MIC status to maintain access to official credit are not driving the estimations.

3.2.1 Dependent Variable

To model the proportion of external borrowings coming from markets rather than official creditors each year, the dependent variable is the annual percent of new external debt that comes from bond markets and commercial banks rather than official multilateral and bilateral creditors.

$$DV = \frac{MarketBorrowings\_USDamount}{(MarketBorrowings\_USDamount + OfficialBorrowings\_USDamount)}$$

Higher values thus indicate more market use. See Table 3.2 for data sources. Although the total amount borrowed is the denominator, this does not automatically mean more borrowing leads to a smaller share of market financing. In practice, as summarized in Chapters 1 and 2 then detailed in later case study chapters, EMs typically co-finance from a variety of official sources to meet large financing needs should they prefer to do so. Statistically, the full range of possible outcomes in this variable (0% to 100%) is observed in the data (see descriptive statistics in Table 3.3).

Figures 3.1, 3.2, and 3.3 show examples of variation in this dependent variable across countries listed in Table 3.1, grouped by region. These plots indicate not only annual and over-time variation between countries, but also year-over-year variation in external borrowings within countries. Reducing concern about selection bias, it is significant that across- and within-unit variation in external borrowing proportions is observable across unit types: variation is observed in

Table 3.2 Variable Information and Country Income Level Coding

Variable Name	Source	Coding Notes
DV	WDI	DT.COM.PRVT.CD/DT.COM.DPPG.CD
WorkingClassParty	V-Party	v2pagroup
Left	DPI	GOV1RLC
Credit Rating	Bloomberg	Best of S&P, Moody's, and Fitch ratings. Coded using sovereign's year-end long-term credit rating. AAA = 1, so lower values are better ratings. If unrated by all three agencies, to avoid losing observations these are coded as Caa3 for Moody's and CCC- in S&P and Fitch. This follows research estimating most unrated countries would fall between Moody's Ca and Caa2, or Fitch/S&P CCC and CC- (Ratha, De, and Mohapatra 2011, 304). This makes intuitive sense, reflecting the likelihood that an unrated country is more creditworthy than one in default, but still relatively risky and low-speculative grade.
USIrates	Ballard-Rosa et al. 2021	Average of annual US Interest rates
Growth	WDI	NY.GNP.MKTP.KD.ZG; GNI growth, annual %
Inflation	WDI	FP.CPI.TOTL.ZG
Deficit	WDI	GC.TAX.TOTL.GD.ZS—GC.XPN.TOTL.GD.ZS; both as % of GDP.
Crisis	Syst Crisis Dataset	Crisis = 1 if country in crisis at any point in the calendar year
Debt Service	WDI	DT.TDS.DPPG.GN.ZS; % of GNI
Reserves	WDI	FI.RES.TOTL.DT.ZS; % of Total External Debt
Democracy	V-Dem	v2x_regime
Rule of Law	V-Dem	v2x_rule
Property Rights	V-Dem	v2xcl_prpty
Debt Service	WDI	DT.TDS.DPPG.GN.ZS; % of GNI
PolCycle	DPI	yrcurnt
UN_Usalign	UN voting database	Annual UNGA voting alignment between borrower and US
UN_CHNalign	UN voting database	Annual UNGA voting alignment between borrower and China
MIC status	World Bank	History of income group for each country-year coded using World Bank file OGHIST.xsl, available here as of Dec. 2021: https://datahelpdesk.worldbank.org/knowledgebase/articles/378834-how-does-the-world-bank-classify-countries

Table 3.3 Descriptive Statistics

	N	Mean	Min	Max	SD
Full cases using V-Party					
DV	601	0.37	0.00	1.00	0.35
WorkingClassParty	601	0.26	0.00	0.75	0.17
CreditRating	601	12.65	6.00	19.00	3.60
USIrates	601	4.13	1.80	8.55	1.71
Growth	601	4.35	−15.91	31.67	4.37
Inflation	601	23.08	−3.75	7481.66	306.17
Deficit	601	−6.79	−28.47	5.75	5.57
Crisis	601	0.08	0.00	1.00	0.27
DebtService	601	2.80	0.12	16.54	2.11
Reserves	601	60.25	1.53	2191.31	147.12
Democracy	601	1.70	0.00	3.00	0.74
RuleOfLaw	601	0.49	0.04	0.96	0.24
PropRights	601	0.79	0.24	0.96	0.12
PolCycle	601	1.93	0.00	6.00	1.45
UN_USalign	601	0.35	0.12	0.72	0.11
UN_CHNalign	601	0.86	0.63	0.98	0.08

	N	Mean	Min	Max	SD
Full cases using DPI					
DV	686	0.35	0.00	1.00	0.34
Left	686	0.28	0.00	1.00	0.45
CreditRating	686	13.08	6.00	19.00	3.70
USIrates	686	4.28	1.80	8.55	1.78
Growth	686	4.21	−19.73	31.67	4.68
Inflation	686	38.05	−3.75	7481.66	336.17
Deficit	686	−7.06	−28.47	5.75	5.56
Crisis	686	0.08	0.00	1.00	0.27
DebtService	686	3.02	0.00	16.54	2.43
Reserves	686	56.46	0.15	2191.31	138.46
Democracy	686	1.59	0.00	3.00	0.80
RuleOfLaw	686	0.48	0.04	0.96	0.23
PropRights	686	0.78	0.24	0.96	0.12
PolCycle	686	1.84	0.00	6.00	1.47
UN_USalign	686	0.35	0.12	0.72	0.11
UN_CHNalign	686	0.86	0.63	0.98	0.08

countries that were MICs through the entire timeframe of the sample; countries that exited MIC status and graduated to HIC status over that timeframe; countries that were not MICs in early years but joined this group of countries in later years; and countries that did not borrow externally every single year.

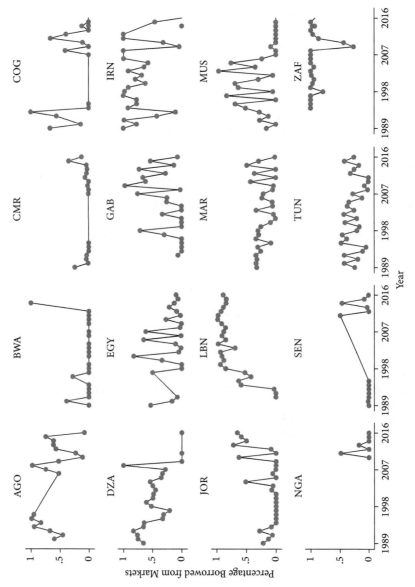

Figure 3.1 Example Variation in EM External Borrowing (Africa and Middle East)

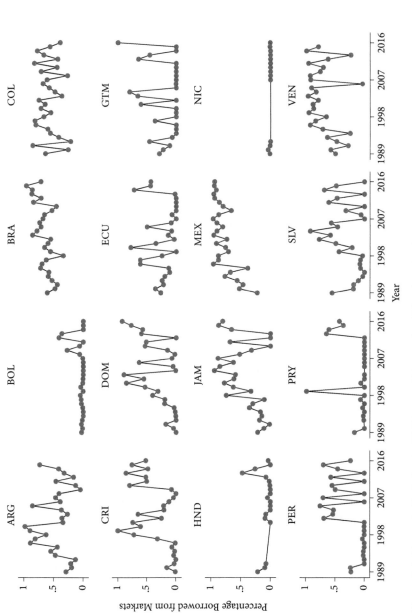

Figure 3.2 Example Variation in EM External Borrowing (The Americas)

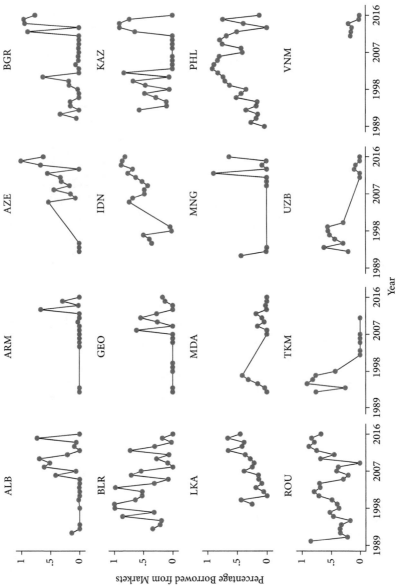

Figure 3.3 Example Variation in EM External Borrowing (Europe and Asia)

3.2.2 Independent Variables

This chapter uses two explanatory variables. The first and primary variable captures the relative importance of domestic working classes, including labor and the poor, to a governing party's political base. This is coded using the Varieties of Party Identity and Organization dataset (V-Party). V-Party codes a variety of characteristics about major political parties in many countries since 1900, including their core political constituencies.

On a 0–1 scale ranging from no support to essential support, V-Party's Party Support Group variable (v2pagroup) codes the 'core membership and supporters' of a party (Lührmann et al. 2020, 31). This chapter's main analysis uses the average importance of urban and rural labor and middle classes including peasants, family farmers, and unions to a political party (v2pagroup_8, v2pagroup_9, v2pagroup_10, v2pagroup_11) to construct a variable reflecting the relative importance of working classes to a governing party (*WorkingClassParty*). Other constituency combinations are used in robustness checks, as discussed below. This includes constructing an elite version of this party support variable to confirm such a constituency is associated with an increased likelihood of more official borrowing (i.e. the inverse of *H1*).

WorkingClassParty includes only governing parties, coded as heads of government or leaders of governing coalitions in V-Party (v2pagovsup = 0). *WorkingClassParty* scores are brought forward until there is a change in governing party or a change in the party's coding. If multiple parties are simultaneously coded as v2pagovsup = 0 in V-Party, then the average of these parties' *WorkingClassParty* scores is used to capture the degree to which working-class constituencies are central to all parties leading the government.[1]

H1 expects that the more important these working-class constituencies are to a governing party, the more government will use markets to meet its annual external borrowing needs. Higher values of *WorkingClassParty* should lead to proportionally more market use rather than official creditor use when borrowing abroad each year.

The second variable is the left–right partisanship of government, using the Database of Political Institutions (DPI) (Beck et al. 2001). DPI codes countries according to the *economic policy* platform of the governing party (Cruz, Keefer, and Scartascini 2018, 6), coding for the executive party in presidential systems and most powerful legislative party in parliamentary systems. This makes DPI a common tool for capturing economic policy preferences (for a recent application in sovereign debt see Ballard-Rosa, Mosley, and Wellhausen 2022). Despite shortcomings in application, particularly outside of the rich world

---

[1] There are only seven cases of this in EMs/MICs over the sample timeframe.

(Rudra and Tobin 2017, 296), it provides a useful alternative measure for testing *H1* after *WorkingClassParty*. Below, *Left* = 1 if DPI codes the government as left and 0 if right, dropping governments DPI codes as centrist or ambiguous to ensure the variable clearly matches the theory's emphasis on the importance of working classes vis-à-vis elites to a governing party.

To confirm that dropping centrists, ambiguous parties, and the subsequently lower N is not responsible for the relationship between *Left* governments and annual external borrowings identified below, robustness tests use the variable *Center-Left*. This pooling is based on the logic that centrists' broader political bases should make their borrowing preferences more similar to left than right parties. For example, the more interventionist or 'undisciplined' items a centrist governing party has in a budget or party platform, the less that government can use official credit without threatening to affect its space to implement these policies. Ambiguous parties are then added to the control group (*Center-Left* = 0). Results persist.

Given multiple explanatory variables of interest, it is useful to confirm that they are statistically correlated in the expected direction and so consistently identifying aspects of partisan politics in a manner that makes them comparable and useful for this study. Of 1,521 MIC country-year observations with both *WorkingClassParty* and *Left* coded by V-Party and DPI, regressing the *Left* dummy variable on the continuous *WorkingClassParty* variable indicates a significantly positive relationship between an increase in working-class importance in V-Party and being coded as a left-leaning government in DPI ($.52$, $p>.000$).

Notably the coefficient becomes larger when regressing *Center-Left* rather than *Left* ($.60$, $p>.000$). This lends credibility to the logic of pooling the center with the left in robustness checks of DPI results. The positive correlation between *Left* and *WorkingClassParty* also remains when using only the complete-case observations that include all control variables and make it into the sample used in the fully specified models below (see Table 3.4).[2]

3.2.3 Control Variables

Lagged dependent variables control for the degree to which borrowing is simply habitual, or a function of past relationships with various creditors. Other economic and political controls account for push and pull factors central to sovereign debt: global market conditions, international political relationships with major official creditors, national economic fundamentals, sovereign debt positions, sovereign credit ratings, and domestic institutions.

---

[2] Correlations are available from the author on request, or by using the data in replication files in Cormier (2023c).

3.2.3.1 Market conditions, creditworthiness, and economic fundamentals

USIRates controls for the amount of liquidity available to developing countries (Zeitz 2022). This is coded using replication data from related work on liquidity's conditioning effects on sovereign borrowings (Ballard-Rosa, Mosley, and Wellhausen 2021). *Credit Rating* is the best rating a country has from Moody's, S&P, or Fitch that year, coded using Bloomberg. A code of 1 means the country is rated as AAA, so higher values reflect less creditworthiness and should mean less market use. *Crisis* must also be controlled for since official credit is likely necessary if facing a debt, currency, or banking crisis that year (Laeven and Valencia 2012).

A number of economic fundamentals inform creditworthiness, risk, market access, and thus use of either market sources or official creditors (see for example Hernández, Mellado, and Valdés 2001; Mosley 2003, 126; Gelos, Sahay, and Sandleris 2011; Koepke 2019, 533–534). *Growth* may increase market use while *Inflation* and *Deficit* may lead to less market use, insofar as the market discipline literature would expect these pull factors to determine market access. Debt portfolios and repayment capacity are controlled for with *Debt Service* and *Reserves*. Higher debt repayment levels may limit further market access and high reserve levels may alter the perceived trade-off between official and private options. These data are drawn from the World Development Indicators (see Table 3.2 for specifics).

3.2.3.2 Political factors

Democracy, *Rule of Law*, and *Property Rights* control for the democratic advantage thesis, which argues more democratic countries should have better access to markets and thus use them more (Schultz and Weingast 2003; Biglaiser and Staats 2012; Beaulieu, Cox, and Saiegh 2012). This data is coded using the Varieties of Democracy dataset (Coppedge et al. 2016).

PolCycle is the number of years until the next election. There are competing expectations about the role of political business cycles in this context, with different arguments about whether governments reduce or expand deficits in election periods (Drazen 2001; Kaplan 2013; Franzese and Jusko 2009). Both possibilities may have implications for EM borrowing decisions. DPI provides this data, coded as 0 in an election year and the number of years until the next planned election otherwise. DPI codes countries experiencing regime change or other outlier events that make it impractical to score this variable for a given year as '-999.' To avoid losing observations these are coded as zeros for the main analysis below, reasoning that such circumstances imply there is no reliable timeline for a forward-looking political business cycle and the incentive to spend for those in power is acute. A robustness test simply drops these observations rather than recoding them. This decreases the N to 578 but does not affect the findings (see Model 22 in Table 3.9).

UN voting alignment of the borrower with the United States as well as China control for political alignment with major powers, both of which may lead to more or less official borrowings (among a vast literature see Dreher, Sturm, and Vreeland 2015). This data is coded using the UN General Assembly voting database (Bailey, Strezhnev, and Voeten 2017).

3.3 Empirical Strategy

A core argument of this book is that borrowing decisions are a function of annual fiscal policymaking processes. This point affects model specification here. Implicit in Chapter 2's model of the annual EM sovereign debt accumulation process, countries make public budget and borrowing decisions this year (t) that do not take effect until next year ($t+1$). Budget negotiations take place and borrowing strategies are thus designed under the conditions and information known in year t, but borrowings do not become formal until those budgets and funding strategies are implemented in year $t+1$. This means that the dependent variable (annual external borrowings) and *Deficit* must be led by one year because they reflect decisions made during year t but not implemented until the budget takes effect in $t+1$. *PolCycle* is also led by one year because, to the extent that there is a political business cycle, the budget is made with an eye to what year in the cycle that budget is used. Remaining variables, accounting for conditions and information under which fiscal and borrowing decisions are made, are included at their year t values. The main model of EM foreign borrowing used below is:

$$DV_{(t+1)} = ExplanatoryVariable_{(t)} + DV_{(t)} + Same-Year\ Controls_{(t)} + Deficit_{(t+1)}$$
$$+ Political\ Cycle_{(t+1)} + Year\ Effects_{(t)} + Country\ Effects + \varepsilon$$

3.3.1 Modelling Strategies

The chapter uses a variety of estimation strategies. First, a fractional dependent variable, measuring the percentage of annual external borrowings that come from market rather than official sources, requires use of probit and logit models. These nonlinear models do not include unit fixed effects to avoid the incidental parameter problem (Greene 2004), and instead use errors robust to unit clustering. Second however, because this chapter uses marginal effects to make inferences, linear Ordinary Least Squares (OLS) and Generalized Method of Moments (GMM) models can still be used to recover estimations using unit fixed effects despite the fractional dependent variable (Papke and Wooldridge 2008, 130). This view and approach allows for controlling unobserved unit heterogeneity despite the fractional dependent variable. A combination of OLS, GMM, logit, and probit model estimations are presented below, with consistency across estimations the threshold for evidence in favor of *H1*.

3.3.2 Post-Treatment Bias

It is possible that, given standard expectations about the policy preferences of left-leaning parties with working-class constituencies, controlling for deficit and inflation may induce post-treatment bias (Montgomery, Nyhan, and Torres 2018) when estimating the effect of, and making inferences about, the partisan explanatory variables of interest in these models. It is also possible that insofar as left-leaning governments get worse credit ratings as has been shown in the rich world (Barta and Johnston 2018), using ratings as controls may also introduce post-treatment bias. For theoretical and empirical reasons, however, this is not a concern here.

In a theoretical sense, at least in the context of a study of external borrowing preferences and outcomes, assuming post-treatment bias due to deficit and inflation control variables is problematic. Inflation is shaped by capital flows, exchange rate policy, and exogenous structural events as much as partisan preferences. Nor is it safe to assume that left-leaning governments successfully sponsor inflation or have less independent central banks (Way 2000). Credit ratings may be lower for left-leaning governments, but to the extent that this is the case, the argument of the paper is that despite and controlling for this, they still use proportionally more market finance. Meanwhile, deficits are shaped not only by partisan spending preferences but tax and revenue generation capacity, tax policy itself, budget rules, and other domestic as well as global exogenous factors.

In a statistical sense, a correlation matrix of these variables in Table 3.4 shows small coefficients, indicating minimal relationships between the partisan explanatory variables and the potential post-treatment bias-inducing controls (see bolded cells in Table 3.4). Moreover, the directions of these relationships are not always consistent across the V-Party and DPI constituency variables (see *Inflation*).

Table 3.4 Correlation Matrix of Potential Post-Treatment Bias-Inducing Controls

	WorkingClassParty	Left	CreditRating	Inflation	Deficit
WorkingClassParty	1				
Left	0.2754	1			
CreditRating	**0.0096**	**0.004**	1		
Inflation	**−0.0012**	**0.0453**	0.0835	1	
Deficit	**−0.0934**	**−0.0649**	0.1332	0.018	1

This eases concern that these control variables significantly bias the partisan relationship to external borrowing estimated in the models below.

3.4 Results

Table 3.5 reports estimations where *WorkingClassParty* is the explanatory variable, capturing the relative importance of working classes to a governing party's political constituency. *H1* expects that the more important these constituencies are to a governing party, the more likely government will be to use a greater proportion of market finance to meet its external borrowing needs that year.

All Table 3.5 estimations lend support to *H1*. Model 1 is a simple OLS correlation. Model 2 is an OLS model with all control variables, unit effects, and year effects. Model 3 is a GMM estimation using collapsed lags as instruments. Model 4 is a fractional probit model, removing unit fixed effects to avoid incidental parameter bias but making errors robust to unit clustering. Model 5 is the same with a logit function.

Figure 3.4 then plots the predicted marginal effect of observed values of *WorkingClassParty* on the proportion of borrowing likely to come from markets rather than official creditors. As is clear, the more important that working classes are to a governing party, the more likely that government is to use a greater proportion of market rather than official sources to fulfill external borrowing needs. This is evidence in favor of *H1*, explained by such constituencies incentivizing government to incentivize DMOs to prioritize market instruments and avoid official creditor conditions, despite higher costs and shorter maturities.

Table 3.6 reports the same series of estimations using the alternative *Left* variable, capturing the categorical economic policy preferences of the governing party. All models estimate a greater proportion of *Left* government external borrowings come from market rather than official sources each year. Figure 3.5 plots the coefficients of these dummy variables to visualize how across models, the average marginal effect of being left-leaning is to use a greater proportion of market finance when borrowing externally.

These statistically significant estimations suggest government partisanship is a substantively important determinant of annual external borrowings by EMs. This also implies partisanship is a significant determinant of variation in the composition of EM sovereign debt structure over time. The point estimations in Figure 3.4 suggest that the governing parties most dependent on working-class political support borrow nearly 25% more from markets each year than do governments that have the least allegiance to working classes. According to the point estimates in Figure 3.5, the average effect of being left-leaning varies between 10 and 55 annual percentage point increases in use of markets rather than official creditors. These are substantively significant annual shifts in external borrowing

Table 3.5 Modeling the Effect of Working-Class Constituencies on EM External Borrowings

Model	OLS 1	OLS 2	GMM 3	Probit 4	Logit 5
WorkingClassParty	0.275***	0.179*	0.371**	0.568**	0.951**
	(0.055)	(0.105)	(0.187)	(0.268)	(0.463)
Dvlag		0.131**	0.391	1.533***	2.532***
		(0.056)	(0.247)	(0.193)	(0.325)
CreditRating		−0.007	−0.017	−0.059***	−0.100***
		(0.006)	(0.011)	(0.018)	(0.031)
USIrates		−0.012	0.003	0.027	0.050
		(0.015)	(0.010)	(0.032)	(0.054)
Growth		0.000	−0.003	−0.004	−0.008
		(0.003)	(0.003)	(0.011)	(0.020)
Inflation		−0.000	−0.000**	−0.000*	−0.000
		(0.000)	(0.000)	(0.000)	(0.000)
Deficit		−0.003	0.001	−0.001	−0.003
		(0.004)	(0.003)	(0.008)	(0.014)
Crisis		−0.047	0.005	0.075	0.120
		(0.051)	(0.045)	(0.124)	(0.211)
DebtService		0.004	0.003	0.011	0.018
		(0.009)	(0.014)	(0.026)	(0.043)
Reserves		0.000	−0.000	−0.001	−0.002
		(0.000)	(0.000)	(0.001)	(0.002)
Democracy		−0.054	−0.021	−0.048	−0.085
		(0.036)	(0.028)	(0.080)	(0.137)
RuleOfLaw		0.236	0.083	0.244	0.409
		(0.169)	(0.103)	(0.267)	(0.451)
PropRights		0.083	0.041	−0.004	−0.011
		(0.184)	(0.129)	(0.428)	(0.742)
PolCycle		0.008	0.007	0.023	0.037
		(0.008)	(0.011)	(0.030)	(0.051)
UN_USalign		0.251	0.272**	0.208	0.307
		(0.451)	(0.112)	(1.132)	(1.878)
UN_CHNalign		−0.174	0.118	0.192	0.255
		(0.467)	(0.249)	(1.365)	(2.273)
N	1153	595	595	595	595
Year Fes	NO	YES	YES	YES	YES
Country FEs	NO	YES	YES	NO	NO

Notes: * p<0.1, ** p<0.05, *** p<0.01
Robust Standard Errors in 1–3; Cluster-Robust Standard Errors in 4–5; Constants suppressed
Dependent Variable, Deficit, and PolCycle led one year (see DGP discussion)

associated with government partisanship. Such annual partisan effects on EM external borrowings compound each year to help explain variation in sovereign debt structures across EMs over time.

Table 3.6 Modeling the Left Partisan Effect on EM External Borrowings

Model	OLS 6	7	GMM 8	Probit 9	Logit 10
Left	0.064**	0.176***	0.234***	0.321***	0.540***
	(0.026)	(0.054)	(0.084)	(0.121)	(0.205)
DVlag		0.061	0.305	1.297***	2.150***
		(0.072)	(0.192)	(0.231)	(0.404)
CreditRating		−0.009	−0.019***	−0.068***	−0.117***
		(0.007)	(0.007)	(0.016)	(0.029)
USIrates		0.019	0.029*	0.076	0.135
		(0.024)	(0.015)	(0.058)	(0.096)
Growth		−0.000	−0.001	0.007	0.013
		(0.004)	(0.004)	(0.014)	(0.026)
Inflation		−0.000**	−0.000***	−0.000*	−0.001
		(0.000)	(0.000)	(0.000)	(0.000)
Deficit		0.001	0.002	−0.001	−0.004
		(0.006)	(0.004)	(0.010)	(0.018)
Crisis		−0.038	−0.009	0.027	0.065
		(0.068)	(0.077)	(0.226)	(0.391)
DebtService		−0.034***	−0.018*	−0.030	−0.047
		(0.013)	(0.010)	(0.031)	(0.057)
Reserves		0.000	−0.000**	−0.004***	−0.007**
		(0.000)	(0.000)	(0.001)	(0.003)
Democracy		−0.060	−0.019	−0.134	−0.234
		(0.042)	(0.039)	(0.098)	(0.174)
RuleOfLaw		0.126	0.264*	1.202***	2.065***
		(0.188)	(0.142)	(0.286)	(0.492)
PropRights		0.165	−0.001	−0.583	−1.026
		(0.223)	(0.098)	(0.483)	(0.858)
PolCycle		0.017*	0.017	0.079**	0.132**
		(0.010)	(0.012)	(0.036)	(0.063)
UN_USalign		0.933	0.277	1.523	2.550
		(0.742)	(0.194)	(1.818)	(3.104)
UN_CHNalign		0.080	−0.109	1.643	2.755
		(0.623)	(0.345)	(1.837)	(3.117)
N	694	364	364	364	364
Year FEs	NO	YES	YES	YES	YES
Country FEs	NO	YES	YES	NO	NO

Notes: * $p<0.1$, ** $p<0.05$, *** $p<0.01$
Robust Standard Errors in 6–8; Cluster-Robust Standard Errors in 9–10; Constants suppressed
Dependent Variable, Deficit, and PolCycle led one year (see DGP discussion)

Across both tables, frequently significant control variables include the lagged dependent variable and credit ratings. The lagged dependent variable performs as expected, indicating past borrowing decisions affect current borrowing decisions.

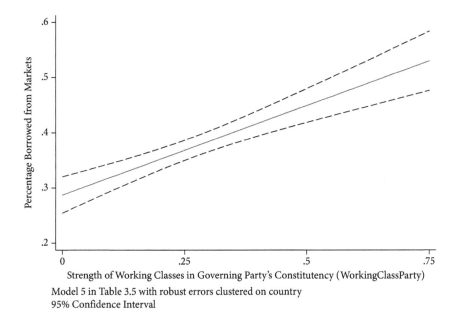

Model 5 in Table 3.5 with robust errors clustered on country
95% Confidence Interval

Figure 3.4 Predicted Marginal Effect of Working-Class and Poor Constituencies on EM External Borrowing

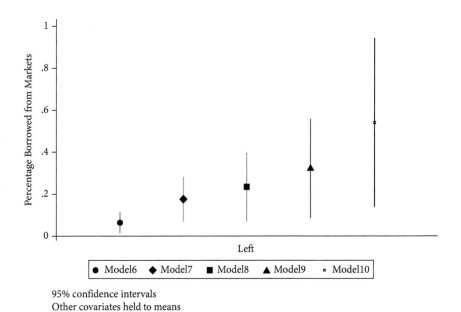

95% confidence intervals
Other covariates held to means

Figure 3.5 Average Marginal Effect of Left Partisanship on EM External Borrowing

Credit ratings also perform as expected, with worse credit ratings associated with less market use and more official credit (recall AAA is coded as 1 in the credit rating variable, so higher values of this variable indicate worse ratings).

Rule of law is sometimes associated with significantly more market use in one table 3.6), but not the other (3.5) nor in the robustness tests below (Tables 3.7, 3.8, and 3.9). Meanwhile, democracy and property rights are never statistically significant and change signs depending on the specification. This leaves application of democratic advantage arguments to understanding sovereign debt accumulation muddled at best, inconsistently associated with annual EM external borrowings.

Occasionally significant macroeconomic fundamentals include inflation, debt service, and reserves. They are sometimes associated with less market use and more official credit, but these relationships are inconsistent and often substantively insignificant. Political business cycles are sometimes statistically significant in Table 3.6, but are never significant in Table 3.5 nor the robustness tests in Tables 3.7–3.9. That EMs are sometimes (though rarely) associated with more market use when farther out from elections is not consistent enough of a relationship to yield any inferences from these tables (compare expectations between Kaplan 2013; Drazen 2001; Franzese and Jusko 2009).

3.4.1 Robustness Tests

These estimations and inferences are robust to several different modelling decisions, including use of alternative variables and sample subsets.

Table 3.7 estimates the effect of the relative importance of elite economic constituencies to a governing party. This tests the inverse of *H1*: the more important that elite economic classes are to a governing party's core political constituency, the more likely they should be to not resist official creditor conditions and thus use more official credit to take advantage of their lower rates and longer maturities. To construct this variable, *EliteParty* uses the average importance of the aristocracy and business elites (v2pagroup_1 and v2pagroup_3, respectively) in the V-Party variable to code the relative importance of economic elites to a governing party. Figure 3.6 shows the predicted effects of elite constituencies over the range of scores observed in the *EliteParty* variable, with increasing use of official creditors predicted when economic elites are more important to the governing party.

This is an important robustness test because the comparative importance of working and elite classes to a governing party cannot be inferred by the inverse of the other variable. Since V-Party's extensive constituency coding goes

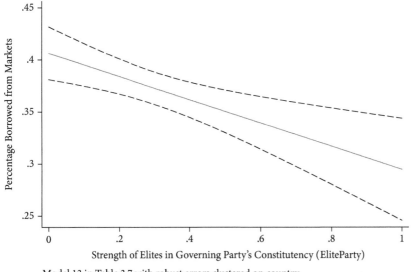

Model 13 in Table 3.7 with robust errors clustered on country
90% Confidence Interval

Figure 3.6 Predicted Marginal Effect of Elite Constituencies on EM External Borrowing

beyond economic classes, it is not the case that *1—WorkingClassParty* captures the importance of elite classes (i.e. equals *EliteParty*). That elite constituencies are associated with external borrowings in the direction expected by the inverse of *H1* adds credibility to the argument that these classes have opposing borrowing preferences.

Table 3.8 reports estimations of robustness tests using additional alternative explanatory variable constructions and specifications. Models 14 and 15 drop V-Party's middle-class groups from the *WorkingClassParty* variable, ensuring that nothing about including family farmers and other small businesses is solely responsible for the main findings. Models 16 and 17 add governments coded as centrist in DPI and pools them with left governments, adds governments coded as unclear in DPI and pools them with nonleft governments, and shows that dropping these observations and the lower N is not driving the relationships estimated in Table 3.6.

Table 3.9 estimates models using sample subsets based on theories of or observations about sovereign debt that may plausibly affect the partisan relationship to external borrowing. Model 18 drops countries about to graduate to high-income in the next two years, so potentially selecting into MIC status. Model 19 drops all IDA recipients, countries which may use more official credit because they

Table 3.7 Modeling the Effect of Elite Constituencies on EM External Borrowings

Model	OLS 11	Probit 12	Logit 13
EliteParty	−0.113***	−0.272*	−0.453*
	(0.041)	(0.163)	(0.275)
DVlag		1.546***	2.552***
		(0.186)	(0.313)
CreditRating		−0.057***	−0.097***
		(0.017)	(0.028)
USIrates		0.020	0.039
		(0.034)	(0.057)
Growth		−0.001	−0.001
		(0.010)	(0.020)
Inflation		−0.000*	−0.000
		(0.000)	(0.000)
Deficit		−0.007	−0.012
		(0.008)	(0.014)
Crisis		0.078	0.122
		(0.125)	(0.210)
DebtService		0.021	0.037
		(0.026)	(0.042)
Reserves		−0.001	−0.002
		(0.001)	(0.002)
Democracy		0.016	0.025
		(0.089)	(0.153)
RuleOfLaw		0.122	0.204
		(0.291)	(0.491)
PropRights		0.115	0.216
		(0.426)	(0.742)
PolCycle		0.026	0.042
		(0.031)	(0.052)
UN_USalign		−0.014	−0.124
		(1.115)	(1.849)
UN_CHNalign		0.483	0.649
		(1.330)	(2.204)
N	1153	595	595
Year FEs	NO	YES	YES
Country Fes	NO	NO	NO

Notes: * $p<0.1$, ** $p<0.05$, *** $p<0.01$
Robust Standard Errors in 11; Cluster-Robust Standard Errors in 12–13
Dependent Variable, Deficit, and PolCycle led one year (see DGP discussion)

have a slightly different borrowing menu with qualitatively different options than most EMs (access to extra-concessional credit from the World Bank and other official creditors). Model 20 drops crisis countries to ensure the results are not driven by crisis countries using official creditors as lenders of last resort. Model 21 drops nondemocracies to ensure there is nothing unique about democracies or nondemocracies, and the role of partisanship in them, that is driving the main

Table 3.8 Probit and Logit Models of Alternative Explanatory Variables

Model	Probit 14	Logit 15	Probit 16	Logit 17
WorkingClassPartyAlt	0.392*	0.667**		
	(0.205)	(0.337)		
Center-Left			0.210**	0.342**
			(0.091)	(0.154)
Dvlag	1.539***	2.544***	1.549***	2.561***
	(0.190)	(0.320)	(0.173)	(0.293)
CreditRating	−0.057***	−0.096***	−0.050***	−0.083***
	(0.018)	(0.030)	(0.017)	(0.028)
USIrates	0.023	0.043	0.017	0.032
	(0.033)	(0.055)	(0.033)	(0.057)
Growth	−0.003	−0.005	0.004	0.007
	(0.011)	(0.020)	(0.009)	(0.017)
Inflation	−0.000*	−0.000	−0.000	−0.000
	(0.000)	(0.000)	(0.000)	(0.000)
Deficit	−0.002	−0.004	−0.005	−0.009
	(0.009)	(0.015)	(0.007)	(0.012)
Crisis	0.063	0.100	0.166	0.267
	(0.127)	(0.216)	(0.106)	(0.181)
DebtService	0.016	0.027	−0.007	−0.009
	(0.026)	(0.043)	(0.026)	(0.043)
Reserves	−0.001	−0.002	−0.001	−0.002
	(0.001)	(0.002)	(0.001)	(0.002)
Democracy	−0.044	−0.078	−0.005	−0.005
	(0.078)	(0.134)	(0.064)	(0.108)
RuleOfLaw	0.282	0.472	0.198	0.315
	(0.273)	(0.461)	(0.259)	(0.432)
PropRights	−0.049	−0.077	0.120	0.229
	(0.435)	(0.754)	(0.382)	(0.678)
PolCycle	0.023	0.035	0.040	0.065
	(0.030)	(0.051)	(0.027)	(0.047)
UN_USalign	0.250	0.363	−0.038	−0.136
	(1.151)	(1.907)	(1.217)	(2.023)
UN_CHNalign	0.271	0.358	−0.104	−0.289
	(1.403)	(2.331)	(1.316)	(2.171)
N	595	595	680	680

Notes: * p<0.1, ** p<0.05, *** p<0.01
Cluster-Robust Standard Errors in all models
Dependent Variable, Deficit, and PolCycle led one year (see DGP discussion)

Table 3.9 Probit Models of Sample Subsets

Model	Drop graduates 18	Drop IDA recipients 19	Drop crisis countries 20	Drop nondemoc-racies 21	Drop PolCycle Outliers 22
WorkingClassParty	0.796**	0.564**	0.578**	0.598*	0.611**
	(0.338)	(0.268)	(0.281)	(0.327)	(0.277)
DVlag	1.463***	1.526***	1.589***	1.383***	1.560***
	(0.213)	(0.192)	(0.196)	(0.285)	(0.191)
CreditRating	−0.044**	−0.059***	−0.050***	−0.091***	−0.059***
	(0.022)	(0.018)	(0.017)	(0.032)	(0.019)
USIrates	0.021	0.026	0.032	0.087*	0.021
	(0.044)	(0.032)	(0.032)	(0.049)	(0.032)
Growth	−0.016	−0.004	−0.003	−0.023	−0.006
	(0.018)	(0.011)	(0.011)	(0.021)	(0.011)
Inflation	−0.000	−0.000*	−0.000*	−0.000*	−0.000*
	(0.000)	(0.000)	(0.000)	(0.000)	(0.000)
Deficit	−0.004	−0.001	0.002	−0.009	0.001
	(0.009)	(0.008)	(0.009)	(0.014)	(0.009)
Crisis	−0.073	0.065	0.000	−0.430**	0.063
	(0.143)	(0.124)	(.)	(0.173)	(0.124)
DebtService	−0.025	0.012	0.009	−0.011	0.009
	(0.026)	(0.026)	(0.028)	(0.038)	(0.027)
Reserves	−0.001	−0.001	−0.001	−0.003	−0.001
	(0.001)	(0.001)	(0.001)	(0.002)	(0.001)
Democracy	−0.043	−0.048	−0.043	−0.195	−0.136
	(0.084)	(0.080)	(0.082)	(0.216)	(0.098)
RuleOfLaw	0.060	0.256	0.327	−0.242	0.429
	(0.329)	(0.265)	(0.267)	(0.353)	(0.268)
PropRights	0.170	−0.023	−0.039	1.439	0.013
	(0.464)	(0.424)	(0.437)	(0.885)	(0.421)
PolCycle	0.025	0.021	0.020	0.031	0.009
	(0.040)	(0.031)	(0.032)	(0.048)	(0.033)
UN_USalign	−0.038	0.175	−0.108	−1.429	0.500
	(1.483)	(1.121)	(1.172)	(1.553)	(1.135)
UN_CHNalign	−0.212	0.154	−0.247	0.144	0.546
	(1.876)	(1.349)	(1.369)	(1.920)	(1.384)
N	425	593	548	368	578

Notes: * $p<0.1$, ** $p<0.05$, *** $p<0.01$
Cluster-Robust Standard Errors in all models
Dependent Variable, Deficit, and PolCycle led one year (see DGP discussion)

estimations. Model 22 drops outlier observations where DPI codes *PolCycle* as '-999' due to significant political uncertainty, rather than including them as zeros as is done in the main analysis. Results persist.

3.5 Conclusion

This chapter statistically tested the argument that an EM's annual external borrowings are significantly determined by government partisanship. Governing parties with working classes as core constituencies and left-leaning economic policy preferences are likely to use more market finance than official credit, proportional to external financing needs.

This theory and evidence puts limits on expectations that left-leaning borrowers are disciplined into using less market-based finance (Mosley 2003, chap. 4; Kaplan 2013), counters arguments that left-leaning governments prefer to avoid markets in the first place (Bunte 2019), and adds to a growing literature on sovereign borrowing preferences (Ballard-Rosa, Mosley, and Wellhausen 2022; Zeitz 2022). More broadly, the study is evidence that partisan politics are central to understanding variation in sovereign debt structure in the EM asset class. Annual partisan effects on external borrowings compound over time to explain variation in external public debt composition across EMs.

One limitation to these statistical tests is that they cannot control for the characteristics or roles of DMOs in the borrowing process. Another limitation is that they do not illustrate the causal mechanism. In this sense, the chapter's statistical tests are tests of the observable implications of the book's model of public debt accumulation (detailed in Chapter 2). The next three chapters supplement these statistical tests with four process-tracing case studies of borrowing outcomes in South Africa, Botswana, Peru, and Thailand over the timeframe of the data used in this chapter. These cases trace the causal process by which we can understand the statistical relationship between government partisanship and annual external borrowings across EMs identified above.

4

South Africa and Botswana

4.1 Introduction

South Africa and Botswana used different external borrowing strategies from the late 1980s through the mid-2010s. South Africa prioritized bond markets while Botswana almost strictly used official credit (see Figure 4.1). Varied borrowing strategies may be expected because, other than being neighbors and one-party democracies, the two EMs have little in common. But many of the ways in which the two contrast would lead one to expect the *inverse* of observed borrowing outcomes. Higher growth, lower debt levels, and superior credit ratings give reason to expect that Botswana would use markets more than South Africa. However, this was not the case. Moreover, outside of a 2009 and 2010 South African government guarantee of a World Bank loan to a state-owned company, nor did structural conditions like global financial crises or historically low interest rates in the rich world in the 2010s lead to consistent convergence in borrowing strategies.

Instead, the partisanship of each country's dominant political party explains how these countries borrowed in this period. South Africa's left-leaning African National Congress (ANC) ensured its DMO avoided conditionality by using bond markets, preventing externally imposed adjustment on core ANC constituencies including labor, the poor, and the public sector. Meanwhile, Botswana's right-leaning Botswana Democratic Party (BDP) ensured its DMO used official creditors because conditions align with BDP policy preferences in the first place and the party preferred to bring cheaper, longer-term external credit onto national accounts. This makes government partisanship central to the two countries' annual external borrowings and thus sovereign debt accumulation over time.

ANC and BDP constituencies, and their effect on each sovereign's external borrowing strategies, are detailed below. Each country's fiscal laws, debt laws, and borrowing processes are outlined, illustrating how legal and institutional frameworks create space for government partisanship to be an important determinant of sovereign external borrowing decisions.

One-party dominance in South Africa and Botswana provides straightforward between-case comparative material for tracing partisanship's effect on EM external borrowing strategies. Subsequent chapters analyze Peru and Thailand, where changes in government partisanship over time provide contexts for testing the partisanship argument in countries exhibiting within-case variation in

How Governments Borrow. Ben Cormier, Oxford University Press. © Ben Cormier (2024).
DOI: 10.1093/oso/9780198882732.003.0004

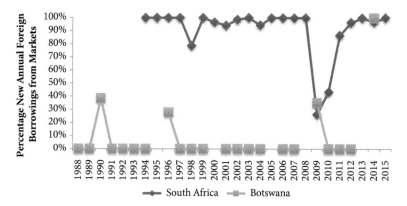

Figure 4.1 South Africa and Botswana Annual Foreign Borrowings

Source: World Development Indicators and author's calculations
Note: Financial embargo on Apartheid South Africa means no foreign borrowing before 1994

the explanatory variable, as well as within-case variation on other important dimensions like regime type.

4.2 South Africa

The dominance of the left-leaning ANC from the end of Apartheid in 1994 through the mid-2010s led the South African state to avoid official creditors when borrowing externally. ANC fiscal and labor policy preferences clash with conditionality, incentivizing use of bond markets. This section first describes elements of ANC partisanship that have informed this borrowing preference. The section then traces how the laws and institutions that underpin South Africa's annual borrowing process create space for government partisanship to affect borrowing. While independent state-owned enterprises (SOEs) used official creditors in 2009-2010 and guarantees of those loans brought some official credit onto the Treasury balance sheet, the central government has consistently used markets for its external financing needs due to the ANC's partisan politics.

4.2.1 ANC Partisanship

The end of Apartheid in 1994 marks a watershed moment for any analysis of South African political economy. This is true of external borrowing as much as any policy area. From 1985 to 1994, South Africa faced an embargo on both official and private external finance. The embargo ended with Apartheid, and the ANC immediately had access to both official and private external resources after it won the first post-Apartheid elections in early 1994. Indeed, Figure 4.2 shows

Botswana				South Africa			
Year	Fitch	Moody's	S&P	Year	Fitch	Moody's	S&P
1989	/	/	/	1989	/	/	/
1990	/	/	/	1990	/	/	/
1991	/	/	/	1991	/	/	/
1992	/	/	/	1992	/	/	/
1993	/	/	/	1993	/	/	/
1994	/	/	/	1994	BB	Baa3	BB
1995	/	/	/	1995	BB	Baa3	BB+
1996	/	/	/	1996	BB	Baa3	BB+
1997	/	/	/	1997	BB	Baa3	BB+
1998	/	/	/	1998	BB	Baa3	BB+
1999	/	/	/	1999	BB	Baa3	BB+
2000	/	/	/	2000	BBB–	Baa3	BBB–
2001	/	A2	A	2001	BBB–	Baa2	BBB–
2002	/	A2	A	2002	BBB–	Baa2	BBB–
2003	/	A2	A	2003	BBB	Baa2	BBB
2004	/	A2	A	2004	BBB	Baa2	BBB
2005	/	A2	A	2005	BBB+	Baa1	BBB+
2006	/	A2	A	2006	BBB+	Baa1	BBB+
2007	/	A2	A	2007	BBB+	Baa1	BBB+
2008	/	A2	A	2008	BBB+	Baa1	BBB+
2009	/	A2	A	2009	BBB+	A3	BBB+
2010	/	A2	A–	2010	BBB+	A3	BBB+
2011	/	A2	A–	2011	BBB+	A3	BBB+
2012	/	A2	A–	2012	BBB+	Baa1	BBB
2013	/	A2	A–	2013	BBB	Baa1	BBB
2014	/	A2	A–	2014	BBB	Baa2	BBB–
2015	/	A2	A–	2015	BBB–	Baa2	BBB–

/ = No Rating
Data from Bloomberg
Accessed December 12–14, 2016

Figure 4.2 South Africa and Botswana Sovereign Credit Ratings

all three major ratings agencies rated South Africa by the end of 1994. Interviews 57 and 61, bureaucrats involved with national debt strategy in the 1990s, recalled the eagerness of foreigners to invest immediately after the end of the Apartheid embargo. Multilaterals and bilaterals also became available but were not used to any substantive degree, as discussed below (see also Thompson 2001, 280).

The ANC is a left-leaning party that, to a significant degree, sees the state as a tool for transferring power and resources to South Africa's previously oppressed racial majority. To be sure, domestic business and international capital interests constrained implementation of some of the ANC's original economic agenda. These influences led some post-Apartheid trade and monetary components of ANC economic policy to follow the neoliberal economic orthodoxy of the time

(Thompson 2001, chaps 8–9; Handley 2008, chap. 3). But such interests did not keep the ANC from pursuing left-leaning aims in other important economic policy areas. Two of these areas, labor policy and fiscal policy (Handley 2008, 79–83), were particularly influential on South Africa's external borrowing.

With respect to labor policy, it is important to note labor's central place in the ANC constituency. The ANC is one of three legs of the 'tripartite alliance,' the other two being the Congress of South African Trade Unions (COSATU) and the South African Communist Party (SACP). ANC electoral success depends on these alliance partners, which is why increasing COSATU and other union frustration with the ANC in the later 2010s was seen by some observers as the biggest threat to the party's grip on power since 1994 (Calland 2013, chap. 8). The importance of labor to the ANC is why the party has long supported strong unions and wage protections, particularly in the country's enormous public sector (Handley 2008, 81–83; Thompson 2001, chap. 9; Bassett and Clarke 2008). Crucial for this study is that South African unions, including the COSATU leg of the tripartite alliance, explicitly want government to avoid official creditors because they are perceived to threaten pro-labor policies like union rights, wage protections, and sponsoring a large public sector.

This pressure has been evident throughout the post-Apartheid period. In 1996 the COSATU president called on government to prioritize financial alternatives to the IMF and World Bank because their loans 'have had a devastating impact on the lives of working people' (Gomomo 1996). The sentiment continued into the 2010s, as COSATU's official policy in 2012 was to 'shift away from the failed solutions offered by the current hegemonic financial institutions, such as the IMF and the World Bank and the African Development Bank' (COSATU 2012, 38). In 2017 a COSATU spokesperson said during an interview that 'our position has always been to stay away from the World Bank and the IMF . . . because they will make [the government] privatize, reduce wages, [and spend less]' (Interview 52).

Labor and thus ANC resistance to conditionality is not a secret to official creditors or state bureaucrats. All government and lender interviewees agreed that official creditors 'are a no-go' because ANC leaders would resist external involvement in labor or any other policy area (quote from Interview 48). Concern about loss of control over various policies make use of official creditors 'more trouble than it is worth' for the Treasury's debt managers (Interview 41). A dozen different interviewees noted conditionality gave rise to control and trust concerns within the ANC. Even if a particular ANC minister is open to official creditors or if bureaucrats think official credit 'may be a good way to expand resources,' they are 'constrained by two of the three legs' of the tripartite alliance (Interviews 51 and 45, respectively).

With respect to fiscal policy, from 1994 the ANC engaged in a variety of large state-led developmental programs to address the socioeconomic inequalities inherited from the Apartheid era. While Nelson Mandela's and Thabo Mbeki's

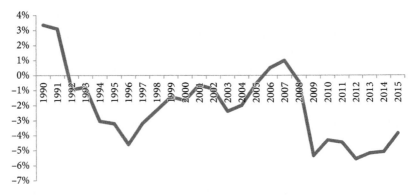

Figure 4.3 South Africa Fiscal Deficit (Rev-Exp)

Source: International Monetary Fund and author's calculations

market-pleasing management of spending frustrated some ANC wings, the ANC has still been a consistent deficit spender. Figure 4.3 shows South Africa ran primary fiscal deficits in all but two years since 1994.

Figure 4.3 also shows deficit levels increased substantially after Jacob Zuma took office in 2009. The Zuma years brought new levels of deficit spending to facilitate a 'big-tent' approach meant to reinvigorate the party's association with a variety of tripartite alliance coalition members (Calland 2013). Multiple public employee wage hike bills overseen by Zuma's ANC in support of COSATU and a large civil service (see for example Reuters 2010; Herskovitz 2010) put particular strain on the budget (Rossouw 2016). New levels of corruption also reflected the patrimonial pattern of state spending in support of ANC supporters under Zuma (on repercussions of this after Zuma left office, see The Economist 2021).

The importance of these core constituencies to the ANC explains why all interviewees noted that reversing this spending trend would be politically difficult. Although a commodity boom increased revenues from the mid-2000s to the early 2010s, South Africa still ran deficits, as a result of persistently increasing spending. When revenues fell, ANC fiscal policy did not tighten but rather implemented 'sustained public spending increases' (Republic of South Africa National Treasury 2009a, 14). In short, the ANC's fiscal approach consistently leads to large deficits and financing requirements that official lenders would subject to conditionality negotiations if the government attempted to use official creditors.

4.2.2 The Budget: Setting the Financing Requirement

Constituents' class-based material interests and economic policy preferences underpin ANC left-leaning partisanship. They in turn determine ANC external borrowing preferences because official creditors would threaten, and are perceived to threaten, pro-labor policies, loose fiscal policies, and the large public sector that is partially sustained by both policies. Most importantly here, the South African fiscal policymaking process ensures these partisan considerations are a main determinant of external borrowings. This is because legal constraints on the fiscal process, which might constrain budgetary spending, debt, or borrowing, are minimal in South Africa. This section explains why ANC policy preferences are a primary determinant of the financing requirement the Treasury's DMO must fund each year, and thus the creditors used to fund it.

A starting point is that South Africa does not have a legal limit on total or annual debt. The Public Finance Management Act states that only the National Treasury and SOEs can borrow, but it does not provide any legal constraints on debt levels or financial instruments. An ostensible constraint is an expenditure ceiling target introduced by Treasury itself in 2012 (Republic of South Africa National Treasury 2014b, 33). While some bureaucrats hope the 'spending limit acts as a debt limit,' the ceiling is not binding (Interview 47). It is a 'flexible' or 'soft' guideline Treasury cannot refer to as more than a point of persuasion (Calitz, Siebrits, and Stuart 2016, 339). In fact, the ceiling increased each year from 2012 through at least 2017, suggesting the ceiling is more of a response to ANC fiscal policy than a constraint on it.[1] While 'the goal is always to stay within the ceiling,' keeping spending within that level depends on the willingness of ANC policymakers (Interview 46). Indeed, some express concern that public debt problems are becoming intractable in South Africa because Treasury has been complacent in not fighting for more formal legislation (Interview 48).

Nor does South Africa have a formal law about debt composition. In the 2010s a self-imposed guideline at Treasury emerged—that no more than 20% of all new annual debt can be foreign (Interview 43) while in practice Treasury aims for 10% (Interview 46). This signals how fluid such informal guidelines are. These numbers also signal how important the domestic market is for the South African government. During Apartheid, as the nation faced embargos on external finance, the state needed to deepen domestic capital markets to have any financial resources. This is discussed more below, but is useful to note here because the relative depth of domestic financial markets (for an EM) created resources, knowledge, and comfort with bond markets that has limited any sense within the DMO that South Africa needs laws that formally regulate debt or borrowing.[2]

Given minimal legal constraints, ANC fiscal policy preferences are the main determinant of annual public revenue, expenditure, and financing requirements. Ministers and MPs, mostly part of the dominant ANC, compete for resources in

[1] See Chapters 3 and 4 of South Africa's National Government Budget Reviews since 2012 to compare ceilings (or, for example, Republic of South Africa National Treasury 2017a, iv).
[2] Interviews 41, 42, 43, 46, 47, 48, 49, 57, 58, 61 all noted DMO staff comfort with markets has suppressed pushing for formal laws that go beyond these informal guidelines.

drafting and authorization phases of the budget process, making the South African budget a political process where it is hard to decrease spending (Interview 46; see also Republic of South Africa Parliament 2011, 19–27). While the size of the pie increased most during the Zuma years, the ANC has generally overseen high spending and normally hands Treasury large annual borrowing requirements (see Figure 4.3).

Treasury's impact on the politics of the budget process is also limited. All interviewees agree the primary job of Treasury is simply to fund the budget, no matter what the borrowing requirement ultimately is. Treasury can consult on debt risk during budget talks, but they are ultimately passive recipients of financing needs. The limited role of Treasury in the budget process reifies the space that ANC politics have to be the primary determinant of government's annual financing requirements.

4.2.3 The ALM: Deciding How to Finance the Budget

Once a budget for the coming year is passed, Treasury's DMO, the Asset and Liabilities Management (ALM) division, has until November to devise a funding strategy (Interview 43). The ALM's official mandate is to manage debt 'only by cost factors.'[3] But if cost was the only consideration, South Africa would use more official credit overall and particularly in its external borrowings. As argued throughout, ANC partisanship explains why this has not been the case.

The ALM uses an informal hierarchy of sources to finance the budget (Interviews 43, 47, 48, 49). Domestic bond markets are the preferred source.[4] Short-term Treasury bills are the second option. External financing options are the third. At the time of this research, a small retail bond market made up 1% of South African debt to round out the government's debt portfolio. Most important here is that after maximizing use of domestic options, the ALM 'will get down to an amount we need to get offshore' to fulfill its borrowing requirement (Interview 46).

When considering external financing, the ALM prefers to issue bonds.[5] There are four reasons for this preference, all of which make clear how ALM borrowing decisions are primarily shaped by fiscal demands and political expediency. In other words, despite the ALM's mandate to optimize borrowing costs and minimize sovereign debt risk, ALM borrowings are constrained by ANC partisan politics. The four reasons the ALM prefers bonds and avoids official creditor

---

[3] Interview 58, who also noted borrowing decisions were made by the central bank until the mid-1990s and the ALM was established to separate borrowing policy from monetary policy.

[4] It is sometimes cheaper for South Africa to borrow domestically than from even official creditors. For example, the World Bank's swap mechanism costs mean Bank loans are sometimes 'still not cheap enough' compared to borrowing domestically, depending on other factors (Interview 47).

[5] Interview 47 noted that drawing on foreign reserves is a funding option the ALM has rarely used, with the levels at which this is appropriate being a matter of debate.

options are: avoiding conditionality, noninvolvement with fund distribution, debt management and revenue shortfalls, and a technical comfort with market instruments that developed in the ALM over time.

First, as detailed above, core ANC constituencies and thus the ANC explicitly resist official credit. For the ALM this means borrowing from multilateral or bilateral creditors for the 'price benefit . . . is more trouble than it is worth' due to the political transaction costs that would come with accepting conditions (Interview 41).

All current and former officials interviewed on both creditor and government sides of South African public debt emphasize this ANC preference and effect. On the lender side, World Bank staff note the reputation of conditionality in South Africa remains associated with Structural Adjustment conditions from the 1980s and 1990s. Bank staff argue this as an outdated view of conditionality, but they say the perception plays a central role in keeping the government from borrowing from the Bank—despite the Bank being eager to lend (Interviews 42 and 65). An African Development Bank official said they had never had a serious discussion with the ALM about loans for similar reasons (Interview 68). ALM officials explain that Western bilaterals are not considered beyond grants (typically health related, funding HIV/AIDS efforts being a major example), while Chinese loans are not only slightly more expensive but come with equally problematic consequences as Western lenders (Interviews 41, 43, 45, 46, 47, 48, 49, 51, 52, 57, 58, 59).

This means official lender conditions and reputations keep the ALM in more expensive foreign bonds when South Africa fulfills external borrowing requirements. This is true despite substantial increases in South African sovereign risk and thus the cost for the ALM throughout this period. Most large foreign bond issuances (over US$1 billion) from 2007 to 2016 were issued while South Africa's credit ratings were below investment grade (Figure 4.2) and as rates on benchmark foreign-denominated South African sovereign bonds increased from 2.4% to around 6%.[6] Meanwhile, World Bank loans were available at no higher than the concessional LIBOR-tied loan Eskom received in this period with a nearly three decade maturity (World Bank 2010b). Despite such significant price and maturity differences, the ALM avoids official creditors for political expediency.

Second, use of borrowed funds is not under the ALM's purview. The distribution of borrowed resources is left to ministers and MPs. This means some key benefits of official creditors, namely project-specific lending, technical support, and project monitoring are not immediately relevant to the ALM. As one official notes, 'it doesn't make sense for us to focus on specific projects . . . everything [we borrow] goes into the [National Revenue Fund] and gets taken from the pot . . . It becomes difficult to have discussions about [funding for] specific projects. We look at [borrowing] from a much bigger picture than that' (Interview 46).

---

[6] Data provided by Interview 50.

In other words, using official credit would require becoming involved with polit-ically sensitive details of fund allocation and condition compliance. While official creditors, particularly Western lenders, claim that conditions improve governance, minimize corruption, enhance efficiency, and improve effectiveness of finance, the ALM finds it difficult to take on this political 'slippery slope' (Interview 51). Bond markets require no such ALM intrusion into the domestic distributional politics of fiscal expenditure.

Third, existing debt obligations incentivize use of private external finance. This is even more relevant when revenues fall short of anticipated targets. At a mini-mum, the ALM issues US$1 billion in foreign bonds every other year to rollover existing debt and maintain an updated benchmark in the market (Interviews 43, 44, 45, 47, 48, 49). Revenue shortfalls due to lower than expected growth, tax col-lection problems, falling export prices, a weakening Rand, and corruption give further reason to issue bonds, since the funds arrive immediately and conditions do not have to be negotiated with political ramifications in mind (Interviews 43, 44, 45, 47, 48, 49). Procedural requirements reinforce the controversial nature of official loans, especially compared to the comparatively string-free option of issuing bonds.

Fourth, ALM officials are comfortable with bond market instruments and con-fident in their risk management practices. This likely stems at least somewhat from the development of domestic bond markets during Apartheid and relatively easy access to foreign markets immediately afterwards. Since, ALM officials have felt South Africa can manage price fluctuations and other market exigencies, even when overborrowing (Interview 41). Indeed, despite 'increased risk' due to fiscal positions, financial market volatility, inflation, exchange rates, and credit ratings, the ALM feels it has 'resilient fiscal and debt management policies' so continue to borrow billions annually in foreign markets (Republic of South Africa National Treasury 2017b, 82–83; 93) rather than utilize other sources.

This view is shared by investors, which has helped sustain the supply of mar-ket finance despite deteriorating creditworthiness, fundamentals, and governance. Bankers are confident in the ALM, feeling it 'has done well to avoid' official credi-tors and stay in markets (Interview 50). Even as South Africa credit ratings reached junk status at the end of the 2010s, foreign currency bond issuances remained two to three times oversubscribed in American and European markets (Republic of South Africa National Treasury 2013, 16–17; 2014a, 21–23). ALM confidence is mirrored by investors who claim 'no [investor] is not going to get their money back' from South Africa (Interview 51).

A symbol of persistent investor confidence in the ALM is that South African bond roadshows are nondeal roadshows. While most EMs must issue bonds while presenting to and communicating directly with investors, the ALM has been able to issue bonds whether on the road or not. This has been true since 2012 and persisted through credit rating downgrades (Interviews 47, 48, 49). A pointed case is when President Zuma recalled Finance Minister Pravin Gordhan from a March 2017 London roadshow. The ALM still met with twenty-six investors that day and issued bonds months later, avoiding official creditors despite this public display of political uncertainty.[7] Although the example is from after this study's timeframe, it highlights the persistence of liquidity available to South Africa despite political-economic events in the country, the ALM's use of that market despite increasingly expensive rates and junk bond ratings, and resistance to diversifying with cheaper official options.

Taken together, these four factors lead the ALM to use markets when turning abroad for finance. ANC partisanship, particularly through fiscal and labor policy, prevent the ALM from seriously considering cheaper and longer-term official credit that comes with conditions.

4.2.4 State-Owned Enterprises

It is important to note the ALM (i.e. the central government) is not the only public debtor with foreign debt obligations in South Africa. While South African line ministries cannot borrow outside of ALM processes, large SOEs can. They have their own treasuries that can simply 'borrow with the approval of their Board of Directors' (Republic of South Africa National Treasury 2015, 39). The ALM relationship to SOEs is consultative rather than authoritative (Interviews 41, 43, 46, 47, 48, 49, 53, 62). This lack of control has had negative consequences for sovereign risk overall, and Treasury has long tried to increase influence over SOE borrowing to 'enhance [government's] creditworthiness' (Republic of South Africa National Treasury 2013, 2).

Despite independent decision-making, SOE borrowing affects Treasury through explicit or implicit guarantees (see Republic of South Africa National Treasury 2015, chap. 5). Explicit guarantees include formal government backing for the obligation, ensuring repayment by Treasury in the case of SOE default. SOEs apply for explicit guarantees and Treasury has the authority to reject applications (Interviews 41, 43, 47, 48). If granted, explicit guarantees come with conditions for SOE operations and go on the national balance sheet (Interviews 43, 62). If rejected, SOEs can and often do borrow anyway. This leads to controversial implicit guarantees, since the government would find it difficult not to bail out SOEs in the event of default on a nonguaranteed loan (Interviews 50, 62). For this reason, all SOE borrowings but particularly implicitly guaranteed borrowings 'remain a major risk to the fiscus' (Republic of South Africa National Treasury 2017b, 91).

---

[7] Interviews 42, 43, 44, 45, 46, 47, 48, 49, 50, 51. Interestingly, the effect of the recall on foreign bond interest rates was less substantial than in the domestic market (Interview 43).

While many SOEs have the potential to affect sovereign debt and risk positions, the most important SOE in this context is utility company Eskom. By 2014 Eskom accounted for over 72% of all SOE guarantees (Republic of South Africa National Treasury 2014a, 40). Eskom was historically so creditworthy that Treasury actually borrowed through Eskom, but price and production issues since the 1980s have inverted this relationship (Interview 53). By the mid-2000s and 2010s, Eskom had junk credit ratings, faced higher external interest rates than the central government (7.37% in 2014), and repeatedly exceeded its planned borrowings agreed with Treasury and issued nonguaranteed bonds (Interviews 42, 45, 50, 53, 54, 62; see also Republic of South Africa National Treasury 2014a, 39, 42; 2015, 41).

Eskom was forced to 'look all over the place' for finance in this period (Interview 53). When doing so the SOE found the cheapest option was official creditors, including among domestic options that were more hesitant to lend to Eskom than any foreigner (Interviews 50, 62). Accordingly, in 2009 Eskom borrowed US$2.5 billion from the African Development Bank (AfDB) and in 2010 borrowed US$3.75 billion from the World Bank (Interview 62).[8] The ALM had little to do with these loans other than providing explicit guarantees. As one Treasury official said, '[Eskom has] their own strategy, and if going to [official creditors] is what they feel they need to do, that is what they will do' (Interview 46). Eskom continued to use official creditors from 2010, returning to the AfDB multiple times and borrowing from Japan, Europe, the United States, and China (Interview 62).[9] While it was hoped that official loans would help attract hesitant private capital to Eskom, official credit came to comprise 90% of Eskom's financing during this period (Groenwald and le Cordur 2017; Interview 68).

When explicitly guaranteed, Eskom's use of official creditors brings official debt onto the government's balance sheet. Other SOEs have had this effect as well, with Japan and Europe also lending to other South African SOEs over the years (Republic of South Africa National Treasury 2010, 97). This means that any official credit to South Africa seen in Figure 4.1 is from SOE guarantees. In particular, Eskom's historic World Bank loan is why Figure 4.1 shows a spike in South Africa's official commitments in 2009 and 2010.

This SOE effect on creditor usage is important to emphasize given this book's argument about partisan sovereign borrowing. The ALM carries official debt only due to SOE guarantees, not because it has ever used official creditors to fund central government borrowing requirements. Indeed, the ALM continued to strictly use capital markets even from 2008 through 2010 despite the activities of Eskom

[8] Negotiations largely concluded in 2009 but the Bank's board committed most of the funds in early 2010. Including loans from Bank environmental funds, the World Bank loan reached US$4 billion in total (Republic of South Africa National Treasury 2010, 97; 2009a; 2009b).

[9] This shift away from the World Bank to other official creditors since 2009/10 was not only because of the size of the 2009/10 loan, but because these other lenders would fund further coal projects that the Bank would not (see Eskom 2017).

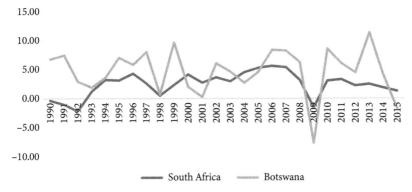

Figure 4.4 South Africa and Botswana Annual Percentage Growth

and despite structural incentives to diversify, including 'access to foreign finance [becoming] much scarcer and more expensive' in that period (Republic of South Africa National Treasury 2009a, 14; 2010, 91).

4.2.5 South Africa Summary

Despite official creditor price and maturity benefits, South Africa's ALM uses bonds when borrowing externally. ANC partisanship explains this foreign borrowing pattern over time. If sovereign borrowing were determined by creditworthiness, South Africa would have been disciplined into using more official credit as credit ratings deteriorated (Figure 4.2), growth slowed (Figure 4.4), and debt levels rose rapidly (Figure 4.5). Alternatively, South Africa may have been disciplined into smaller deficits to continue using markets, but there is no evidence of such a disciplinary effect on fiscal policy (Figure 4.3). Meanwhile, if borrowing were determined by structural factors, the ALM would have used official credit from 2007 to 2010 (Republic of South Africa National Treasury 2009a, 14). But SOEs were the only ones to use official credit in these years. The central government did not. Instead, South Africa's ALM issues bonds because 'at the right price, there will always be a market' and it is politically easier to find that price than use official credit (Interview 47).

4.3 Botswana

Botswana has been called the 'African Miracle' for consistent economic growth based on 'democratic institutions, a prospering private sector, and healthy public finances' (Samatar 1999; Danevad 1995, 381). Despite high inequality, devastating

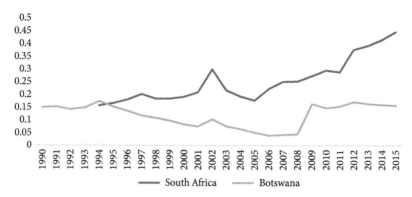

Figure 4.5 South Africa and Botswana External Debt Stocks (Percentage GNI)
Source: Data from World Bank Development Indicators

effects from the HIV/AIDS epidemic, and diamond dependence (Hillbom 2008; Makgala and Botlhomilwe 2017; Lewin 2011, 87–88; Taylor 2004), the country had low-cost bond market access from 1990 to 2015. In fact, Botswana had vastly superior investment grade credit ratings than South Africa throughout this period (Figure 4.2).[10]

Yet Botswana almost strictly used official creditors when turning abroad for finance. Why would Botswana avoid markets despite better fundamentals and market access than South Africa? Botswana's preference for and use of official creditors is explained by the right-leaning partisanship of the country's dominant party, the Botswana Democratic Party (BDP). The BDP's economically conservative political constituency leads to comfort with official creditor conditions that reinforce preexisting 'good' policy preferences (Lewin 2011).

4.3.1 BDP Partisanship

The BDP has controlled Batswana politics since independence in 1966 (Poteete 2012). The party's roots lie in ethnically homogenous rural areas dominated by the cattle industry. From independence, patrimonial transfers shored up party support from cattle industry elites (Danevad 1995, 389). The discovery of diamond deposits led to enormous new government revenues by the mid-1970s, and in the 1980s the BDP began using these funds to diversify the economy. These efforts took the form of transfers to manufacturing and service sector entrepreneurs,

---

[10] Interview 82 noted the Botswana Ministry of Finance and Economic Development resisted offers for ratings from rating agencies themselves, as well as central bank pressure to get ratings, until 2000. The offers, central bank pressure, and the high investment-grade ratings they immediately received when Moody's and S&P rated the country indicate low-cost market access.

which on top of economic diversification also aimed to obtain 'the political loyalty of an increasingly diversified economic elite' (Danevad 1995, 389–93).

It is difficult to overstate the political effect of Botswana's unparalleled diamond revenues. While efforts to diversify the economy have had limited effects on the country's overall economic production profile (Good 2005; Hillbom 2008; Lewin 2011, 87; Makgala and Botlhomilwe 2017, 55–58), diamond-funded transfers have allowed the BDP to ensure support from elites across sectors (Good 2005; Von Soest 2009). Prioritizing elite constituents has led to substantial inequalities and 'suggest the majority of the population . . . only constitute a limited source of political pressure' on the BDP (Danevad 1995, 395). Minimal nonelite political voice characterizes the period of BDP party dominance under study here (Good 2003; Cook and Sarkin 2010; Makgala and Botlhomilwe 2017). Even those who laud Botswana's economic development admit BDP national development strategies are designed 'in the interests of the dominant class' (Leith 2005, 40, referencing and aligning with Samatar 1999).

Elite core constituencies incentivize the BDP to consistently implement right-leaning, open economic policy. The most important here are fiscal and labor policies, which stand in stark contrast to South Africa's ANC fiscal and labor policy preferences. Fiscal conservatism is a main reason the BDP is sometimes criticized for overseeing 'growth without structural change and development' (Hillbom 2008, 193). Labor has long been juxtaposed as in conflict with the BDP, as far back as speeches made by BDP founder and Botswana's first President Seretse Khama (Khama 1971). These are discussed in turn below.

Figure 4.6 shows the BDP regularly implements fiscal surpluses. Supporters argue BDP prioritization of saving over spending is 'prudent fiscal policy' providing 'macroeconomic stability' (Lewin 2011, 85–86). In practice, savings allow for accumulation of reserves the state uses to smooth effects of diamond market downturns. The BDP maintains such high savings that reserve levels reached twenty-five months of import cover in the 1990s and, while trending to half that level by the 2010s, BDP-led economic ministries see nine months of import cover as the lowest acceptable reserve level.[11] These high saving thresholds give Botswana fiscal and financial cushions that are 'exceptional in the developing world' (Danevad 1995, 387).

Despite diamond wealth, such large surpluses and reserve levels are not inevitable. They are a policy choice. This choice reflects the BDP's conservative aims of 'withholding some of the benefits from the economy during the booms . . . to insulate it from the busts' (Lewin 2011, 86). In the event that negative revenue trends make surpluses difficult to maintain, the Ministry of Finance and

---

[11] Interviews 72, 80, 81, 82. These economic ministries include the finance ministry and central bank. Reserve data, measured by months of import cover, can be found via the World Bank's WDI database.

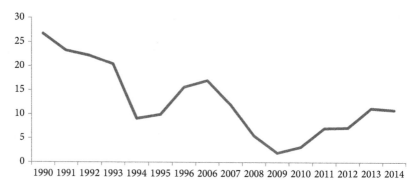

Figure 4.6 Botswana Central Government Fiscal Balance

Source: International Monetary Fund and author's calculations
Note: IMF data missing between 1997 and 2005 and in 2015

Economic Development's (MFED) plan under the BDP is to either 'cut Government expenditure by postponing projects or downsizing the public service, or to enhance the revenue base by eliminating tax expenditures' (Republic of Botswana Ministry of Finance and Economic Development 2016, vii, para 7).[12] In other words, despite massive reserve levels, spending is to be cut *before* reserves are touched. BDP prioritization of fiscal sustainability and minimizing the role of the state in the economy is official policy (Interviews 72, 79, 80, 81, 82).

Predictably, this approach to fiscal policy and reserves has been central to left-leaning party criticism of BDP-led government (Taylor 2003; Makgala and Botlhomilwe 2017; see also Danevad 1995, 399–401, who pointed to similar trends in the early 1990s). These opposition parties argue the BDP's overemphasis on surpluses has kept the government from investing in broad-based development, leading to worsening inequalities, unnecessary unemployment, and an undereducated population unprepared for a future without diamonds (Good 2003; Taylor 2003; Hillbom 2008; Cook and Sarkin 2010; Lewin 2011, 87–88; Makgala and Botlhomilwe 2017). This frustration is not only due to low spending but also allocation of spending, in particular military expenditure (Beaulier and Subrick 2006, 112; Interviews 72, 73, 74). There is political pressure to increase spending and direct it to other pro-poor and pro-labor ends than what the BDP prioritizes, but the BDP prioritizes the interests of its elite constituencies.

Partisans in the state and private sector know the BDP is 'accused of being conservative' despite having 'no hard budget constraint' (Interviews 81 and 72, respectively). While this means the government could spend more, some claim spending more would have minimal effect because the state does not have the

---

[12] Interview 82 noted this was the first formal debt strategy, but reflects how the same fiscal preferences have been held across multiple generations of civil servants under the BDP.

capacity to effectively spend (Leith 2005; Lewin 2011; Botlhale 2015, 415). Regardless, it is clear that Botswana has an unusual amount of financial resources and fiscal space for an EM. The BDP's minimal deployment of these resources is a savings-oriented fiscal policy choice that supports an elite political base.

Directly related is BDP labor policy and relationship with unions. The BDP has long sought to minimize labor in national politics. Indeed, as far back as 1971, President Khama encouraged unions to accept that Botswana could only develop if mining profits were 'mainly re-invested and not consumed' (Khama 1971, 12), defending fiscal conservatism to the group most likely to challenge it. Khama also outlined the political implications of not accepting such policy, saying the BDP would 'keep the channels of communication open' between government and labor only if labor and their 'minority interests' do not seek gains 'by direct involvement in the political arena' (Khama 1971, 9–10). The BDP's interest in minimizing labor's role in politics has been explicit since the country gained independence.

BDP opposition to labor continued through the 1990s and 2000s, manifest in legal restrictions on unions. Unions are difficult to legally register, general strikes are 'categorically impossible' (there has never been a legal strike in Botswana due to legal frameworks and intimidation), union officials cannot work full-time, and workers are not protected from shop closures (Taylor 2003, 226). The BDP's contentious relationship with labor continued through the 2010s (Poteete 2012, 87; Makgala and Botlhomilwe 2017, 69–70).

Together, BDP fiscal and labor policies reflect the party's elite economic constituents and preference for policies that reflect their interests. This provides a clear and succinct contrast to the South African ANC's left-leaning constituencies and policy preferences in these areas.

Elite constituencies also explain other BDP policies and approaches to governance. Open trade has been the norm since the early 1900s. Openness to FDI and foreign ownership in key areas of the economy is exemplified by the fact that mining company Debswana was initially a fully private South African firm and remains part-owned by foreigners (Leith 2005, 68–70, 61–63, note 7). The BDP also favors privatization. Botswana's public sector is among the smallest in Africa (Lewin 2011, 86–87), stemming from the BDP's early efforts to bring private sector elites into its political constituency rather than sponsor state-owned competition that would threaten private sector income (Danevad 1995, 393; Hillbom 2008). With respect to monetary policy, although the Botswana Pula is pegged to the South African Rand, the IMF and World Bank support the peg as a tool for managing prices and inflation in a small economy (International Monetary Fund 2002b, 23; Lewin 2011, 86). Good governance is central to Botswana's economic reputation, with transparency and rule of law credited by those who claim Botswana has avoided the resource curse (Robinson and Parsons 2006; Beaulier and Subrick 2006; Beaulier 2003; Lewin 2011).

4.3.2   Fiscal Rules Written by the BDP Reinforce Conservatism

The BDP's economic policies reflect the interests of its elite constituents and set the stage for Botswana's use of official creditors. However, laws and institutional arrangements may also affect borrowing. This section considers these possibilities. It concludes that any fiscal laws or rules are products of BDP preferences in the first place, and borrowing preferences reflect BDP prioritization of fiscal sustainability and risk management over other possible priorities.

Botswana's only debt law is that total outstanding public debt is limited to 40% of GDP, half of which can be external (Republic of Botswana Ministry of Finance and Economic Development 2016, 23, para 55).[13] This is well above national debt levels and thus seen as irrelevant in practice (Interview 72, 77, 78, 80). Indeed, official BDP government documents explain that the law was written to conform with 'international best practice' and 'given the modest level of debt in Botswana, the need for public debt law is not considered necessary' (Republic of Botswana Ministry of Finance and Economic Development 2016, 23–24).

The BDP sets additional informal fiscal and debt rules in the party's policy platform, the National Development Plan (NDP), which is updated in six- to seven-year intervals. For example, spending is limited to 30–40% of GDP, with the exact ceiling varying by NDP iteration (Interview 80). Such variability reinforces how these are internal party guidelines rather than legally enforceable restrictions or externally set rules (see Republic of Botswana Ministry of Finance and Economic Development 2016, v, paragraph 2 for an example). Reflecting concern about fiscal efficiency and state capacity for productive investment, the NDP always includes a rule that only 30% of debt can go toward new projects rather than recurring expenditures (Interviews 77, 78, 80). Finally, the NDP sets a debt cap for each line ministry (Interviews 77, 78). While some (including, perhaps surprisingly, the IMF)[14] want the BDP government to implement looser fiscal rules to allow for a large-scale investment program, many within the MFED resist this due to concerns about the medium- and long-term risks of financing such a program, as well as fears about losing oversight of line ministry finances and projects (Interviews 68, 77, 78, 80, 81, 82).

Since Botswana's fiscal rules are direct products of the BDP's policy platforms, they are not exogenous institutional constraints that force the BDP-dominated parliament to produce budgets and fiscal policy it would not produce otherwise. In contrast to South Africa, line ministries have firm control over the few SOEs that exist and no budget or financing decisions take place outside of MFED processes (Interviews 72, 73, 77, 78, 79, 80). Such a centralized budget process in Botswana

---

[13]   See also Part IV of the 2005 Stock, Bonds, and Treasury Bills Act.
[14]   Interview 80 noted the IMF asked in multiple years of Article IV meetings why the 30% limit on new-investment debt is not higher (see also Republic of Botswana Ministry of Finance and Economic Development 2016).

ensures the BDP can manage all components of fiscal policy according to its preferences. Moreover, laws were implemented not in reaction to risks but to match best practices and thus do not present hard constraints on actual spending or debt levels, making BDP policy the clear primary determinant of budget and borrowing decisions.

4.3.3 Borrowing Process and Choices

After parliament passes a budget, Botswana's DMO (the Office of Budget Analysis and Debt Management) considers whether there is a need to borrow. Given Botswana's persistent surpluses, the DMO is normally not interested in general budget support and mostly considers financing for specific projects. On a case-by-case basis, the DMO determines whether projects in the budget are best paid for by revenue, reserves, or borrowed funds. In practice, borrowing is most likely when a line ministry proposes borrowing for one of its projects or if the DMO receives financing offers as spending plans are made public (Interviews 68, 77, 78, 81).

Borrowing decisions are made by the DMO in coordination with line ministries. The process is the same regardless of whether the external source of credit is official or market based (Interview 77). Officials say the DMO may accept ministries' lender suggestions or force them to use the DMO's preference (Interviews 77, 78, 81). Either way, the choices are almost always official creditors, with a few cases since 1990 of line ministries requesting guarantees of commercial bank loans for SOEs. Indeed, any market flow for Botswana indicated in Figure 4.1 is a guarantee of a foreign bank loan to SOEs. Once the DMO chooses a financier, parliamentary approval is required but there is 'very little debate' at this stage and MPs 'just want to see a presentation.'[15] This signals how policy alignment across the executive and legislative branches of government under the BDP allows the DMO substantial control over use of official creditors.

Botswana's hierarchy of borrowing preferences is different from South Africa's. Drawing on reserves is the first consideration, official external credit is the second choice, domestic debt is less common but possible, and private external debt is a last resort. In fact, at the time of fieldwork in 2017, the DMO had never issued an external bond and never borrowed from banks for central government use (i.e. for non-SOE use; Interviews 72, 73, 74, 77, 78, 80, 81, 82). This chapter's main question is why Botswana prefers official over market external finance while South

---

[15] Interviews 77, 78. Interviews 68 and 81 noted that a guarantee for a SOE (Botswana Development Corporation) was rejected by parliament in 2016, a first in their recollection. Interviews 72 and 79 noted this was likely due to increased salience and concern about guarantees in 2016, when Barclays called in a government guarantee to mining company BCL and a $US800 million guarantee for Botswana Power Corporation. This signals a possible shift in the politics of guarantees after 2015.

Africa prefers the opposite, but it is useful to note the role of reserves and domestic markets.

Botswana's high reserve levels make drawdowns a relatively risk-free option. But as noted above, the BDP policy of protecting these high reserve levels means other sources of finance are often sought despite abundant reserves (Interviews 72, 82). Moreover, since the central bank holds reserves and technically sells them to the MFED, drawing down reserves is not entirely up to the MFED and may be controversial. This hurdle gives the MFED further reason to not use reserves, especially if reserve levels are trending downwards (Interviews 72, 82). Meanwhile, Botswana's domestic capital markets are 'immature' and more expensive than external credit, with domestic rates normally around 7–8% and official credit rates between 1.5–5%.[16] Civil servants and bankers note that the government resists issuing long-term domestic debt that would deepen the market (Interviews 72, 73, 74). There are contrasting views about this approach to sovereign debt management. Some consider this prudent given the uncertainty that comes from diamond dependence, while others worry that using official lenders means the DMO is unable to take advantage of the chance to develop bond markets during good times that can minimize risk in the long run.[17]

But why does Botswana prefer official rather than market instruments when making external borrowings? Crucially, all interviewees emphasize Botswana has some of the best bond market access across EMs, saying the DMO 'is always told to issue,' that foreign bankers 'knock on [the government's] door all the time,' and that there 'is all sorts of demand' for external bonds.[18] Botswana's investment-grade credit ratings corroborate this (Figure 4.2).

This means Botswana does not issue because of lack of market access. Rather, the DMO has 'no interest at all' in bond markets due to 'macro policy and government priorities' (Interviews 77 and 72, respectively). This was consistent from 1990 to 2015. Tellingly, the MFED saw no need to obtain credit ratings in the 1990s, despite pressure from investors as well as the state's central bank to get them. Once the MFED gave in and received high ratings, both raters and the central bank then pushed for bond issues. But the DMO continued to resist (Interviews 80, 82). Market avoidance continued through the era of low global interest rates in the 2010s (Figure 4.1).

The DMO uses official credit because it provides price and maturity benefits, includes repayment flexibility, reinforces BDP macroeconomic priorities, and

---

[16] Interviews 72, 73, 74, and quote from 79. Interview 72 noted prices. Interviews 77, 78, 80, and 81 say this means external loans are normally cheaper even including exchange rate risk, while Interview 72 disagreed.

[17] Interviews 65, 72, 73, 74, 75, 79 on the latter, Interview 80 on the former. Interview 81 suggested that after 2015 the MFED began to focus on developing domestic markets for the long term, not as a financial resource for the short term.

[18] Quotes from Interviews 81, 73, and 77 respectively, and all interviewees concurred.

brings technical assistance. First, the DMO finds official loan terms beneficial. These benefits do not only include lower interest rates and longer maturities than bond markets, though that is the primary benefit. In addition, the DMO finds it can shop among official lenders for longer maturities, can repay official loans early if they prove unnecessary, and assumes official creditors will be open to restructuring if exchange rate or revenue problems arise.[19] In sum, the DMO finds official creditors allow them to 'borrow sustainably' in comparison to markets (Interview 81). As another senior government official said, there are 'stories about the benefits of issuing [bonds, but we] just don't buy it' (Interview 80).

Second, BDP policy preferences align with official creditors' standard prescriptions, encouraging their use. Most obviously, this means the DMO does not face resistance from BDP elite constituents about using official creditors that may intervene in domestic policy (Interviews 65, 73, 74, 79). In fact, related not just to policy but the price and term benefits noted above, long-tenured senior officials trust the hands-on behavior of official creditors more than they do markets (Interviews 80, 81). As one banker said, the 'conservative' DMO 'likes working with [official creditors'] economists' (Interview 73).

Ideological alignment also leads to smooth negotiations. Since Botswana is not desperate to borrow, since official creditors like the World Bank are eager to lend to EMs, and since official creditors concerned with borrowers' domestic policy trust Botswana will pursue 'good' policy, the DMO has the power to negotiate conditions to the point where they essentially reflect existing government policy (Interviews 79, 82). This gives the DMO 'more power over [official creditors] than markets,' leading one official to say borrowing from them is 'easy' (Interviews 81 and 77, respectively). Again, this leads some to worry that such easy official borrowing leads to short sighted debt management, and a missed opportunity to develop market benchmarks and relationships during Botswana's good times (Interviews 65, 72, 73, 74, 75, 79).

The third benefit is technical assistance. The DMO values foreign involvement in projects because it increases capacity, efficiency, and effectiveness of projects (Interviews 77, 78, 80, 81, 82). While this brings bureaucratic delay, resistance to large-scale investment at the national level means the DMO does not mind official lenders' relatively slow processes (Interviews 80). Others note Botswana's landlocked position means some projects are regional, making coordination through official lenders appealing (Interview 56). Finally, DMO officials perceive bond roadshows to be just as time-consuming and costly as these delays (Interview 80).

An exception has been Chinese-funded projects. Officials say that while these loans are tied to Chinese companies and workers, the major issue in their

---

[19] Interviews 65, 72, 73, 74, 75, 77, 78, 79, 80, 81, 82. Interviews 68, 73, and 74 said Chinese bilateral finance had been tried across various projects but was now avoided due to ineffectiveness (not price or different conditionalities).

experience is that Chinese-funded projects were not completed on time or on budget (Interviews 68, 73, 74). This perceived ineffectiveness of bilateral Chinese loans across a variety of sectors has become publicly salient and criticized by MPs, leading some bureaucrats to claim the DMO 'will never use them again' (Interview 81). Regardless of fluctuations in China's role as a lender, the DMO has continued to use official credit rather than issue bonds. And it is notable that in the Botswana context, resistance to Chinese loans was not a reaction to the effect of Chinese labor and firms on Batswana labor or small firms, but a sense that Chinese projects were less successful than Western projects.

Botswana's preference for official credit is thus largely explained by BDP partisanship. First, tight fiscal policy reflects a broader emphasis on macroeconomic stability, leading the DMO to value official creditors' interest rates and maturities (as well as repayment flexibility). Second, the BDP's economic policy preferences mirror the aims of official creditors' loan conditions, making use of official credit uncontroversial within the party or the MFED. Third, technical assistance and foreign involvement is seen by the MFED to reinforce good governance and efficiency. BDP politics create the space for the DMO to use official creditors when borrowing.

4.4 Comparison and Conclusion

Botswana consistently used official credit from the late 1980s through 2015. Global and national economic factors commonly associated with market access and use did not negate the BDP's preference for and DMO use of official credit. First, Botswana continued to use official options as global interest rates reached historic lows in the 2010s. The 2014 datapoint in Figure 4.1 reflects a guarantee of a loan to a SOE, not central government borrowing. Otherwise, Botswana relied on official lenders. Second, Botswana's persistent growth, surpluses, and strong credit ratings suggest Botswana could issue bonds at some of the lowest rates in the EM class (Figure 4.2). Persistent invitations from investors and pressure from its own central bank to issue highlight this. But Botswana's DMO, constrained by BDP partisans, resisted. In contrast, South Africa issued bonds despite junk ratings and high borrowing costs. Economic indicators such as low growth and high debt levels, nor related high interest rates, did not determine borrowing decisions as much as ANC partisanship.

In the end, without considering the role and effect of partisan politics, it would be difficult to see why market instruments and obligations wound up on South Africa's rather than Botswana's balance sheet, and why official credit wound up on Botswana's rather than South Africa's balance sheet. Partisan-determined annual external borrowings explain variation in the composition of the countries' sovereign debt structures from the 1990s through mid 2010s.

The next chapters consider the effects of partisanship in other EM borrowers: Peru and Thailand. They are important third and fourth cases because government partisanship changed multiple times in each country in recent decades, allowing for within-case tests of the partisan argument. As will be shown, as various parties with different economic constituencies and policy preferences governed in Peru and Thailand, partisanship remained central to explaining how these EMs borrowed abroad each year from the 1980s through the mid-2010s.

5

Peru

5.1 Introduction

Chapter 4 traced the partisan effect on external borrowing in a comparison of South Africa and Botswana. This chapter traces the partisan effect on external borrowing in Peru. Peru is a valuable third case for two reasons. First, Peru's governing parties, and the partisan leanings of those parties, changed multiple times from 1990 through 2015. This allows for a within-case test of partisan effects on EM external borrowings, adding to the between-case comparison in Chapter 4.

Second, Peru's DMO is a unit within a notoriously independent and influential set of national economic ministries. The General Directorate of Treasury and Indebtedness (DTI—*Dirección General de Endeudamiento y Tesoro Público*), located within the Ministry of Finance and Economics (MEF—*Ministerio de Economía y Finanzas*), makes Peru's sovereign borrowing decisions. The MEF is a powerful ministerial 'island of efficiency' that uses its influence to promote 'neoliberal' policies in many areas of Peru's economy despite the election of successive center-left governments since the early 2000s (Crabtree and Durand 2017, chap. 4). If this book's model of sovereign debt accumulation based on politically constrained DMOs is credible, the effect of government partisanship on external borrowing should persist despite an influential MEF and DTI. Indeed, given MEF's conservative economic policy preferences and the outsize influence Peru's economic ministries have on policy in most areas of Peru's macroeconomy, one might expect Peru to have used official creditors when turning abroad for finance regardless of government partisanship.

Figure 5.1 shows this was not the case. When conservative parties were in power after 1990, Peru's MEF used official credit. But when governing parties had working-class constituencies and comparatively left-leaning economic policy preferences, the MEF could not strictly use its preferred official creditors. Left governments forced the MEF to issue foreign bonds it would prefer not to issue because these parties' policy preferences meant they resisted official creditor conditions and associated effects on their core constituents.

This does not mean that MEF preferences are entirely irrelevant. The MEF explicitly prefers official credit not only for lower prices and technical assistance, but also because MEF can 'use conditions to reform line ministries' and tie the

How Governments Borrow. Ben Cormier, Oxford University Press. © Ben Cormier (2024).
DOI: 10.1093/oso/9780198882732.003.0005

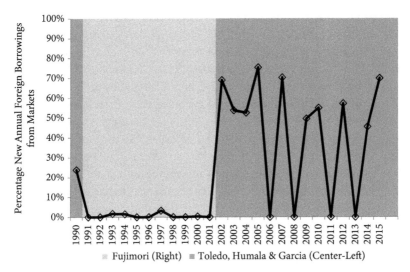

Figure 5.1 Peru Annual Foreign Borrowings

Source: Data from World Bank Development Indicators, calculations by author. Partisanship from Beck et al. 2001
Note: The 2001 elections were later in the year, making Toledo's first budget and borrowing FY 2002

hands of future governments that MEF officials fear 'will be [more] anti-market'.[1] Without MEF influence and preferences, Peru may have used more private external finance in years of left governments because market demand for Peruvian debt is 'huge ... [foreign investors] always [say Peru] could issue more'.[2]

But the election of successive and increasingly left-leaning governments from the early 2000s through 2015 also meant the MEF did not use its preferred official creditors for many budget items and projects. Under left governments 'there are lots of voices pushing for more bonds [rather than official credit], including ministers of line ministries' (Interview 95). This is because 'line ministries do not want a nanny' (Interview 87) and condition-free bonds whose funds arrive rapidly and without scrutiny helps match the financing demands of left-leaning parties' spending programs (Interviews 92, 93, 98, 99, 100). Through the budget and due to their economic policy preferences, left-leaning governing parties constrain MEF and keep it from borrowing as it would otherwise.

---

[1] Quotes from Interview 92, but everyone interviewed listed some of these preferences and reasons, especially Interviews 86, 87, 88, 91, 95, 97, 99, 100. On project loans, all MEF and official lender staff interviewees noted the role official creditors have in project needs in Peru. On program loans, see World Bank documents (2015a, 13 for example).
[2] Quote from Interview 88. Corroborated by many, especially Interviews 92, 95, 99, 100. Interviews 99 and 100 noted that foreign demand for Peruvian debt is traditionally higher than domestic demand, and global bond issuances are typically oversubscribed.

A summary was given by two former senior MEF officials: many at the MEF '[want] to take even more from [official creditors],' but increasing spending and pressure from left-party policies and ministers forces bonds to be used more than many at the MEF would like (Interview 95). This leads another official to predict that that the MEF will be unable to keep bonds from constituting a consistently higher proportion of Peru's external debt structure in the foreseeable future, as they suspect left-leaning parties will continue to win elections (Interview 92). In short, despite a MEF with explicit preference for official credit, the more left leaning the governing party, the more likely Peru is to use markets when borrowing.

This chapter details this argument by tracing the annual borrowing process in Peru. The next section outlines how laws do not substantively constrain spending or creditor choices. The third section describes the points of partisan political influence on annual borrowing decisions through the fiscal policymaking process. The fourth section traces Peru's external borrowings since 1990, showing the effect of government partisanship on Peru's sovereign debt accumulation as different parties won elections and despite the preferences of the MEF.

5.2 Setting the Financing Requirement: Budgets and Politics

In Peru, Congress passes budgets and the MEF's DTI is responsible for financing it. It is important to consider whether fiscal or debt laws constrain partisan spending and borrowing preferences through this process. Peruvian fiscal and debt laws do set caps on spending and debt, but Congress regularly passes exceptions. Nor do debt laws say anything about which creditors can be used. This flexible legal framework around the budget, debt, and borrowing creates space for partisanship to be a primary determinant of annual financing requirements and borrowing decisions.

5.2.1 The 1999 Fiscal Law

The first relevant law is the 1999 Fiscal Prudence and Transparency Act. No formal fiscal law existed before 1999. As detailed below, Alberto Fujimori's 1990–2000 government pursued austerity, privatization, and Washington Consensus–informed fiscal policies that constrained spending without any formal law. The law was passed by the conservative government in 1999 (and not before) to institutionalize such policies in the aftermath of the Asian Financial Crisis and in the face of looming elections in 2000 (Interviews 86, 88, 89, 90, 98).

While the 1999 law sets a 1%-of-GDP limit on fiscal deficits, the law also allows Congress to pass annual exceptions that raise the limit. In practice, the exceptions have allowed deficit spending to increase up to 4% of GDP in some years

(Lledó et al. 2017, 61). These exceptions have expanded the deficit in times of both necessity and political controversy. For example, exceptions pass uncontroversially in response to natural disasters such as those caused by el Niño events. But exceptions are controversial when used inconsistently by Congress with respect to economic cycles. At times Congress has denied exceptions intended to create room for countercyclical fiscal policies during low growth periods, but passed exceptions during growth periods when some find the spending pro-cyclical. Interviewees gave various interpretations of these episodes, but the general point is that 'fiscal rules change so much [that they recently have become just] whatever government says,' signaling the political rather than legal nature of government spending in Peru (Interview 95). Despite the ostensible 1%-of-GDP deficit limit, spending levels are largely a function of the policy preferences of the governing party.

5.2.2 Annual Indebtedness Laws

Within the parameters of the 1999 Fiscal Law, Congress passes three laws each November that set national spending, revenue, and borrowing plans for the coming year. The borrowing component (the 'Indebtedness Law,' or *Ley de Indeudamiento*) plans how much borrowing will come from foreign and domestic sources. However, the borrowing law does no more than cap the amount to be borrowed that year. It does not set a limit on total outstanding foreign debt, nor does it constrain choice of creditor in meeting these financing requirements (Interviews 92, 99, 100). While the MEF sets internal benchmarks for how it would like the composition of sovereign debt structure to evolve, these do not have the effect of law (Interview 92).

Once annual borrowing amounts are set, MEF is ostensibly delegated the authority to finance the budget without further Congressional involvement. The only instance where Congress is formally brought back into the picture is if an emergency arises (el Niño events or other natural disasters, for example) or if either domestic or external financial resources dry up and the other must be increased beyond the initial plan. However, in these cases (the latter of which had never happened as of fieldwork in 2017), Congress only has the purview to consider the nominal amount to be borrowed, not the source of financing to be used (Interviews 92, 99, 100). As discussed in the next section, it is cabinet that typically maintains formal oversight of debt accumulation from this stage onward.

In sum, Peruvian fiscal and debt laws are flexible. Spending limits are easily and regularly overridden, minimizing legal constraints on partisan spending preferences. Once budgets are finalized and financing requirements go to the MEF, there are no legal restrictions on which external creditors are used.

5.3 Borrowing Process and Politics

After the annual budget's financing requirement is finalized, the MEF's DTI begins gathering financing options and decides how to borrow. Once creditors are decided upon, the MEF writes a 'supreme decree' outlining the purpose, terms, conditions, and evaluation plans for each borrowing operation. The decrees then go to cabinet for approval. While many at the MEF see their formal role in borrowing as a source of power and potential tool for reforming line ministries, borrowing still must not infringe on items included in the budget or other government policy priorities. Indeed, borrowing requires negotiation with line ministries and their corresponding cabinet-level political appointees if borrowing might alter their spending and project plans. This is because, as just noted, cabinet approval is required of all borrowing decrees.

5.3.1 Line Ministries and Cabinet

Because line ministries cannot borrow on their own, MEF attempts to use its position in the borrowing process to influence not only whether a ministry gets finance, but the source of that finance and the conditions that come with it (Interview 92). All interviewees agreed MEF tries to use official credit to improve technical capacity, drive reform, and affect policy in the rest of the economy. In the eyes of one official who has worked in both the state and official lenders, 'the MEF wants [official creditors to be] a nanny' (Interview 87). Given the MEF's technocratic history, it is not surprising it sees conditions as a tool that makes official credit appealing (see Crabtree and Durand 2017).

However, depending on the economic policy preferences of the government in power, line ministries and government push back on MEF preferences because 'line ministries do not want a nanny' (Interview 87). The strongest view of this relationship, offered by some associated with line ministries, is to claim that ministries, cabinet, and thus government have the power to choose creditors for projects because MEF needs cabinet approval. At the least, cabinet approval of borrowing plans does make ministers and government veto players, forcing MEF to account for government's borrowing preferences when constructing annual borrowing plans (Bunte 2019, 141). Indeed, even those in the MEF who advocate for use of official creditors and conditions admit 'negotiation of conditions previous to the supreme decree [and cabinet approval] is an issue' for MEF (Interview 92). Others agree 'there are lots of voices pushing for more bonds [rather than official credit], including ministers of line ministries' under left-leaning governments (Interview 95).

These politics underpin why multilateral lenders are concerned that Peru's official borrowings have become limited over time. Some multilateral staff claim Peru has come over time to only accept conditions that reflect 'policies government has already achieved' (Interview 88). This is why, despite official creditor interest in providing large loans to Peru, major projects and programs have become rare. Instead, Peru's relationships with multilaterals have come to often take the form of small technical arrangements designed to maintain relationships rather than provide the financial basis for large projects or programs.[3]

Implicit here is that conditions are harder for MEF to force through under successive left-leaning governments, despite the MEF '[wanting] to take even more from [official creditors]' (Interview 92). Indeed, some in the DTI claim their task is largely to attempt to 'maintain balance' between these external financing options as best they can because 'some prefer multilaterals, some markets' (Interviews 99, 100). Over time, increasing government preference for bonds has limited the MEF's ability to use its preferred official credit.

5.3.2 SOEs and Other Guarantees

Guarantees are not a major issue for Peru's MEF and DTI because there are few SOEs after Peru's privatization drive in the 1990s.[4] One exception is national oil company PeruPetro, which by law maintains the ability to borrow on its own. However, to obtain a government guarantee, they must negotiate with and get approval from the MEF on a loan-by-loan basis. PeruPetro can and sometimes does borrow if the MEF says no, but this is not seen as a major source of risk as it is in South Africa (Interview 92). In this respect, Peru is similar to Botswana. These countries have few SOEs due to past privatization and maintain substantial oversight over the debt of SOEs that do exist.

5.4 Peru Foreign Borrowing from 1990 to 2015

Although the MEF ostensibly holds formal authority over Peru's financing decisions, annual foreign borrowings and the composition of Peru's external sovereign debt structure from 1990 through 2015 can only be fully explained by accounting

---

[3] Interviews 84, 85, 87, 88, 92, 95, 97. The three major multilaterals in Peru are the World Bank, the Inter-American Development Bank (IDB), and the Development Bank of Latin American and the Caribbean (CAF).

[4] Interviews 99, 100 also noted subnational guarantees are not an issue because subnational government entities cannot borrow on their own.

for changes in government partisanship. The most dramatic shift in Peru's foreign borrowing strategy over this period was in 2002, the year of Peru's first bond since 1928 (Rossini and Santos 2015, 24). This was the first year and budget of President Alejandro Toledo's government, which included working classes and the poor as core political constituencies. Toledo accordingly moved left of predecessor Alberto Fujimori's explicitly conservative economic program to support these constituents. Despite persistence of monetary and trade orthodoxy, and despite prior and later points where issuing bonds may be expected instead, Toledo's broader coalition of working-class and poor constituents is key to explaining the timing of the change in Peru's borrowing strategy in the early 2000s. Since Toledo, the role of bonds has only increased as governments have represented even more expansive left-leaning constituencies, leading official credit to become less central to Peru's sovereign debt structure over time.

5.4.1 The Late 1980s

Alan Garcia was elected president in 1985 and explicitly pursued anti–Washington Consensus economic policies until the end of his term in 1990. Particularly relevant to this study was overt rejection of IMF conditionality, default on foreign debt by limiting repayments to 10% of exports, and pro-cyclical stimulus spending. Despite some early economic success, by the 1990 elections Peru was in an extreme economic and debt position (see Aggarwal and Cameron 1994, 66–76). Notable indicators include negative growth (–9% in 1988), inflation (3,000% in 1989 and 7,000% in 1990), and unemployment (formal employment dropped to 11% in 1990). This led to national revenue shortfalls and an inability to meet even the self-imposed 10%-of-exports debt repayment limit (Crabtree and Durand 2017, chaps 2–4).

This meant that by 1990, Peru was locked out of markets and was struggling for lender-of-last-resort credit from official creditors (Crabtree and Durand 2017, chaps 2–4; Aggarwal and Cameron 1994, 70–75). Coherent solutions were beyond the capacity of an increasingly fragmented left (Crabtree and Durand 2017) and the economic problems led to a decline in established programmatic party politics (St. John 2010, 3–4; Levitsky 1999). This created the space for a new economic program and the concentration of political power to implement it under 1990 election winner Alberto Fujimori (Aggarwal and Cameron 1994, 75).

5.4.2 Alberto Fujimori (1990–2000)

Fujimori was elected in 1990 by campaigning against the Washington Consensus program of his opponent (Conaghan 2005, 17; Stokes 2004, 2). But this campaign rhetoric did not match Fujimori's policies once in office. One reason for the shift was that implementing Washington Consensus policies helped Fujimori limit foreign criticism of what would become his authoritarian politics. Another reason for the shift was insistence on such policy by economic officials from the International Financial Institutions (IFIs), the US, Japan, and other lenders given the economic challenges facing the country in 1990. Finally, since Garcia's policies had contributed to Peru's dire economic position and fighting domestic terrorism was the primary political issue, there was little domestic resistance to or focus on neoliberal economic policies at the time (on all of these points see Conaghan 2005, chap. 1; Levitsky 1999; Wise 2003, 179; Stokes 2004, 69–71; St. John 2010, 2–6).

Fujimori's switch to conservative economic policy began prior to taking office. Before his inauguration, Fujimori ostracized left-leaning campaign advisors and named technocrats from the IFIs and the domestic business community to top economic positions. This allowed the MEF to accumulate a significant amount of autonomy, sidestep the possible moderating influences of legislative or other ministerial forces, and unilaterally implement Washington Consensus policies. The MEF was able to sustain its economic program through Fujimori's full decade in office (Crabtree and Durand 2017, chap. 4; Stokes 2004, 70; Wise 2003, chap. 6).

Particularly relevant here is that austere fiscal policy was central to the Fujimori years. Reductions in public employment levels and wages, subsidy elimination, and social program cuts decreased government spending. Privatization and new taxes simultaneously increased revenue. Some targeted spending took place to mollify rural groups, but Fujimori's fiscal policy was overtly tight (Schady 2000). The focus on austerity continued throughout the 1990s, allowing Peru to achieve surpluses by 1996 (Rossini and Santos 2015, 14–17; Wise 2003, 190).

Such persistently austere fiscal policy informed the Fujimori government's external borrowing strategy of strictly using official creditors: 'fiscal consolidation . . . [meant that] public sector borrowing requirements were covered with privatization receipts [and] multilateral lending. . . with no need for borrowing in international capital markets' (Rossini and Santos 2015, 20).

To be sure, IMF last-resort lending was central to avoiding economic collapse from 1990 to 1992 and reinforced Fujimori's economic program. But strict use of official creditors throughout the remainder of Fujimori's decade in office was not a foregone conclusion. The government could have easily issued bonds, especially during Fujimori's second term from 1995 to 2000. Sovereign bond market access was evident by then, signalled in the obtainment of credit ratings comparable to South Africa (Table 5.1). In fact, credit ratings in the late 1990s under Fujimori were stronger than or equal to what they would be when Fujimori's successor ultimately issued bonds in later years. Moreover, re-election campaigns provided

Table 5.1 Peru Sovereign Credit Ratings

Year	Fitch	Moody's	S&P
1989	/	/	/
1990	/	/	/
1991	/	/	/
1992	/	/	/
1993	/	/	/
1994	/	/	/
1995	/	/	/
1996	/	/	/
1997	/	/	BB
1998	/	/	BB
1999	BB	Ba3	BB
2000	BB	Ba3	BB–
2001	BB–	Ba3	BB–
2002	BB–	Ba3	BB–
2003	BB–	Ba3	BB–
2004	BB	Ba3	BB
2005	BB	Ba3	BB
2006	BB+	Ba3	BB+
2007	BB+	Ba2	BB+
2008	BBB–	Ba1	BBB–
2009	BBB–	Baa3	BBB–
2010	BBB–	Baa3	BBB–
2011	BBB	Baa3	BBB
2012	BBB	Baa2	BBB
2013	BBB+	Baa2	BBB+
2014	BBB+	A3	BBB+
2015	BBB+	A3	BBB+

Note: / = No Rating
Source: Data from Bloomberg. Accessed December 12–14, 2016.

potential political incentives to issue in these years. But despite reasons and opportunities for using bond markets, the Fujimori government's conservative economic policy preferences explain Peru's strict use of official credit in the 1990s seen in Figure 5.1.

First, Fujimori's re-election campaigns in 1995 and 2000 did not encourage a shift away from fiscal austerity, general economic conservatism, or conditional official credit because this would not have served core constituencies. In 1995 some geographically targeted spending took place, but this relatively small program did not affect Fujimori's general economic program (Schady 2000). In fact, when research in the planning stage of the program showed the allocated funds would be insufficient, Fujimori became personally involved to ensure there would not be any debt issued to increase program resources (Interview 101).

While that 1995 election took place in the context of a still weak economy and Peru had yet to obtain sovereign credit ratings, this changed by the 2000 elections. The government could have used its newly stable economic position and creditworthiness to issue bonds and increase condition-free pre-election spending. But instead it passed the 1999 Fiscal Rule referred to earlier in this chapter, symbolic of the sincerity with which the Fujimori government and its capital-oriented constituents took conservative economic policy. Figure 5.2 shows a small dip into deficit territory in 1999 and 2000, but this was due to revenue problems after a general economic slowdown more than any significant spending increases (Interview 98; see also Rossini and Santos 2015, 22–24).

Second, the 1990s included multiple debt restructuring events where the Fujimori government could have begun prioritizing bond markets rather than official creditors. The issue here is not whether entering markets was prudent or not—the point is that if the Fujimori government wanted to draw on capital markets, it could have. But it did not do so.

One clear possibility was borrowing after the Brady Bond program in 1997. Brady Bond restructuring took place after Peru achieved high growth from 1993 to 1997 and surpluses in 1996 and 1997 (Figure 5.2). Subsequently, Peru obtained a credit rating from Standard & Poor's (S&P) in 1997 (Table 5.1). Although sub-investment grade, it was in line with the sovereign risk assessments characteristic of many EMs. And the act of obtaining a credit rating suggests that markets for Peruvian debt were on the minds of both the MEF and investors. Indeed, 1997 was not the first year that Peru 'normalized relations with all external creditors,' highlighting that policy moves throughout the decade were designed to get Peru back into capital markets (Rossini and Santos 2015, 20–22; also Interviews 98, 99, 100.). This all suggests that Peru could have accessed bond market or commercial bank finance in 1997. But it did not.

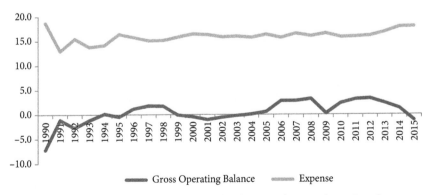

Figure 5.2 Peru Central Government Fiscal Balance and Expenditure Levels (Percentage of GDP)

Source: Data from IMF Government Finance Statistics. Accessed November 8, 2017

Why did Peru not utilize this market access in 1997? One interviewee said the MEF resisted bonds because (1) they were comfortable with official creditors and (2) foreign investors were available but they were 'not the type of investors Peru wanted' (Interview 98). Another interviewee agreed with this, saying issuing 'could have happened but it would not have been smart' (Interview 92). And this is precisely the point. It was Peru's choice. The Fujimori government had market access and decided it did not fit their preferences, instead choosing to continue using official creditors after the economy had grown and stabilized by the late 1990s. To be sure, as various crises hit emerging markets elsewhere in 1997, the government may have had further reason to avoid foreign capital markets. But the sequence of these events suggests these events reified rather than determined the Fujimori government's borrowing preferences.

The end of the 1990s provided another clear opportunity to issue bonds. After S&P gave Peru its first credit rating in 1997, Peru obtained ratings from the other two major agencies by 1999 (Table 5.1). This means that after crises in other EMs in 1997–1998, Peru was even better positioned to utilize market instruments. But Peru continued to resist doing so. One multilateral interviewee suggested Peru did not issue in these years because the ratings were sub-investment grade (Interview 88). However, as shown below, not only did later governments issue before Peru reached investment grade, they issued when both S&P and Fitch rated Peru *lower* than they had rated Peru under Fujimori. This is why one former MEF official feels Peru should have shifted to a market-based financing strategy at the end of the Fujimori years, to set a benchmark for future issuances while under a conservative government (Interview 98).

In sum, Peru could have used bond markets in the latter half of the 1990s—particularly before and after the Asian Financial Crisis—but chose not to. Instead, the Fujimori government strictly used official credit that reinforced its macroeconomic preferences and came at lower prices.

5.4.3 Alejandro Toledo (2001–2006)

The neoliberal approach to economic policy and strict use of official creditors continued through Fujimori's third election in 2000. But an accumulation of political oppression and corruption charges soon led to Fujimori's resignation and exile. A transition government briefly took over before Alejandro Toledo won the 2001 election (St. John 2010, chap. 1; Barr 2003, 1165–1166; Crabtree 2001).

Toledo campaigned on populist economic policy promises, though his government did continue Fujimori's economic policies in some important ways. For example, once elected, Toledo sought to shore up market confidence in a left-of-Fujimori leader by naming people preferred by foreign and domestic business and finance to lead the MEF and other economic ministries. In this sense, powerful economic ministry 'islands of efficiency' in the Peruvian state (the MEF, the central bank, and the tax ministry) were maintained after Fujimori. And particularly with respect to monetary and trade policy, policy continued as they had under Fujimori (Crabtree and Durand 2017; St. John 2010, 35).

But outside of monetary and trade policy, Toledo implemented policy changes that reflected a comparatively center-left political constituency and brought about a subsequent shift in Peru's external borrowing. In particular, more spending on different priorities and a softer approach to privatization led Toledo's government to rely more on expensive but condition-free market finance for external borrowing needs. Indeed, Toledo's small but important set of economic policy changes from the Fujimori years help explain why Peru began to issue bonds on global markets during Toledo's first year rather than before or after.

First, privatization revenues that helped bring back budget surpluses in the 1990s had slowed by the time Toledo took office (Rossini and Santos 2015, 25). After considering further privatization, Toledo changed course to '[signal] a move to the left' (Barr 2003, 1166). Such moves led some MEF and other market-oriented ministers to resign from Toledo's government, broke privatization plans supported by the IMF, and in part were responsible for a credit rating downgrade early in Toledo's term (Barr 2003, 1165–1169; St. John 2010, 39–40; also see Table 5.1). This negatively affected the revenue side of Toledo-era budgets, alongside low overall growth (Interview 98).

Second, Toledo pursued a new set of spending priorities designed to support a broader political constituency than Fujimori, making Toledo's fiscal policy decidedly less conservative than Fujimori. Toledo increased public sector employment and wages, invested public money in roads and energy, and increased education spending (St. John 2010, chap. 3). Business community opposition and MEF influence limited the scope of some of these efforts, with a few of Toledo's initial program ideas delayed until the *Programa Juntos* spending plan began in 2005 (el Comercio 2011; also Interview 101). But there is no question that, from the beginning, Toledo had a looser approach to spending than Fujimori designed for a comparatively left-leaning coalition of political constituents (Barr 2003, 1165–1166; St. John 2010, 35).

This increase in spending on such constituencies despite revenue problems helps explain Peru's first foreign bond in 2002 (Toledo's first fiscal year). Slow growth, countercyclical fiscal policy, a few high-profile anti-privatization moves, and subsequent credit rating downgrades may make it surprising that Peru would begin to access markets at this time. To be sure, the MEF was able to secure financing from a combination of multilateral and bilateral lenders in 2001 to help fund some components of Toledo's targeted spending efforts (St. John 2010, 37). But Toledo's general shift left from Fujimori in these policy areas is key to explaining why markets were first used in 2002, and not before or after. In the words of one former MEF official, Peru 'had to use bonds to help finance Toledo's spending' (Interview 98). Toledo's partisan fiscal policy underpinned external borrowing choices.

The same official recalled how difficult it was to convince long-term members of the MEF to support the bond issue. Some new Toledo-era officials wanted to issue in order to increase reserves, restructure existing debt more than had been achieved under Brady Bonds, and begin building relationships and yield curves with a view to long-term market-based government financing and debt management strategies. But the preference among longer-term MEF staff remaining from the Fujimori era was still to maximize official credit. Only when the World Bank, IMF, investment banks, and a few long-respected members of the Peruvian economic policymaking community began to comment publicly that bond market risks could be managed did 'new people convince older people [at the MEF] that [bond] markets can be good' (quote from Interview 98, corroborated by Interview 101; see also Rossini and Santos 2015, 24–25). This illustrates the tension between Peru's bureaucratic 'islands of efficiency' like the MEF and left-leaning governments, and how political interests are a primary determinant of sovereign borrowings and debt structure despite DMO preferences.

After the initial bond issuance, a commodity price boom in the early 2000s contributed to high economic growth through the rest of Toledo's time in office. This had a positive impact on government revenues and helped fund the various spending initiatives Toledo had financed in his first year with debt (Interview 91). This economic and revenue growth minimized the need for new large bond issues and also minimized official creditor pushback on Toledo's fiscal policy. These two conditions meant the MEF could use official creditors in the context of the boom (Interview 87) alongside bonds (Interview 98). But Toledo's shift left made combined use of both markets and official credit necessary in the first half of the 2000s.

5.4.4 Alan Garcia (2006–2011)

Alan Garcia, the president who rejected the IMF and purposefully defaulted on foreign debt in the late 1980s, won the 2006 election (The Economist 2006). While he followed Toledo by installing a business-friendly economic team, Garcia did not leave his 1980s anti–Washington Consensus credentials behind. In fact, some understand Toledo's left-leaning policies as a politically necessary reaction to Garcia's re-emerging left-leaning influence and followership in the early 2000s (Barr 2003, 1169; St. John 2010, 39–40; Interview 98). Indeed, once in office, Garcia maintained and expanded Toledo's spending (Interviews 98, 99, 100).

The commodity boom continued through 2008, meaning revenues could pay for expanded spending levels in Garcia's first years in office. In 2007, bonds were issued to restructure rather than meet new financing needs (Interviews 99, 100).

However, reflecting partisan resistance to official creditor conditionalities that was also evident in Garcia's politics in the late 1980s, Garcia's government simultaneously began to explicitly resist budget support and policy loans from multilaterals and bilaterals, preferring to restrict use of official credit to projects (Interviews 84, 87). This restriction ensured conditionality mainly shaped components of the project (Interviews 84, 87, 88), rather than Peru's overall economy in ways that might adjust the position of Garcia's relatively broad center-left political constituency (see Navia and Velasco 2003, 268 for a discussion of second-generation reforms that were central to budget support policy loans). MEF and DTI foreign borrowing preferences were increasingly constrained as Garcia pushed economic policy further left.

In 2008, uncertainty given the Global Financial Crisis led Peru to use official financing entirely (Figure 5.1), despite receiving investment grade credit ratings from Fitch and S&P the same year (Table 5.1). In 2009, a sharp drop in commodity prices affected Peruvian government finances. Despite the dip in revenues and low growth in the aftermath of 2008 and 2009, the Garcia government not only sustained but increased spending, pursuing a large countercyclical infrastructure investment plan. External financing was imperative for this infrastructure and social spending plan because a domestic bond at the end of 2007 was undersubscribed, shifting emphasis further onto external resources in the following years (Interviews 99 and 100).

In the event, Peru issued bonds in 2009 and 2010 to fulfill this borrowing requirement. Following increased restrictions on use of official credit in Garcia's early years, the government now issued bonds despite lingering market uncertainty after the crisis and MEF preference for official credit for such infrastructure projects. Without partisan concern about official creditor conditionality, Peru's MEF would have likely continued prioritizing official credit. Instead, official credit became a mere supplement to the Garcia government's prioritization of bonds, relegated to a tool that 'helped diversify [from over-exposure to market]' (Interview 99). Moreover, by 2011, Peru paid back outstanding *official* credit first to move itself further away from World Bank and Inter-American Development Bank commitments.[5]

5.4.5 Ollanta Humala (2011–2016)

After losing to Garcia in 2006, Ollanta Humala was elected president in 2011. Despite a campaign that emphasized populist economic rhetoric, concessions to business and cabinet appointments that omitted left-leaning advisors from

---

[5] Interview 84. The smaller CAF maintained a more significant lending relationship with Peru than these two larger development banks.

the campaign meant Humala continued the post-Fujimori pattern of mismatch between campaign rhetoric by successful candidates and some limits to implementation of such policy once in office (Avilés and Rosas 2017, 162–170; Interviews 86, 88, 92, 98.).

But also consistent with the post-Fujimori governments, Humala continued to move Peru further left than predecessors with respect to fiscal policy. Government spending on both social programs and infrastructure increased as promised during the campaign (Reuters 2011). A return of the commodity boom after the Global Financial Crisis allowed these spending increases to be covered by revenue gains.[6] This meant that spending increases did not threaten Peru's fiscal position, so there was little controversy about spending increases at the time. Ratings agencies even cited Humala's social and capital spending as reason for upgrading Peru in 2011, a stark contrast to downgrades for such policy in previous years (Cordeiro 2011).

However, the commodity boom ended by 2014 (Gauss 2014, 3; The Economist 2014). This led to a sharp revenue decrease and subsequent fiscal deficits due to the spending established in the first half of Humala's term. In reaction, the government pursued countercyclical policy that both cut taxes and increased spending (Kozak 2014; Interview 92). Figure 5.2 shows spending increased to new levels in 2014 and a rapid move into deficit by 2015. Accordingly, sizable and urgent financing requirements emerged in the second half of Humala's term (Interviews 92, 99, 100).

To be sure, the end of the commodity boom underpinned this change in fiscal position. But the effect was severe only because Humala followed through on spending promises despite these economic conditions. In other words, the political necessity of maintaining spending levels was central to the size and substance of Peru's post-boom deficit and financing requirements. For example, public wages, health, and education spending increases were maintained due to strikes and other pressure from the left (Interviews 86, 92; for examples of events reflecting pressure from left constituents for sustained public spending see Reuters 2012; Taj and Wade 2012). Other governments with other political constituencies may not have pursued the same post-boom spending levels as Humala.

This spending, in turn, informed foreign borrowing. Boom-driven growth allowed the MEF to utilize low volumes of official credit in 2011–2013 to meet comparatively small financing needs, the exception being the 2012 US$500 million fixed-rate, forty-year bond, the lowest interest rate the country had attained at that point.[7] The issuance was a debt management operation that allowed the MEF

---

[6] All interviewees pointed to the role of the commodity boom in creating uncontroversial spending room in these years.

[7] The MEF website publicly lists headline details of all sovereign foreign Peru bonds. See https://www.mef.gob.pe/contenidos/deuda_publ/bonos/externos/bonos_globales_emitidos.pdf. This was last accessed in October 2022. Saved data is available from the author if links are inaccessible.

to extend maturities and take on fixed, lower interest rates compared to existing debt (Interviews 92, 99, 100).

But after the commodity boom, in 2014–2015, market instruments again became central to Peru's external debt accumulation because official credit that did not include conditions had been maximized. In 2014, Peru issued another version of the 2012 US$500 million bond noted above.[8] Condition-free fulfillment of new financing requirements was central to the new issue, as well as helping to further restructure outstanding debt and benchmark at acceptable rates in anticipation of further issuances by the Humala government (Aquino 2014; Interviews 92, 99, 100).

In 2015, Fiscal Law exceptions were passed (Interviews 92, 97) and Peru had moved into fiscal deficit (Figure 5.2). This helps explain the issuance of three large bonds, in both USD and EUR, totaling over US$3bn in value.[9] Interest rates were again favorable, but the MEF's preferred strategy of emphasizing official creditors was untenable given resistance to conditions that might undermine the size and purpose of the borrowing. As one MEF official observed, the government 'had to finance all this infrastructure and social spending . . . [that would be] political suicide [to stop]' (Interview 95). A multilateral official agreed it would be 'wishful thinking' to think such fiscal policy and subsequent borrowings would change anytime soon (Interview 98). Indeed, the former MEF official cited in this chapter's introduction said the situation meant bonds had to be central to the state's external financing strategy—official creditor conditions and the political transaction costs of trying to agree to such conditional loans under successive and increasingly left-leaning governments meant bonds were unavoidable (Interview 92).[10]

Despite a powerful MEF preferring official creditors, Peru was in deficit and prioritizing bond markets to meet foreign financing needs. The MEF felt powerless enough in the context of government's spending and borrowing that some of the 2015 bond proceeds were used to pre-finance future budgets at current borrowing costs. In other words, the MEF was worried about increases in Peru's future borrowing price due to worsening fundamentals, but certain about the need to issue bonds in the future given Peru's leftward political trend (Interviews 92, 99, 100).

5.5 Conclusion

The relationship between government partisanship, annual external borrowing choices, and sovereign debt accumulation over time is evident in Peru. MEF preferences cannot explain borrowings, as they are constrained by government

---

[8] There was also a sizable domestic issuance.

[9] See MEF website cited at footnote 7.

[10] As a corollary, the official expects that fiscal rules will continuously be overridden to create room for these governments' spending.

partisanship. Nor can sovereign risk fully explain Peruvian external borrowings. Neither obtaining credit ratings, achieving investment grade ratings, nor strong or weak economic fundamentals determined if Peru issued bonds or how much they prioritized bonds compared to official creditors each year. Peru issued bonds with weaker credit ratings under left-leaning governments in the early 2000s rather than with stronger credit ratings under conservative 1990s governments. Despite ostensible MEF influence and accounting for variation in creditworthiness, Peru's annual external borrowing choices and the accumulation of an increasingly bond-oriented external sovereign debt structure from 1990 to 2015 was to a significant degree determined by government partisanship

6

Thailand

6.1 Introduction

Thailand provides a fourth case with more within-unit change in partisanship than Peru. While government partisanship in Peru trended from right to left from 1990 to 2015, Thailand's governments over this period oscillated between conservative parties and left-leaning populist parties. Such variation provides context for a demanding within-case test of partisanship's effect on annual external borrowings.

Thailand also provides a case of within-unit change on other dimensions theoretically relevant to this study. For example, some of these changes in government partisanship occurred through military coups instead of democratic elections. This allows for a within-unit qualitative test of the argument that a partisan effect on borrowing does not depend on regime type, adding to the evidence in the Chapter 3 quantitative tests. Thailand's central role in the Asian Financial Crisis (AFC) also makes it an important case for assessing whether and how major economic crises limit or affect this book's partisan model of public debt accumulation. Finally, Thailand strategically developed its domestic public bond market over this period, providing a financial resource for the state that could affect external sovereign borrowing strategies.

Yet the partisan effect on external borrowing was evident in Thailand from 1990 to 2015 through government changes, military coups, pre-crisis and post-crisis eras, and development of the domestic bond market. Before the AFC in 1997, right-leaning parties used official creditors despite strong growth and investment-grade credit ratings. From 1998 to 2000 the conservative Democrat party continued prioritizing official credit despite a large 1998 bond issue designed to benchmark for Thailand's return to markets, rapid credit rating improvements in 1999 and 2000, and salient popular pressure to avoid official credit in response to frustrations with the IMF's crisis loan conditions. Thailand did not prioritize markets until the comparatively left-leaning Thai Rak Thai (TRT) party won the 2001 elections by explicitly campaigning against the Democrat's close relationship with official creditors and austere economic policies. From TRT's first years in government through at least 2015, the state's external borrowing choices depended on whether partisan descendants of the TRT or partisan descendants of the conservative Democrats were in office. Conservative descendants of the Democrats returned to their favored official creditors while populist TRT descendants, with

How Governments Borrow. Ben Cormier, Oxford University Press. © Ben Cormier (2024).
DOI: 10.1093/oso/9780198882732.003.0006

working classes as consistent core constituents, avoided official creditors in various ways. This was true regardless of whether these parties took office through democratic elections or military coups.

As noted, in the background is Thailand's successful development of its domestic public bond market over this period. In a strategic effort to minimize exposure to foreign debt in absolute terms following the AFC, the Thai DMO spent the 2000s deepening demand for local-denominated government debt. By the early 2010s the effort was so successful that most public borrowing occurred in Thai Baht rather than foreign currencies (Interview 21), and in 2013 and 2014 the Thai government did not borrow externally (Figure 6.1). By 2015, only 6.2% of outstanding Thai public debt was external, making the country an 'outlier' among EMs (Interview 1).

Of immediate relevance for this study is that successful local deepening did not negate the partisan effect on foreign borrowing. Conservative parties added official foreign credit to the national balance sheet despite significant domestic financial depth in the early 2010s (see 2015 in Figure 6.1), partly to minimize borrowing costs and partly to limit future government policy autonomy. In contrast, left-populist parties relied on markets when borrowing abroad, while simultaneously minimizing foreign borrowing altogether and issuing most bonds in local currency because this increases policy autonomy even in comparison to foreign bonds (see Ballard-Rosa, Mosley, and Wellhausen 2022). So the partisan effect on

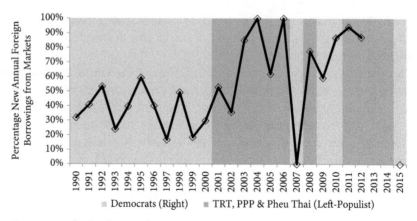

Figure 6.1 Thailand Annual Foreign Borrowings

Source: Data from World Bank Development Indicators, calculations by author. Accessed November 8, 2017
Note: Beck et al. 2001 label all parties in Thailand after 2001 as nonright, reflecting the relative populism and looser fiscal policy of all parties after TRT. In the quantitative chapter they are coded per Beck, but a level of detail is added here to highlight how the only times Thailand was likely to return to official creditors in a substantial way after the TRT years is when Democrats were in power (including after the domestic market had become the primary source for government finance in the late 2000s into the 2010s)

foreign borrowing outcomes withstands deepening of domestic resources. However, this evolution in Thai public debt structure by the mid-2010s also highlights how domestic financial resources can decrease the importance of foreign public debt obligations in an EM's sovereign debt structure in absolute terms. This gives rise to important questions for further sovereign debt research, discussed in the concluding chapter.

As in previous chapters, Thailand's fiscal and debt laws are outlined to establish the legal framework within which budgets are set and borrowing decisions take place each year. The remainder of the chapter traces changes in government partisanship and Thailand's annual external borrowings from 1990 to 2015.

6.2 Fiscal and Debt Laws

Thailand has a reputation for technocratic economic management. Until the 1990s, military rulers allowed economic ministries to operate with little political interference. Economic technocrats used this space to implement pro-globalization policies so adeptly that a mid-1990s World Bank book called the country a 'macroeconomic miracle' (Warr and Bhanupong 1996; see also Stifel 1976; Pasuk and Baker 1999, 195–198; Hewison 2002, 1–4).

The end of military rule from 1988 to 1992 also meant the end of such insulated technocratic control over Thailand's macroeconomy (Apichat 2002; Suchitra 1998, 161–164; MacIntyre 2001, 96–101; Baker and Pasuk 2014, 255; Pasuk and Baker 1999, 201). Policymaking processes became more subject to domestic political interests than before, as power was transferred 'to elected politicians rather than technocrats or generals' (Baker and Pasuk 2014, 246–247).

This is a useful starting point because decades of unchallenged technocratic control over economic policy helps explain why formal legal frameworks for budgets and borrowing are minimal in Thailand. For example, national fiscal laws are nonexistent. Under military rule, the Bureau of the Budget (BOB) internally 'set ceilings for budget expenditures in line with expected revenue and politicians could not change these ceilings,' a formal framework that did not change in the timeframe of this study (Jansen and Choedchai 2009, 329; Root 1998, 64). Even as the AFC hit in 1997, spending was difficult to constrain in this more politicized context partly because there were no clear legal reference points (MacIntyre 2001, 97). Upward pressure on budgets and deficits continued without any new legal constraints since the early 1990s (Interview 20).

Like other EMs in this study, Thai debt regulations comprise flexible laws and informal benchmarks. Most debt limits are set as percentage-of-expenditures, which means they are essentially products of annual spending levels rather than reliable constraints on that spending (Interview 20). Informal guidelines intend for borrowing to not fund more than 20% of government expenditures, but ad hoc exceptions are commonly passed. Multiple state officials (Interviews 20, 26) emphasize that all political parties 'too often' (Interview 30) use such emergency tools to increase spending. While total outstanding debt is capped at 60% of GDP, this limit has not constrained borrowing in practice.[1]

A Public Debt Management Act was passed in 2005 which largely formalized debt management practices that had been habitual and informal.[2] It did not create any new debt laws. Some say the populist TRT party passed the Act in 2005 to gain support from the business class and investors in the lead-up to an election (Interview 30), while others say it was designed to increase confidence in rapidly growing domestic debt markets (Interview 35). Regardless, the Act did not increase formal stringency of fiscal or debt laws in Thailand in ways that added additional constraints on borrowing decisions (Interviews 18, 20, 21, 30, 35). Flexible laws persisted throughout this study's timeframe.

Finally, reflecting the increasing size and role of domestic bond markets by the 2010s, in 2007 the Ministry of Finance set an internal benchmark that no more than 20% of government debt should be external. 2007 was before the domestic bond market fully developed, and in practice the government has remained well under this level since (Interview 1). However, most important here is that no law or benchmark explicitly constrains choice of creditor when the government does turn abroad for finance.

6.3   Borrowing Process

Before 1997 external borrowing was controlled by multiple entities, but after the AFC, a single Public Debt Management Office (PDMO) became responsible for borrowing.[3] The PDMO works on financing once budget items are finalized, meaning the PDMO simply 'has to [fund] what government wants' (Interview 26). This is why, although highly regarded by various financial actors for technical capacity and professionalism,[4] the PDMO's work is inevitably constrained by the partisan politics that determine what is in annual budgets and the subsequent financing requirements.

The PDMO produces an annual borrowing plan each September. The plan is reviewed by a Debt Management Committee of economic ministers and approved by cabinet before being included in the final budget submitted to the prime minister and MPs for approval (Interviews 1, 20, 26). Crucially, ease of approval has historically varied by the partisanship of the governing party. In particular, the

---

[1] Interviews 17 and 21 also note there is a lower internal target of 50% within the finance ministry.
[2] See section 3 of the Act, which highlights the variety of debt laws and finance ministry roles codified in piecemeal laws going back to 1944.
[3] Interviews 26 and 35 said this new PDMO essentially consolidated external and domestic debt management operations into one unit.
[4] This view is shared across official and private interviewees, both previous and current.

populist TRT party and its descendants politicize multilateral credit options and explicitly work to keep the PDMO from using them. Lender and domestic intervie-wees agree TRT made the PDMO's work 'a whole new game.'[5] As detailed below, political interference in annual foreign borrowing decisions is in some ways more explicit and public in Thailand than in other countries in this study.

6.3.1 PDMO Borrowing Options and Criteria

The PDMO 'compares costs' when borrowing (Interview 26). All interviewees noted that by the 2010s this typically meant maximizing domestic resources before turning abroad to complete financing requirements. While external borrowing 'gradually' decreased in absolute terms by the 2010s because of this (Interview 24), the PDMO remained interested in external finance 'for emergenc[ies] or for invest-ment projects in which the lender offers preferential terms or technical knowledge' (Interview 1). So despite deep domestic markets by the 2010s, the PDMO still finds external finance carries benefits under certain conditions. And of course, before successful deepening of the local bond market, external finance was central to government borrowing.

When turning abroad, the PDMO faces the same trade-off as other EMs. As just noted, the PDMO sees value in official creditors' below-market prices and tech-nical assistance in projects. Line ministries will include official credit in budget proposals if they see a benefit (Interviews 11, 20, 26)[6] and most lender and gov-ernment interviewees emphasize Thailand values the benefits of official lenders' project loans (Interviews 8, 9, 11, 17, 18, 19, 20, 24).[7] In addition, from a debt management perspective, although official lenders cannot lend large amounts in Thai Baht (Interviews 1, 2, 8, 9, 24), the PDMO values how official creditors are typically more open to early repayment and other restructuring plans than private investors.[8]

But as with all official credit, these benefits come at the cost of accepting con-ditions. Official creditor conditions are widely politicized and controversial in Thailand because they became salient during the AFC and have remained so since. Even acknowledging some expansion from strictly Washington Consensus–style structural adjustment loans after the 1990s, labor, environmental, and transparency standards remain practical points of contention (Interview 16).

[5] Quote from Interview 20, corroborated by Interviews 1, 2, 8, 9, 11, 16, 17, 18, 19, 24, 30.
[6] Interview 24 claimed Thai companies 'can build a road with their eyes closed,' but most intervie-wees indicate and the data suggest SOEs and the PDMO clearly see productivity value-add in official creditor project loans.
[7] Some suggest multilateral creditors' executive boards resist giving nonproject budget support to Thailand anyway (Interviews 1, 24).
[8] Although Interview 18 also noted a few instances in the 2000s and 2010s when official creditors tried to convince the PDMO not to repay debt early.

Meanwhile, all lender and debt management interviewees highlight that concerns about autonomy infringement by official creditors creates high reputation costs for any Thai government if they use official credit. Regardless of PDMO valuation of official loan prices, conditions, and technical support, the governing party must be open to using official creditors for the PDMO to ultimately do so. Indeed, some parties have become overtly involved with borrowing processes to keep the PDMO from using official credit and the PDMO has had trouble finalizing official loans if and when new populist leaders come into power in the middle of negotiations (Interview 26).

6.3.2   Politics and PDMO Foreign Borrowing Decisions

Throughout the 1990s, Thai public borrowing was technocratic, with minimal executive influence and no legislative oversight (Interviews 18, 19, 20, 24, 26, 30). But after the populist TRT party won the 2001 elections, borrowing became a 'whole new game' (Interview 20) where 'political transaction costs' (Interviews 8, 11) began to 'constrain' PDMO borrowing decisions (Interview 24). In other words, many sense that borrowing was 'traditionally technical and parties listened to bureaucrats, but TRT changed that' (Interview 19). TRT was specifically interested in eliminating use of official creditors, a political position drawn from its campaign against Democrats' close association with them coming out of the AFC. All interviewees noted this explicit and specific TRT interest (on how TRT used criticism of official creditor conditionality to gain political support, see Choi 2005; Hewison 2005; Baker and Pasuk 2014, 263–265).

TRT interventions in the borrowing process in the name of avoiding official creditors were both informal and formal. Informally, PDMO staff at all levels were forced out or left the ministry if they did not agree with TRT's approach to external creditors or fiscal policy more generally (Interviews 11, 16, 17, 18, 19, 20, 24). This allowed TRT to informally impose a US$1 billion limit on official credit flows with little pushback from remaining PDMO staff (Interview 26). Moreover, while those remaining at the PDMO were open to using this limit, there was pressure not to (Interviews 20, 26), including from TRT leader Thaksin Shinawatra, who wanted to 'personally manage and limit' PDMO staff relationships with official creditors (Interview 30).

Indeed, one former multilateral official recalled Thaksin appearing unannounced at a PDMO meeting with their development bank and ending the meeting despite PDMO interest in borrowing (Interview 19). Another official creditor staffer said maintaining a relationship with Thailand under TRT was 'almost not worth it' (Interview 24), while another described the relationship of their multilateral and Thailand as 'broken' in the Thaksin years (Interview 11). PDMO interviewees also recall a new level of interest in borrowing among MPs and cabinet members, many of whom were TRT partisans and thus interested in scrutinizing use of official credit as a way of aligning with Thaksin. Justifying official creditor loans came to involve 'high political transaction costs' for the PDMO (Interviews 17, 18, 20, 21, 23, 26).

Such explicit but informal efforts to minimize use of official creditors was formalized in Section 190 of the 2007 Constitution, which gave multilateral loans the status of treaties.[9] While this did not include bilaterals like the Japan International Cooperation Agency (JICA), this meant multilateral loans must go through a different approval process than other forms of finance: the PDMO now had to propose multilateral loans to Parliamentary committees in hearings broadcast on public television (Interviews 11, 20, 26). The PDMO '[had] to explain to the public' why official creditors were being used, which was 'difficult' because MPs would 'express a lot of emotion' and 'invent . . . claims about sovereignty and autonomy even if [they were] not true' (Interview 26). MPs used the hearings as an 'opportunity to make noise about protecting people' (Interview 26) and show that they resist 'being run by foreigners' (Interview 24). In practice, multilateral price and technical benefits were overwhelmed by the 'hassle' (Interview 11) of this new 'exhausting' process (Interview 26).

Notably, the 2007 Constitution was passed after a military coup removed TRT from office. So this shift to treaty status and the subsequent requirements for agreeing to multilateral loans was not done by the TRT or Thaksin. Instead, and somewhat paradoxically, the idea of treating multilateral loans as treaties came from the finance ministry. Pushback on using official credit had become so ingrained in Thai politics that finance ministry and PDMO bureaucrats suggested this clause in an attempt to increase transparency, appease politicians, and ideally make it more viable to use official credit moving forward (Interview 23). This intended effect did not come to pass.

6.3.3 SOEs

SOEs came to use external finance more than central government during this period, making SOEs central to understanding Thailand's external sovereign debt structure. By December 2015, SOEs accounted for THB 267 billion in outstanding external debt while the central government accounted for THB 81 billion in external debt. Again, by this time, most central government debt, THB 4 trillion, was domestic (Thailand PDMO 2018).

Unlike some other countries in this study, Thailand's SOEs are part of the central government's routinized budget process (Kriangchai 2009, 52; Warr and Bhanupong 1996, 93; Interviews 1, 18, 20, 26). When borrowing, there is a

---

[9] All interviewees noted the subtle importance of this change.

law limiting SOE guarantees or on-lending to 20%-of-expenditure (Interview 1). Within this cap the PDMO can decide whether or not to explicitly guarantee foreign SOE debt obligations, though they tend to do so. In the post-AFC years, 85% of SOE debt was explicitly guaranteed, and Interview 18 says this level has been at a minimum maintained and likely increased since the early 2000s (International Monetary Fund 2004, sec. 19).

With such explicit central government backing, SOEs have used both official and private external finance. For example, Thai Airways has long used external bond markets (Interview 1). But at times the PDMO will offer to only guarantee an official loan for Thai Airways, incentivizing the SOE to use an official loan to restructure its debt portfolio, as it did in the 2010s to fund new airplanes (Interviews 1, 18). This exemplifies the substantial control the PDMO has over SOE borrowing decisions and debt accumulation in Thailand.

6.4 Thai Foreign Borrowing from 1990 to 2015

This section traces Thai government external borrowing in four phases: pre-AFC (mostly Democrats), from the AFC through 2001 (Democrats), from 2002 through 2006 (TRT), and from 2007 through 2015 (various coup and elected governments descendant from either the Democrats or TRT). Each subsection details the economic context of the period, governing party political constituencies and partisanship, and annual borrowings. Throughout periods partisanship remained central to external borrowings, even as external debt became a smaller component of Thai sovereign debt structure in the final years of this study.

6.4.1 Pre-AFC (1990–1996)

Thailand experienced an economic boom from the late 1980s through 1996 (Warr 2005, 3–14). High growth and orthodox economic policies led to investment-grade credit ratings throughout the period (see Table 6.1). The Thai private sector used this market access to take on high levels of foreign direct and portfolio investment throughout the boom (Warr 2005, 3–13). Yet the PDMO continued to use more official credit than bond markets despite clear market access in these years (Figure 6.1).

Prioritizing official credit is explained by the conservatism of Democrats, the dominant party in these years (Baker and Pasuk 2014, 253–255; King 1996). Integrative macroeconomic policy characterized much of the economy, and conservative economic ideology was especially evident in fiscal policy. Figure 6.2 shows consistent surpluses in these years, which meant official creditor conditions would not push back on or alter government's preexisting fiscal policy or

Table 6.1 Thailand Sovereign Credit Ratings

Year	Fitch	Moody's	S&P
1989	/	A2	A–
1990	/	A2	A–
1991	/	A2	A–
1992	/	A2	A–
1993	/	A2	A–
1994	/	A2	A
1995	/	A2	A
1996	/	A2	A
1997	/	Ba1	BBB
1998	BB+	Ba1	BBB–
1999	BBB–	Ba1	BBB–
2000	BBB–	Baa3	BBB–
2001	BBB–	Baa3	BBB–
2002	BBB–	Baa3	BBB–
2003	BBB	Baa1	BBB
2004	BBB	Baa1	BBB+
2005	BBB+	Baa1	BBB+
2006	BBB+	Baa1	BBB+
2007	BBB+	Baa1	BBB+
2008	BBB+	Baa1	BBB+
2009	BBB	Baa1	BBB+
2010	BBB	Baa1	BBB+
2011	BBB	Baa1	BBB+
2012	BBB	Baa1	BBB+
2013	BBB+	Baa1	BBB+
2014	BBB+	Baa1	BBB+
2015	BBB+	Baa1	BBB+
2016	BBB+	Baa1	BBB+

Note: / = No Rating
Source: Data from Bloomberg. Accessed December 12–14, 2016

other macroeconomic preferences. Politically, such policies were supported by the Democratic coalition of powerful urban and rural business elites (among many reviews see Hewison 2000, 196–201).

This helped sovereign debt accumulation be seen as a simple technocratic, or somewhat apolitical, issue at the time. 'Parties listened to bureaucrats' about borrowing in this period (Interview 19) and debt managers used this space to '[borrow] from [official] sources such as the World Bank, because these funds would be closely monitored and supervised' (Warr and Bhanupong 1996, 94, corroborated by Interviews 19, 20, 24.). In the context of democratization following the end of military rule in the early 1990s, technocrats saw official creditor conditions as a tool for increasing the returns to spending increases they felt the public sector did

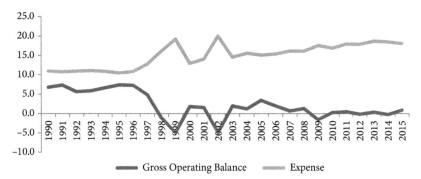

Figure 6.2 Thailand Central Government Fiscal Balance and Expenditure Levels
Source: Data from IMF Government Finance Statistics. Accessed November 8, 2017

not have the capacity to use effectively.[10] If market rates were unusually cheap at a certain time then the bureaucrats did issue bonds, as they did once in the United States and once in Japan in this period (Interview 18). Commercial banks were also used if cheaper, though the Thai private sector tended to use banks and the government tended to use bonds (Interview 18).

In short, the investment-grade Thai government could have easily accumulated a majority of its external debt from market sources in the 1990s before the AFC (and the private sector did so, providing important context for the AFC). But the Democrat's economic policy preferences gave debt managers space to prioritize official credit in these years, which the PDMO used to take advantage of cheaper loans with conditions they thought enhanced the economic benefits of external finance.[11]

6.4.2 The AFC and Post-AFC Democrats (1997–2001)

Many point to floating the Thai Baht on July 2, 1997 as the beginning of the AFC, but the buildup extends into 1996 (for summary timelines and analyses, see Nabi and Shivakumar 2001, chap. 3; Warr 2005, 14–32; MacIntyre 2001, 96–101). Democrats briefly lost leadership of the governing political coalition in 1996, but the onset of the crisis brought the Democrats back to leadership in November 1997 without elections because the coalition 'wanted the Democrats and their technocrat team to return and manage the economy' (Baker and Pasuk 2014, 260).

---

[10] Interviews 11, 18, 19, 20, 26, and 30 discussed how civil servants were (and remain) skeptical about the lack of public sector capacity to use borrowed money efficiently and effectively.

[11] Also important to keep in mind is that the domestic market did not develop until much later. External credit was the primary financing option in the 1990s.

Before the Democrats took office again the IMF had already arranged a US$17.2 billion bailout package, aggregating a variety of multilateral and bilateral funds. Bailout conditions included allowing insolvent banks to fail, fiscal surpluses, privatization in a number of sectors, a new Value-Added Tax, increasing foreign exchange reserves, and monetary policy changes that included floating the Baht (Nabi and Shivakumar 2001, chaps 3–4; International Monetary Fund 1997a; 1997b). While 'Democrats lobbied the IMF to adjust the details. . . . [in] general, the Democrats cooperated with the IMF' once back in government (Baker and Pasuk 2014, 260). Indeed, the second IMF Letter of Intent in November 1997 began by stating '[the] new government . . . has reconfirmed its full commitment to the economic program specified in the [first Letter of Intent] of August 14, 1997' (International Monetary Fund 1997b). This emergency package is why most external finance in 1997 was from official sources, despite coming at the end of the fiscal year (Figure 6.1).

The economic crisis continued into 1998, which makes it significant that Figure 6.1 also shows a return to markets in 1998. This reflects bond issues via more creditworthy SOEs on foreign markets as a way to 'immediately increase reserves and creditworthiness' (Interview 18). For example, a US$300 million bond was issued in 1998 by the country's utility SOE. The loan was partially guaranteed by the World Bank's IFC arm, which brought the credit rating to 'A3/A–, significantly above' Thailand's crisis-era junk rating (World Bank 1998, 2; also see Table 6.1). Other external borrowing in 1998 continued to be official credit associated with the IMF-led bailout.[12]

Post-crisis recovery began by 1999 and the Democrats remained in government until 2001 (Nabi and Shivakumar 2001, chap. 8; Warr 2005, 13). In those years, the only other uses of private external credit were for SOEs—the Democrats did not issue a foreign bond for the central government budget, strictly using official creditors (Interviews 1, 8, 9, 16, 17, 18, 20, 24, 26, and 35). In other words, any use of private external finance in Figure 6.1 before 2001 is SOE debt. This signals Thailand had bond market access, but the PDMO sought to avoid this option when meeting the central government's financing needs.

Democrat avoidance of markets may seem inevitable because the crisis had just ended. But their persistent commitment to fiscal austerity (and other conservative economic policies dictated by the IMF bailout) and official creditors was not predetermined. The party committed to these fiscal and borrowing policies 'despite gradual erosion of support [for them over these] three years' (Baker and Pasuk 2014, 260). It would have been politically popular to pursue fiscal expansion once

---

[12] It is interesting to note that the aftermath of the crisis was also when Thailand began to issue domestic public debt. Avoiding 'original sin' became an obvious benefit over time, but an initial motivation for this was to 'fiscalize' THB 1.4 trillion of nonperforming loans accumulated by the Financial Institutions Development Fund during the crisis (Nabi and Shivakumar 2001, 30–31; Bank of Thailand 2002; International Monetary Fund 1998b, secs 7, 18).

the crisis subsided by 1999. It also would have been politically popular, if comparatively expensive, to resist conditionality by using re-established credit market access to issue bonds like the SOEs. But the Democrats and their PDMO did neither, which, as discussed later, is central to the rise of a new populist political opposition in these post-crisis years and their subsequent electoral success in 2001.

First, looser fiscal policy after the crisis was not only possible but advocated for by the IMF and World Bank. The IMF promoted countercyclical spending by 1998 (Baker and Pasuk 2014, 258; Hewison 2002, 12; International Monetary Fund 1998a) and, while Democrats implemented a stimulus in 1999, World Bank staff 'proposals for an even larger fiscal stimulus . . . were rejected' and 'the impact would have been larger if it had been implemented earlier' (Nabi and Shivakumar 2001, 43, 59, 67–68). While this may be 'revisionist' World Bank history insofar as Bank calls for expanded social safety nets were not as clear as claimed later (Hewison 2002), the central point is that the Democrats pursued either as much or even less fiscal expansion and social spending than advocated for by the IFIs. Tight fiscal policy was a partisan policy choice, not a conditionality, by 1999. Moreover, Figure 6.2 shows the Democrats still ran surpluses by 2000.

Second, whether prudent or not, the Democrats could have used private external finance from 1999 to 2001. SOE use suggests some level of market access as early as 1998, and Thailand was upgraded to investment grade rather quickly after the crisis (by Fitch in 1999 and Moody's in 2000; see Table 6.1). But the Democrats did not use this market access. While funding for the Democrat's relatively small stimulus efforts 'had to be foreign-financed,' this was done through official creditors (Interviews 1, 8, 9, 16, 17, 18, 20, 24, 26, 35; Nabi and Shivakumar 2001, 55).

Again, the issue is not whether using bond markets after 1998 would have been wise. The point is that the Democrats chose to avoid this option, and the Democrats faced political repercussions for their commitment to official finance. Indeed, views of the Democrats' external borrowing strategy at the time range from admiration (for long-term perspective despite political backlash) to criticism (for shortsightedness). Some suggest that the Democrats simply found markets too expensive at the time (Interview 21). Emphasis on costs rather than policy autonomy benefits leads some to say Democrats knew official credit 'did not help politically but put the country on a good path.'[13] Others say the party was not so altruistic, knew the policies would be criticized, and tried to say from the outset that the policies were dictated by the IMF (Interviews 8, 35) but 'had problems explaining' this (Interview 21). Still others suggest Democrats actually 'did not understand' there was a political backlash to using official creditors and associated policies (Interview 30).

---

[13] Quote from Interview 17. Interviews 8, 9, 11, 16, 19, 21, 24 took a similar perspective.

Regardless of perspective, the fact is that the Democrats' preferred official creditors from after the AFC through 2001 and the PDMO borrowed accordingly. It may be true that despite the political implications, future spending levels and welfare state expansion in Thailand were only possible because the Democrats' post-crisis policy choices led to stability in the long run (Interviews 8, 18, 21, 24). Yet they remain policy choices. Fiscal and other macroeconomic policy, as well as foreign borrowing choices, could have been otherwise after the AFC and particularly from 1999 onwards. If the Democrats were not aligned with official creditor policy prescriptions generally, had other economic policy preferences, or if they were only concerned with the political ramifications of using official creditors, they could have implemented different policies and borrowed from sources that would allow them to do so. But they did not. And ultimately, the Democrats lost the January 2001 elections to a new left-leaning economically populist party largely 'because of their association with IMF-mandated policies' (Baker and Pasuk 2014, 262–263).

6.4.3 Thai Rak Thai (2001–2006)

Even if the Democrats gave 'markets, the international financial institutions, and bilateral partners confidence regarding Thailand's commitment and its ability to stay the course' in 1997 (Nabi and Shivakumar 2001, 37), their economic policies created space for a new populist party to emerge and compete for voters domestically. Thai Rak Thai (TRT) cohered the 'nationalistic reaction to the crisis . . . embrac[ing] the theme of self-strengthening to manage globalization' (Baker and Pasuk 2014, 262–263; Hewison 2010, 122). The poor, labor, and some domestic businesses, the economic groups hurt most by Democrats' commitment to elite constituencies, conservative economic policies, and sustained IFI-sponsored post-crisis adjustments, created a new left-leaning populist political coalition based on anti-integration economic policy and ideology. Business sought to combat foreign ownership and exposure, the poor sought welfare state expansion, and long-repressed labor sought new political access and voice (Baker and Pasuk 2014, 262–263; Warr 2005, 40–43; Dempsey 2000, 392–393; Hewison 2002; 2004, 508–512, 515; 2005; Jayasuriya and Hewison 2004, 572, 582–583; Hewison 2010, 121; Choi 2005; Ammar 2011, 75; Brown 2007).

Once in office, TRT set out to minimize technocratic influence in the economy, making 'appointments in the senior bureaucracy and state enterprises to intimidate officialdom into submissiveness' (Baker and Pasuk 2014, 263). This included the PDMO, as anyone who 'expressed concern [about TRT] was removed or resigned' (Interview 20). TRT economic preferences came to immediately shape Thai economic policy, including sovereign borrowing and debt accumulation, despite being policy areas relatively insulated from overt political interference under the Democrats.

Fiscally TRT emphasized social spending, reflecting the interests of its constituents, and was farther left than any previous Thai government (Hewison 2004; 2010; Interviews 8, 9, 11, 19, 20, 24). Major programs included block grants to villages and universal healthcare (Hewison 2004, 516; Ammar 2011, 75–77; Baker and Pasuk 2014, 263). While Figure 6.2 shows TRT ran small surpluses after a large initial deficit in 2002, this was possible because the Democrats' policies left behind high levels of foreign exchange and privatization proceeds for TRT to draw down (Ammar 2011, 76–77).[14] In addition, some expenses were financed off-budget via banks that were caught in a new 'political envelope [of] government control' under TRT leader Thaksin Shinawatra (Ammar 2011, 76–77; The Nation 2003).

This increased role for the state in the economy also reflects more general movement away from Democrat-type conservative economic policy. For example, while granting a three-year moratorium on farmers' debts, Thaksin mandated more credit be available than the banks were willing to provide independently (Ammar 2011, 75–77; Wichit 2003). The IMF even noted this in its AFC program conclusion, warning 'against the resumption of state-directed lending in recapitalized banks' (International Monetary Fund 2002a). Another well-known example of new levels of populist state intervention in the Thai economy was a scheme where the government kept rice prices artificially high, benefitting rural farmer constituencies (Ammar 2011, 78). Credit and price manipulations show TRT followed through on its populist campaign rhetoric in many key economic areas.

And as in other EMs, these left-leaning economic policies came to shape annual external borrowings. Indeed, TRT and Thaksin explicitly shifted borrowing away from official creditors. As one former PDMO employee noted, TRT wanted to change spending rapidly, direct it to such populist purposes, and the 'PDMO needed private money to do that' (Interview 20). Figure 6.1 shows most external borrowing in the TRT years was from markets.

To be sure, TRT's first years included some official credit. These reflect official loans begun under the Democrats but completed by the PDMO under TRT, such as a US$400 million World Bank budget support loan that was able to support TRT's shift in spending priorities without adjusting them (World Bank 2002; Interviews 16, 19). It is also true that upgrades from all three major ratings agencies in 2003 made markets more appealing to the PDMO than they had been. However, Thailand was investment grade at two of the three major credit rating agencies under the Democrats in 1999 and 2000, so Thailand had been seen as highly creditworthy for some time. Borrowing primarily changed because of TRT's left-leaning

---

[14] In some ways, this reflects the long-run benefits of the Democrat's policies after the crisis, noted by Interviews 8, 18, 21, 24.

partisanship, which took effect most clearly after lingering official loans from the Democrat years were finalized.

TRT borrowing preferences had significant effects on both lender and PDMO staffs. For lenders, the IMF experience signaled what was to come. After declaring 'the IMF had harmed Thailand,' TRT pledged to repay the IMF's AFC bailout early (Hewison 2004, 511; Kazmin 2002). This was achieved in 2003, which Thaksin 'touted ... as one of his proudest moments in office' (Kazmin 2006). Interviewees recalled Thaksin 'on television saying Thailand was free' (Interview 21), and other interviewees recalled similar efforts by Thaksin to politicize repaying the IMF early as a victory for TRT, the Thai economy, and Thai sovereignty (Interviews 8, 18, 19, 24, 30). This political stance affected all official lenders, as concerns about economic and political autonomy meant official creditors took on an inescapable 'stigma' among Thai politicians and the public (Interview 11).

Indeed, the World Bank struggled to lend to Thailand in the TRT years after the lingering Democrat loans were finalized. The Bank tried branding itself as non-threatening to Thai autonomy, for example changing terminology to represent a 'knowledge partnership' rather than a lending relationship (Interview 18). But the Bank–Thai relationship was limited to a 'non-lending' service-for-fees relationship under TRT (World Bank 2006, 9, fn 5; see also 2003, sec. i). Using a relatively small amount of Bank funds in a multi-lender roads project in 2003 was 'almost a favor' for the Bank by the PDMO (Interview 18; see World Bank 2010a, sec. 2).

Similarly, the Asian Development Bank (ADB) was restricted to advisory assistance with the 'absence of an active borrowing program' in this period (Asian Development Bank 2007, secs 1, 9), symbolized by Thaksin delaying the opening of the ADB's Bangkok offices for many years until 2005 (Interviews 17, 21, 21). Japan found by 2006 that '[d]ue to Thailand's policy ... [i]n a practical sense, it can be said that bilateral cooperation through large-scale yen loans is to be terminated' (Government of Japan 2006, sec. 2). China was (and would remain through 2017 fieldwork) unused because the PDMO found it more expensive than other official creditors, required excessive collateral commitments, and was tied to Chinese companies and labor (Interviews, 19, 20, 24, 30).

This indicates the PDMO was significantly constrained by TRT partisanship. Even when financing requirements were small, the rapid shift in priorities made market instruments efficient (Interview 20). Thaksin would 'personally manage and limit' the PDMO's further use of official creditors (Interview 19, 26, 30). Despite the price and technical benefits of official creditors valued by the PDMO, the TRT made the 'political transaction costs' of using them too high (Interviews 11, 26).

TRT focused on avoiding official credit, and Figure 6.1 shows the party largely succeeded. The early 2000s shift away from official credit is primarily explained by the party's partisan-informed borrowing preferences. TRT policy diverged significantly from official creditors' macroeconomic prescriptions. Political concern for autonomy led to overt intervention by TRT in the borrowing process, leading the PDMO to avoid official creditors more than they would have otherwise. It was not credit ratings or improvements in fundamentals that explain the timing of shifts in Thailand's external sovereign borrowing, but partisan politics.

6.4.4 Post-TRT (2006–2015)

In September 2006, a year after TRT won a second election, the military took government by coup 'to adjust the balance of political power by neutralizing Thaksin, reducing the role of elected politicians, and returning power to the bureaucracy' (Baker and Pasuk 2014, 271). This began a period of frequent government change between Thaksin allies and a military–bureaucrat–business class coalition represented by the Democrats. TRT-descendant parties won elections in 2007 and 2011 and Democrats took charge following their military or judicial removals in 2008 and 2014. This meant Thailand had Democrat-led governments from mid-2006 to 2007, from 2009 to mid-2011, and in 2015 (Baker and Pasuk 2014, chap. 9; Hewison 2010; Kitti 2015; 2016).

While government changes did not yield substantial changes to fiscal policy, they did affect external borrowing. On the fiscal side, TRT had set new expectations about the Thai welfare state and 'governments have [since] viewed welfare as essential for winning political support' (Hewison 2010, 130). Although Democrats remained conservative (Hewison 2014, 853–855), some level of state-provided welfare was now part of all party platforms (for a practical example surrounding the 2006–2007 coup government coalition, see Kitirianglarp and Hewison 2009, 467–468). This explains why Figure 6.2 shows expenditures have trended upward since TRT regardless of the specific party in power.

Foreign borrowing decisions, however, did continue to change by governing party. Democrats used official credit and TRT-descendant parties did not. While national and global economic conditions help explain when the PDMO turned outside for finance rather than issue domestic bonds,[15] use of official creditors when turning outside for finance continued only when Democrats were in government. This remained the case despite investors, banks, and ratings agencies encouraging foreign bonds (Interviews 20, 26).[16] 'Borrowing preferences [came to] depend on ministers' and thus the governing party (Interview 17). The Democrats put in economic ministers who 'had better memories of IFIs' (Interview 11) and

---

[15] The substantial development of domestic markets through this time minimized the amount needed from external sources. Interview 1 showed that the size of the domestic public bond market went from 12% to 72% of GDP from 1997 to 2015.

[16] Interview 18 suggested Thailand's credit ratings are good but could be better if Thailand met this demand and issued more foreign currency debt.

had 'interest in official credit' (Interview 16) while parties descendant from TRT did not (Lefevre 2012).

Accordingly, Figure 6.1 shows official creditor use spiked in 2007, 2009, and 2015, the first years of the three Democratic governments in this period. In 2007 the coup led to some nerves in markets which made it a 'bad year [in markets for us]... but there was never a serious liquidity problem' so a return official credit was a choice (Interview 20). Despite persistent liquidity, the Democrats borrowed from Japan even though Japan had considered lending to Thailand 'terminated' due to TRT (JICA 2008; Ministry of Foreign Affairs of Japan 2009; Government of Japan 2006, sec. 2). Meanwhile, the PDMO reinvigorated the formal partnership with the ADB where one had not existed in TRT years, symbolizing the shift in PDMO behaviors and borrowing preferences under Democrats (Asian Development Bank 2007; 2008, 72).

In 2009 and 2010, the PDMO went to the World Bank and ADB for budget support. These loans were not necessary to fund the budget but Democrat ministers who had experience with the banks wanted the funds (Interviews 11, 16, 17, 21, 24). Even Bank staff were surprised at the new interest in traditional loans rather than mere technical assistance (Interview 16). The loans were sought partly because 'while Thailand has good access to financial markets, borrowing from [official creditors] will help Thailand access longer term maturity financing' (World Bank 2010c). The ADB provides similar benefits to the PDMO, which they use under Democrat governments (Interviews 27, 30). The official loans were also partly sought to enhance the relationships with both creditors, and partly to provide a cushion for any lingering effects of the Global Financial Crisis (Interviews 8, 9, 11, 16, 17, 18, 19, 20, 21, 24, 26). Using official credit under the Democrats in these years despite market access and the high political transaction costs given the status of multilateral loans as 'treaties' by this time is strong evidence for the effect of partisanship on external sovereign borrowing in EMs.

In 2015, the Democrats returned to government and used the ADB for project loans (see 'ADB-Supported Projects and Programs' and 'Cofinancing' sections in Asian Development Bank 2016). The loans were again not necessary for financing requirements but enhanced the relationship (Interviews 17, 18, 20, 21, 24, 26). Still, it is telling that the Democrats used official credit again after the TRT-related Pheu Thai party had avoided them from 2011 to 2014. Under TRT-descendant populist parties, resistance to official credit is so strong that a flood crisis in December 2011 did not lead to substantial official credit, despite official lenders offering significant concessional funds (Interviews 8, 9, 19, 20, 26). Although conditions were fewer in number in these years, environmental safeguards and transparency conditions, as well as reputational concerns, remain problematic for parties other than the Democrats (Interview 16).

6.5 Conclusion

Thailand again shows how and why EM annual external borrowings are informed by government partisanship. Before the AFC, conservative technocratic governments used more official than market finance. After the AFC, right-leaning Democrats continued to implement conservative economic policies and use official credit that reinforced those policy preferences, despite clear political costs and the return of market access by at least 1999. External borrowing did not change until the populist TRT explicitly moved Thailand away from official creditors after 2001. To be sure, other factors are important. The AFC required official credit in 1997 and 1998 and the growth of domestic resources gradually reduced the PDMO's need to use external finance in absolute terms. But sole focus on global or domestic economic conditions cannot explain the structure of the foreign debt obligations Thailand accumulated from 1990 to 2015. The PDMO faced different political constraints when making external borrowings, depending on the partisanship of government in a given year.

7

Conclusion

7.1 Introduction

The economic interests and policy preferences of core governing party constituencies help determine the financial instruments EM sovereigns prioritize when borrowing abroad each year. This means core components of external sovereign debt structure in EMs (the cost of external debt, the maturity of external debt, and the conditions attached to that debt) cannot be apolitically managed by DMOs as EM sovereigns accumulate debt over time.

These two interrelated arguments, articulated and tested throughout the book, have implications for research on sovereign debt as well as research on the relationship between political interests, ministerial institutions, and economic policy outcomes. They also have implications for practitioners working on sovereign debt in developing economies. This chapter discusses a number of these implications, then concludes by considering possible future shifts in the global political economy that would alter the trade-off EMs face when borrowing externally and, by extension, the partisan politics of EM external debt accumulation.

7.2 Research and Policy Implications

This book's theory of external borrowing stems from the trade-off EM governments face when turning abroad for finance. The trade-off, at least at the time of borrowing and in the short term, is that official credit is cheaper with longer maturities but comes with controversial conditions while markets are more expensive and shorter term but provide policy autonomy.

This trade-off reframes traditional conceptions about the relationship between globalized financial markets and policy constraints outside of the rich world. Sovereign debt markets are often expected, implicitly and explicitly, to constrain developing country economic policy space or constrain market access for governments with policies that imply the country may be less able or willing to repay debts. But this book shows why, as EMs accumulate sovereign debt, markets represent comparatively *more* space for implementation of their preferred policies compared to other external financing options. That sovereign debt markets are attractive to EMs for reasons of policy autonomy does more than help explain variation in EM public debt structures. The argument sharpens concepts and issues

How Governments Borrow. Ben Cormier, Oxford University Press. © Ben Cormier (2024).
DOI: 10.1093/oso/9780198882732.003.0007

central to the international and comparative political economy of sovereign debt in developing economies, relevant to both research and practice. This includes the following implications, discussed in turn below:

(1) setting limits to disciplinary models of borrower partisan politics in EM sovereign debt markets, highlighting left-leaning partisans are likely to borrow *more* from markets;

(2) showing borrower autonomy, and the politics of demand-side use of markets and official creditors, is central to understanding both sets of flows and thus the composition of EM sovereign debt;

(3) suggesting the demand side helps explain variation in the cyclicality of EM financial flows;

(4) highlighting the importance of distinguishing between price and volume in sovereign debt, and ways to clarify theorization and measurement of flows in the IPE of sovereign debt;

(5) advancing questions about politically feasible DMO effects on public debt structure and sustainability (transparency and diversification);

(6) emphasizing the academic and practical importance of further research on deepening domestic public bond markets;

(7) identifying how and why the role and effect of ministerial institutions like DMOs varies not only across different aspects of public debt structure, but across different areas of the economy.

7.2.1 Demand-Side Limits to Market Discipline

Sovereign debt markets outside of the rich world are often thought to discipline left-leaning governments. Markets may do this by charging higher rates, lending shorter term, or making less capital available to left-leaning EMs than they would EMs with other policy preferences. A corollary is that left-leaning governments may be expected to be disciplined into changing policy to access as much market finance as other governments. But this study shows that (1) left-leaning EMs accumulate proportionally *more* market-based external debt than other EMs in terms of volume and (2) they do this despite any disciplinary prices or maturities and the availability of cheaper official financing sources. In sum: even if markets charge higher rates or otherwise discipline left-leaning political parties and policies in their debt contracts with EM sovereigns, this will not keep left-leaning EMs from taking on those costs and borrowing from markets.

This signals important demand-side limits to theories of disciplinary capital allocation based on borrower partisan politics in EM sovereign debt. Markets do not systematically discipline left-leaning EM sovereigns out of relying on debt markets for financing as they accumulate external debt. EM DMOs use market-based instruments to meet external borrowing needs if the governing party's core political constituencies incentivize it to do so. This point helps explain variation in the trajectory of sovereign debt structure in EMs, and why this can defy disciplinary expectations. Future research can sharpen the literature by taking the differences between disciplinary effects on price and disciplinary effects on volume of flows seriously (see Section 7.2.4 below).

7.2.2 Borrower Autonomy, Domestic Politics, and Sovereign Debt Structure

Relatedly, the book shows the importance of taking borrower autonomy and politically informed borrower preferences during periods of debt accumulation more seriously in studies of EM sovereign debt. When making annual borrowings, EM governments do not need to use market instruments to meet all (or any) of their external financing needs. Official credit is available and can be used to varying degrees, alongside or instead of markets. In turn, official creditor flows are also often a matter of borrower autonomy because borrowing sovereigns 'can say no'.[1] The financial options and corresponding trade-offs EMs face when borrowing bring autonomy, and the politics of how that autonomy is used, to the fore.

This means the external sources of finance EM governments use to add to their national balance sheets each year, and thus the accumulation of a particular external sovereign debt structure over time, are not merely functions of supply-side creditworthiness assessments, capital allocation decisions, or official creditor selectivity. Nor do borrowing governments simply choose the lowest prices and longest maturities available, as the debts that do and do not end up on EM balance sheets often do so *despite* prices and maturities. Borrowing strategies, determined by partisan politics within EM borrowers, are also central to explaining why EMs accumulate relatively more or less expensive, longer or shorter term, and conditional or nonconditional external sovereign debts than others over time.

Studying explanations for variation in the composition of sovereign debt structure is important because, ultimately, the debts that an EM government actually accumulates are what dictate the opportunities, constraints, and risks that sovereign debt provides for an EM's social and economic development prospects. As this book shows, EM use of sovereign debt markets largely hinges on the policies and reputations of the available alternatives, namely the official financial institutions associated with powerful countries. This means political considerations inform foreign economic policy in sovereign debt as much as, if not more than, price-based cost–benefit calculations or market discipline. Further exploration

---

[1] Thanks to Gerry Helleiner for this phrase.

of how domestic borrower politics determine sovereign debt structures would advance interdisciplinary sovereign debt research.

Provocatively, a focus on borrower autonomy implicitly puts a degree of responsibility for debt sustainability on the borrower. Yet politics, including but not limited to the partisan dimension articulated in this book, make strictly technocratic use of this autonomy unlikely. This gives rise to a question: how can sustainable borrowing be ensured if markets do not systematically discipline borrowers and DMOs face domestic political constraints? Suggestions for ways to begin tackling this question are considered below, particularly in 7.2.5 through 7.27.

Lastly, a scoping limitation to this book is that it merely controls for crisis periods and defaults to theorize about and test for the generalizability of partisan effects on borrowing outcomes. But borrowing preferences immediately following defaults or other crises may be subject to nuance not captured here. In particular, the official and market creditor groupings used in this book may be important to deconstruct at more granular levels in such episodes. For example, China may present a qualitatively different option than Western creditors if they are serving a lender-of-last-resort function.[2] The case of Thailand in this book suggests this is *not* the case. Even after one of the most damaging financial crises in modern history, post-crisis Thai sovereign borrowings depended on government partisanship, and China did not alter this. However, in other cases like Ecuador, China had a unique role following a 2008 default (Bunte 2019, 101–105). In that episode, China was a preferred resource for a few post-default years despite being a left-leaning government.[3] In other words, where Thailand's left-leaning government returned immediately to markets upon winning the election after the Asian Financial Crisis, Ecuador's left-leaning government used China before returning to markets about six years after the default. The politics of varied borrowing preferences in post-crisis episodes is a potential topic for future research.

7.2.3 The Cyclicality of EM Sovereign Debt Flows

The ability of borrowing EMs to use or not use markets or official creditors in most circumstances also suggests the importance of demand-side factors in shaping the cyclicality of EM financial flows. Supply-side factors such as investor irrationality, global liquidity, and market structure can lead to pro-cyclical flows, meaning capital is abundant during good times and less abundant when most needed (Bauerle Danzman, Winecoff, and Oatley 2017a; Cormier and Naqvi 2023; Naqvi 2019;

---

[2] Thanks to an anonymous reviewer for prompting this consideration.
[3] Though it is also notable that some officials explicitly identify this approach as short-sighted with respect to future policy autonomy and implications of indebtedness to China (Bunte 2019, 105).

Reinhart and Rogoff 2009). This contrasts with official credit flows which are often counter-cyclical (Galindo and Panizza 2018). But by emphasizing that EM governments do not need to rely on markets or official creditors for all or any of their external financing needs as they accumulate debt, this book suggests why demand-side factors such as partisan politics are likely important to understanding variation in the cyclicality of flows across EMs (cf. Galindo and Panizza 2018).

7.2.4 Clearer Theory and Measurement in the IPE of Sovereign Debt

Advocating for more focus on the politics that explain why countries use different financing instruments each year and build different sovereign debt structures over time also implies the gains to be made by improving the specificity of measurement and theory in IPE of sovereign debt research. A review of the IPE sovereign debt literature reveals muddling of different sovereign debt outcomes and the politics underpinning them.

For example, some studies of the Democratic Advantage use credit ratings as the dependent variable, a proxy for price (Biglaiser and Staats 2012; Cormier 2023b). Others use amount borrowed, a measure of supply-demand equilibrium in flows, to test the same theory (Ballard-Rosa, Mosley, and Wellhausen 2021). This creates inference problems. First is that price does not equal market use, as emphasized throughout this book. This disconnect makes it unclear how studies using different dependent variables to test the same theory ultimately relate to one another. Second is that specifying models theoretically relevant to one type of outcome but applying them to another can lead to misspecification. For example, specifying a model derived from theories of creditworthiness but applying the model to a flow outcome can lead to omitted factors (such as not accounting for annual financing requirements or other fiscal policy measures in a model of flows).

Another example of mismatch between measurement and theory lies in studies of the effect partisanship has on different sovereign debt outcomes, to which this book contributes. Some find a partisan effect on creditworthiness (Barta and Johnston 2018; Cho 2014; Vaaler, Schrage, and Block 2006) leading some to note with surprise that they find no partisan effect on actual flows (Frot and Santiso 2013, 42–44). But this book explains why both may be the case, by being specific about the importance of borrowers' use or nonuse of markets despite rates.

This is not a novel critique (Saiegh 2005), but dissonance in theory and measurement in the IPE of sovereign debt studies remains common. Studies can do better to clearly specify what the dependent variable is, confirm that their theory is relevant to that particular dependent variable, and account for the full list of factors relevant to that particular dependent variable as controls in subsequent models. This will ensure studies control for all relevant variables when making new arguments, omit unrelated variables, and clearly identify what their results do and do not speak to in the literature. In this vein, two rules of thumb implicitly emerge from this book, depending on the outcome variable being considered.

First, the ability of EMs to use or not use market instruments to meet financing needs suggests that selection effects must be taken seriously in any study of EM sovereign debt looking at rates, maturities, or other measures dependent on the instrument existing in the first place. This selection effect also applies to studies of official creditor loans and conditions. Second, when studying capital flow volume or the amount of debt that governments take on each year, fiscally determined financing requirements and partisan politics are minimum requirements for accounting for the demand side of sovereign debt.

7.2.5 DMO Practices and Effects (Transparency and Diversification)

Chapter 2's model of sovereign debt accumulation hinges on the role of EM DMOs in the annual fiscal policymaking process, emphasizing the political constraints they face in managing external debt accumulation through that process. But emphasizing the politicized nature of borrowings and ensuing debt structures does not imply that this is the end of the story for DMOs. Instead, the model gives rise to more specific questions about the ways in which DMOs may affect sovereign debt accumulation, and by extension sovereign debt composition and sustainability, within such first-order political constraints. Given the need to account for the relationship between the annual fiscal policymaking process, partisan politics, and government borrowings, what realistic institutional effects might DMOs have in practice? How might EM DMOs enhance public debt sustainability if markets do not systematically discipline and they face political constraints when making borrowing decisions?

For one, recent research argues that transparent public debt practices enhance sovereign creditworthiness, and thus reduce borrowing costs, regardless of regime type or the degree to which the government is transparent in other areas (Cormier 2023b). This signals the importance of further research on variation in DMO reporting, particularly whether there are more precise political or economic conditions under which DMOs are more or less transparent (World Bank 2021a, 16–18). Since public debt transparency is an area in which the IMF and World Bank find most developing countries 'fall short' (International Monetary Fund and World Bank 2018a, 8), understanding why there is significant variation in sovereign debt transparency has practical implications for improving DMO practices in politically realistic ways that could enhance sovereign debt sustainability (see World Bank 2021a, 19–21).

In addition to enhancing transparency, what else might DMOs realistically do to enhance sustainability within first-order political constraints? The cases in this book suggest that, to the extent possible, mixing or diversifying foreign creditors may yield sustainability benefits for public debt structure. Peru's DMO, for example, occasionally used official credit for projects under left-leaning governments when it was clear they could negotiate conditions that would not adjust or threaten left-leaning governments' economic policies. Meanwhile, other DMOs, such as South Africa's and Botswana's, did not mix foreign creditors over this time period. For South Africa, this contributed to public debt sustainability concerns by the end of the 2010s. For Botswana, this amounted to a missed opportunity to benchmark for future bond issues at uniquely low prices during good times. For both countries, minimal or nonrelationships with the unused source only increases the economic, political, and bureaucratic transaction costs of using that source at future points in time.

To be sure, the capacity to mix creditors is still ultimately a function of partisan politics. Peruvian politics had allowed space for a close relationship between the DMO and official creditors over time and was sufficiently center-left to allow for occasional use of official creditors. In contrast, South Africa's ANC explicitly forbade use of official creditors, and Botswana's BDP was so comfortable with official creditors that the party explicitly resisted bond markets. But to the extent possible, diversification may contribute to sustainable external EM debt accumulation. Given a particular political constellation, EM DMOs may retain significant control over debt accumulation while politicians simultaneously maintain control over national economic policies.[4]

7.2.6 Deepening Domestic Public Debt Markets

Deserving an itemized mention is the importance of domestic rather than external EM sovereign debt. Particularly important is the depth of local currency public bond markets, or the volume and liquidity of the market for local-denominated government debt. The process of deepening local currency public bond markets is an important policy challenge for DMOs. Often, developing countries do not have access to the amount of domestic-denominated financial resources they may want. Outside of a few exceptionally large developing economies, including some now wealthy High Income Countries, most developing country debt accumulated in recent decades remains foreign denominated (see countries in, for example, Aizenman et al. 2021; Dehn 2020, fig. 5). In 2019, China alone made up 47% of the local-currency bond market, while most regions are home to governments that issue between two and five times as much foreign as domestic debt (Dehn 2020, fig. 3).

---

[4] Thanks to Lou Pauly for this summary point.

The political and institutional foundations of deepening local currency government bond markets in developing countries—generating greater demand for local currency instruments—is thus an important policy-relevant research topic. But it is one with a shallow literature (Claessens, Klingebiel, and Schmukler 2007). One way forward is to use this book's model of EM public debt accumulation to locate this debt management challenge within political-economic constraints on public debt. Key is not only to identify the political economy of using what local-denominated market resources are available (Ballard-Rosa, Mosley, and Wellhausen 2022), but *deepening* those markets, particularly where they are minimal or nonexistent.

Moreover, and most related to this book's arguments about external borrowing, is that deeper local currency bond markets may alter the political and economic trade-off that underpins external borrowings. Inversely, efforts to deepen local resources may be affected by the politics of external borrowing strategies. What DMOs can and cannot do to deepen local currency bond markets within political constraints, and how the politics of external borrowing may inform the prospects of local deepening, are important questions for both the literature and practitioners working on sovereign debt in developing economies. Understanding the political and institutional foundations of deepening local bond markets would have profound implications for debt managers and public policy outside of the rich world.

7.2.7 The Varying Role of Institutions in Different Areas of Public Debt and Different Areas of the Economy

As detailed in Chapter 2, one of the book's central arguments is that the role and effect of DMOs is not necessarily comparable across different areas of sovereign debt structure. The maturity structure of a sovereign's market instrument repayment obligations, for example, may be more subject to DMO control than use of markets in the first place. More specificity about the part of the government balance sheet being considered can advance political economy literature on the role and effect of DMOs, and perhaps other institutions, on sovereign debt structure.

Extrapolating this point out to broader comparative political economy, the study is an example of why it is important to consider the extent to which the relationship between political interests and ministerial institutions varies across different areas of economic policymaking. For example, as also discussed in Chapter 2, the role and possible effect of institutions in public debt cannot be easily compared with the role and possible effect of independent institutions in monetary policy. At least in EMs, DMOs are constrained by procedural aspects of the fiscal policymaking process on both the input side (what the financing requirement is and what is being borrowed for, which is shaped by partisan fiscal policy) and the output side (what external borrowing decisions will be ratified by partisan ministers) of borrowing.

This observation has implications for both theory and practice, suggesting paths for future research on the relationship between interests, institutions, and economic policy. In what other areas of economic policy does institutional independence not affect policy outcomes? Might a more explicit focus on procedural aspects of policymaking better specify the role institutions may or may not have in shaping policy outcomes in different areas of the economy? This follows calls for more qualitative studies in developing country comparative political economy and public policy (Bertelli et al. 2020; Centeno, Kohli, and Yashar 2017; Williams 2020), intended to provide both more nuanced and policy-relevant research.

7.3 Looking Ahead

The external borrowing trade-off at the center of this book may or may not be unique to the international financial architecture and character of financial markets available to EMs in the twenty-five years following the end of the Cold War. Were this context to change, the international political economy of EM sovereign external borrowings and debt accumulation would likely change. This section concludes the book by considering what possible future shifts in the character of sovereign debt markets, official creditors, or borrowers themselves might mean for EM external borrowings and sovereign debt.

Supply-side changes in sovereign debt markets and investor behaviors could alter EM market access. In addition to exogenous policy factors that determine the overall amount of credit available to EMs (such as US interest rates), supply-side shifts might not simply change the volume of liquidity available to EMs but the nature of the borrowing trade-off EMs face given that liquidity. These include market structure and legal aspects of sovereign debt contracts.

Market structure, or the practical mechanics of how investors assess and group potential debtors and allocate capital, could significantly change. For example, recent work highlights how global capital allocation decisions are increasingly concentrated in bond index providers (Petry, Fichtner, and Heemskerk 2019). While EMs have the autonomy to issue or not issue bonds, *changes in index inclusion criteria* may alter the incentives or capacity to do so in significant ways. The benchmark foreign currency EM sovereign bond index is J.P. Morgan's EMBIG, with inclusion criteria designed to automatically include virtually all EM foreign-denominated bonds, ensuring the index reflects the character of EM hard currency bonds as an asset class (Cormier and Naqvi 2023). If EMBIG inclusion criteria were to change, say to more stringent criteria in the interest of providing a more sustainable index, this could affect the access EMs have to bond markets. The same effect might come to pass if bond indexes proliferate and asset managers follow more specific indexes for any number of reasons. Similarly, if local currency indexes grew to become more representative of the asset class (Dehn 2020, 5–6), this would increase access to local currency finance and potentially alter use of foreign-denominated instruments.

The legal framework around EM sovereign debt contracts may also change in significant ways. Since this often happens after crises and defaults (Choi, Gulati, and Posner 2012), and given the rise in EM public debt levels and sovereign risk even before the Covid-19 pandemic (Mustapha and Prizzon 2018), it is plausible that some EMs will come to face newly stringent legal terms in sovereign debt contracts in the coming years. Sovereign debt contract language is often assumed to be 'boilerplate' and irrelevant to cost and issuance strategies, but studies show that the law under which a sovereign bond is issued is associated with risk considerations (Choi, Gulati, and Posner 2011). Part of the reason for this is that bonds issued under foreign laws provide investors more recourse than bonds issued under domestic legal regimes (Choi, Gulati, and Posner 2011), which also affects the bond's tradability in secondary markets (Dehn 2020, 5–6). If legal aspects of debt contracts become more of a bargaining item between sovereigns and creditors, this might alter the external borrowing trade-off faced by EMs. For example, it is possible that investors increasingly 'take better precautions' (Choi, Gulati, and Posner 2011) by only holding certain EM debts under the laws of certain countries. This could alter EM incentives to use markets rather than official creditors, making contract terms and legal regimes an important aspect of the international political economy of annual borrowings and ensuing sovereign debt structures.

Meanwhile, the content of official creditor conditionality could alter incentives to use or not use these resources. Most obviously, if labor and working classes in EMs no longer experienced or anticipated a disproportionate amount of adjustment when using official creditors, this would alter the partisan political economy of EM sovereign borrowing preferences. Such a shift would diverge from the inertia observed in recent history. Expansion of policy areas covered by conditionality have not eliminated the centrality of austerity, debt reduction, privatization, increased competition for domestic producers through both market integration and tied supply chain changes, and increased labor competition through more flexible labor markets and tied labor (Babb 2013; Bräutigam 2011, 760; Cormier and Manger 2022; Dreher et al. 2018, n. 9; Huang, Xu, and Mao 2018, 33, 243, 251; Isaksson and Kotsadam 2018b; Kaplan 2021, chap. 3; Kentikelenis, Stubbs, and King 2016b; Weaver 2008). The persistence of such official creditor conditions and effects on specific groups within the borrower underpin this book's theory that parties with working classes as core constituents prefer to avoid official creditors. But if the international politics of conditionality were to change, the domestic politics of EM external borrowings would correspondingly change.

Finally, the political and economic characteristics of EMs themselves may change. A major shift would be a decrease in the political power of labor across or within certain EMs. Such a shift may stem from reshoring efforts by rich countries, increased production capacity in lower-cost Low Income Countries, or technological advancements that limit the availability of many forms of labor on which EM citizens depend for income and political power.

For one EM, a decrease in the political power of labor and the working classes fits this book's theory. The effect would be to increase the probability of using more official credit to meet foreign borrowing needs. But what this book doesn't account for is whether major global production shifts might decrease the political power of labor across the world, leading to new political economic interest groups, new core political cleavages in EMs, and new external borrowing preferences. If the political power and importance of labor decreases on aggregate across EMs, this could affect the politics of external government borrowing preferences across EMs.

Another possible shift could stem from 'democratic backsliding' (Bermeo 2016). To the extent that there is a rise in authoritarian regimes around the world, governments may perceive the external borrowing trade-off differently. For example, authoritarian regimes in Thailand before 1992 and in Peru in the 1990s used close relationships to Western multilaterals and bilaterals, and implementation of 'good' economic policy promoted by these lenders, to avoid foreign criticism of undemocratic politics (see Chapters 5 and 6). In this sense, the role of democratic governance in the politics of foreign borrowing would have less to do with market use (cf. Biglaiser and Staats 2012; Schultz and Weingast 2003) than it would official creditor use. If close economic relationships with official creditors increased space for authoritarian domestic politics, this would change the calculation that EMs may make when borrowing externally. Such effects are controlled for in the models in this book covering the twenty-five years after the Cold War, but if such considerations became more salient in borrowing choices in the future, then this may affect the applicability of this book's argument under such conditions.

As EMs with financing options continue to borrow, and low income frontier markets grow into EMs with more financing options, future work on the politics of sovereign debt accumulation will have to account for whether and the extent to which these and other changes affect the partisan politics of external sovereign borrowing outside of the rich world.

Interviews List (further information available from author on request)

Interview#	Date	Name	Type	Style	How record
1	March 10, 2017	Anonymous	Multilateral	Semi-structured	Live recording
2	April 4, 2017	Anonymous	Multilateral	Semi-structured	Simultaneous notes
3	Jan 12, 2017	Anonymous	Bilateral	Unstructured	Post-event notes (4 hours later)
4	May 26, 2017	Anonymous	Academic	Semi-structured	Simultaneous notes
5	May 29, 2017	Anonymous	Domestic	Unstructured	Email
7	June 1, 2017	Anonymous	Academic	Semi-structured	Simultaneous notes
8	June 1, 2017	Anonymous	Multilateral	Semi-structured	Simultaneous notes
9	June 1, 2017	Anonymous	Multilateral	Semi-structured	Simultaneous notes
10	June 2, 2017	Anonymous	Multilateral	Semi-structured	Email
11	June 2, 2017	Anonymous	Multilateral	Semi-structured	Live recording
12	June 2, 2017	Anonymous	Bi & Multilateral	Semi-structured	Email
15	June 5, 2017	Anonymous	Domestic	Semi-structured	Simultaneous notes
16	June 7, 2017	Anonymous	Multilateral	Semi-structured	Simultaneous notes
17	June 7, 2017	Anonymous	Multilateral	Semi-structured	Simultaneous notes
18	June 8, 2014	Anonymous	Domestic	Semi-structured	Simultaneous notes
19	June 12, 2017	Anonymous	Multilateral	Semi-structured	Simultaneous notes
20	June 13, 2017	Anonymous	Domestic	Semi-structured	Simultaneous notes

Interview#	Date	Name	Type	Style	How record
21	June 15, 2017	Anonymous	Domestic; Multilateral	Semi-structured	Simultaneous notes
22	June 16, 2017	Anonymous	Domestic	Specific Questions	Email
23	June 20, 2017	Anonymous	Domestic	Unstructured	Simultaneous notes
24	June 22, 2017	Anonymous	Multilateral	Semi-structured	Live recording
26	June 27, 2017	Anonymous	Domestic	Semi-structured	Simultaneous notes
27	July 14, 2017	Anonymous	Multilateral	Semi-structured	Live recording
28	July 14, 2017	Anonymous	Multilateral	Semi-structured	Live recording
30	July 26, 2017	Anonymous	Domestic	Semi-structured	Simultaneous notes
31	July 28, 2017	Anonymous	Multilateral	Unstructured	Live recording
33	Aug 4, 2017	Anonymous	Multilateral	Semi-structured	Live recording
34	Aug 7, 2017	Anonymous	Multilateral	Semi-structured	Live recording
35	Aug 16, 2017	Anonymous	Domestic	Structured	Email
39	Aug 2, 2017	Anonymous	Academic	Semi-Structured	Simultaneous notes
40	Aug 4, 2017	Anonymous	Academic	Semi-Structured	Simultaneous notes
41	Aug 7, 2017	Anonymous	Domestic	Semi-Structured	Simultaneous notes
42	Aug 8, 2017	Anonymous	Multilateral	Semi-Structured	Simultaneous notes
43	Aug 8, 2017	Anonymous	Domestic	Semi-Structured	Live recording
44	Aug 11, 2017	Anonymous	Underwriter	Semi-Structured	Simultaneous notes
45	Aug 14, 2017	Anonymous	Foreign Banker	Semi-Structured	Live recording
46	Aug 16, 2017	Anonymous	Domestic	Structured	Live recording
47	Aug 17, 2017	Anonymous	Domestic	Semi-Structured	Live recording
48	Aug 17, 2017	Anonymous	Domestic	Semi-Structured	Live recording
49	Aug 17, 2017	Anonymous	Domestic	Semi-Structured	Live recording
50	Aug 18, 2017	Anonymous	Domestic	Semi-Structured	Live recording

Continued

Continued

Interview#	Date	Name	Type	Style	How record
51	Aug 22, 2017	Anonymous	Domestic	Semi-Structured	Simultaneous notes
52	Aug 23, 2017	Anonymous	Domestic	Unstructured	Simultaneous notes
53	Aug 25, 2017	Anonymous	Domestic	Unstructured	Simultaneous notes
54	Aug 28, 2017	Anonymous	Domestic	Structured	Email
55	Aug 28, 2017	Anonymous	Multilateral	Structured	Live recording
56	Aug 29, 2017	Anonymous	Multilateral	Semi-Structured	Simultaneous notes
57	Aug 29, 2017	Anonymous	Frmr Domestic	Structured	Simultaneous notes
58	Aug 30, 2017	Anonymous	Domestic	Unstructured	Simultaneous notes
59	Sept 4, 2017	Anonymous	Multilateral	Semi-Structured	Simultaneous notes
60	Sept 4, 2017	Anonymous	Multilateral	Structured	Email
61	Sept 4, 2017	Anonymous	Frmr Domestic	Structured	Email
62	Oct 17, 2017	Anonymous	Domestic	Semi-Structured	Live recording
65	Aug 8, 2017	Anonymous	Multilateral	Semi Structured	Simultaneous notes
66	Aug 10, 2017	Anonymous	Multilateral	Semi Structured	Live recording
67	Aug 22, 2017	Anonymous	Academic	Unstructured	Email
68	Aug 29, 2017	Anonymous	Multilateral	Semi-Structured	Simultaneous notes
69	Aug 30, 2017	Anonymous	Domestic	Unstructured	Simultaneous notes
70	Aug 30, 2017	Anonymous	Domestic	Unstructured	Simultaneous notes
72	Sept 11, 2017	Anonymous	Domestic	Semi Structured	Simultaneous notes
73	Sept 12, 2017	Anonymous	Banker	Structured	Simultaneous notes
74	Sept 12, 2017	Anonymous	Banker	Structured	Simultaneous notes
75	Sept 12, 2017	Anonymous	Domestic	Semi Structured	Simultaneous notes
76	Sept 12, 2017	Anonymous	Domestic	Structured	Email
77	Sept 12, 2017	Ms. B. Peter	Domestic	Semi Structured	Live recording
78	Sept 12, 2017	Ms. S. Fologang	Domestic	Semi Structured	Live recording

Interview#	Date	Name	Type	Style	How record
79	Sept 13, 2017	Anonymous	Intl Banker	Semi Structured	Simultaneous notes
80	Sept 14, 2017	Anonymous	Multilateral and Domestic	Structured	Simultaneous notes
81	Sept 15, 10am	Anonymous	Domestic	Structured	Simultaneous notes
82	Sept 15, 2pm	Anonymous	Domestic	Semi Structured	Simultaneous notes
84	Oct 18, 2017	Anonymous	Multilateral	Semi-Structured	Live recording
85	Oct 19, 2017	Anonymous	Multilateral	Semi-Structured	Live recording
86	Oct 23, 2017	Anonymous	Frmr Domestic	Semi-Structured	Simultaneous notes
87	Oct 24, 2017	Anonymous	Frmer Domestic; Multilateral	Semi-Structured	Simultaneous notes
88	Oct 24, 2017	Anonymous	Multilateral	Semi-Structured	Simultaneous notes
89	Oct 27, 2017	Anonymous	Frmr Multilateral; Domestic	Semi-Structured	Simultaneous notes
90	Oct 27, 2017	Anonymous	Frmr Multilateral; Academic	Semi-Structured	Simultaneous notes
91	Oct 30, 2017	Anonymous	Frmr Multilat; Domestic	Structured	Email
92	Oct 31, 2017	Anonymous	Frmr Multilat; Domestic	Structured	Live recording
93	Nov 2, 2017	Anonymous	Frmr Domestic	Structured	Email
94	Nov 2, 2017	Anonymous	Academic	Structured	Live recording
95	Nov 6, 2017	Anonymous	Domestic	Semi-Structured	Simultaneous notes
96	Nov 8, 2017	Anonymous	Domestic	Structured	Simultaneous notes
97	Nov 14, 2017	Anonymous	Multilateral	Semi-Structured	Live recording
98	Nov 30, 2017	Anonymous	Frmr Domestic; Investor	Semi-Structured	Simultaneous notes
99	Nov 30, 2017	Anonymous	Domestic	Semi-Structured	Simultaneous notes

Continued

Continued

Interview#	Date	Name	Type	Style	How record
100	Nov 30, 2017	Anonymous	Domestic	Semi-Structured	Simultaneous notes
101	Dec 1, 2017	Anonymous	Frmr Domestic	Semi-Structured	Simultaneous notes
102	Dec, 2017 Emails	Anonymous	Academic	Structured	Email
109	Feb 23, 2021	Anonymous	Multilateral	Semi-Structured	Email

References

Aberbach, Joel D., and Bert A. Rockman. 2002. 'Conducting and Coding Elite Interviews.' *PS: Political Science & Politics* 35 (4): 673–676. https://doi.org/10.1017/S1049096502001142.

Aggarwal, Vinod, and Maxwell Cameron. 1994. 'Modelling Peruvian Debt Rescheduling in the 1980s.' *Studies in Comparative International Development* 29 (2): 48–81.

Aguiar, Mark, Manuel Amador, Emmanuel Farhi, and Gita Gopinath. 2013. 'Crisis and Commitment: Inflation Credibility and the Vulnerability to Sovereign Debt Crises.' w19516. Cambridge, MA: National Bureau of Economic Research. https://doi.org/10.3386/w19516.

Aizenman, Joshua, Yothin Jinjarak, Donghyun Park, and Huanhuan Zheng. 2021. 'Good-Bye Original Sin, Hello Risk on-off, Financial Fragility, and Crises?' *Journal of International Money and Finance* 117 (October): 102442. https://doi.org/10.1016/j.jimonfin.2021.102442.

Alesina, Alberto, and Roberto Perotti. 1995. 'The Political Economy of Budget Deficits.' *IMF Staff Papers* 42 (1): 1–31.

Alonso, Jose Antonio. 2016. 'AID FOR TRADE: BUILDING PRODUCTIVE AND TRADE CAPACITIES IN LDCs.' United Nations Committee for Development Policy Review Series No. 1 United Nations Committee for Development Policy Review Series No. 1. United Nations Committee for Development Policy Review Series. United Nations.

Ammar, Siamwalla. 2011. 'Thailand after 1997: Thailand after 1997.' *Asian Economic Policy Review* 6 (1): 68–85. https://doi.org/10.1111/j.1748-3131.2011.01181.x.

Anner, Mark, and Teri Caraway. 2010. 'International Institutions and Workers' Rights: Between Labor Standards and Market Flexibility.' *Studies in Comparative International Development* 45 (2): 151–169. https://doi.org/10.1007/s12116-010-9064-x.

Apichat, Satitniramai. 2002. 'The Rise and Fall of the Technocrats: The Unholy Trinity of Technocrats, Ruling Elites and Private Bankers and the Genesis of the 1997 Economic Crisis.' PhD Dissertation, Swansea: University of Wales.

Aquino, Marco. 2014. 'Peru Says Most of $3 Bln in Bonds Sold to Manage Existing Debt.' *Reuters*, October 31, 2014. http://www.reuters.com/article/peru-bonds/update-2-peru-says-most-of-3-bln-in-bonds-sold-to-manage-existing-debt-idUSL1N0SQ1ZR20141031.

Asian Development Bank. 2007. 'Country Partnership Strategy: Thailand (2007–2011).' Asian Development Bank. https://www.adb.org/sites/default/files/institutional-document/32384/files/cps-tha-2007-2011.pdf.

Asian Development Bank. 2008. 'Annual Report 2007.' Manila: Asian Development Bank. https://www.adb.org/sites/default/files/institutional-document/31324/annual-report-2007-vol01.pdf.

Asian Development Bank. 2016. 'Asian Development Bank Member Fact Sheet: Thailand.' Asian Development Bank. http://www.fpo.go.th/FPO/modules/Content/getfile.php?contentfileID=11419.

Asian Infrastructure Investment Bank. 2016. 'AIIB and World Bank Sign First Co-Financing Framework Agreement.' Asian Infrastructure Investment Bank. April 14, 2016. https://www.aiib.org/en/news-events/news/2016/AIIB-and-World-Bank-Sign-first-Co-Financing-Framework-Agreement.html.

Avilés, William, and Yolima Rey Rosas. 2017. 'Low-Intensity Democracy and Peru's Neoliberal State: The Case of the Humala Administration.' *Latin American Perspectives* 44 (5): 162–182.

Babb, Sarah L. 2013. 'The Washington Consensus as Transnational Policy Paradigm: Its Origins, Trajectory and Likely Successor.' *Review of International Political Economy* 20 (2): 268–297. https://doi.org/10.1080/09692290.2011.640435.

Babb, Sarah L., and Bruce G. Carruthers. 2008. 'Conditionality: Forms, Function, and History.' *Annual Review of Law and Social Science* 4 (1): 13–29. https://doi.org/10.1146/annurev.lawsocsci.4.110707.172254.

Bailey, Michael A., Anton Strezhnev, and Erik Voeten. 2017. 'Estimating Dynamic State Preferences from United Nations Voting Data.' *Journal of Conflict Resolution* 61 (2): 430–456.

Baker, Chris, and Phongpaichit Pasuk. 2014. *A History of Thailand.* 3rd ed. Port Melbourne: Cambridge University Press.

Ballard-Rosa, Cameron. 2020. *Democracy, Dictatorship, and Default: Urban-Rural Bias and Economic Crises across Regimes.* Cambridge: Cambridge University Press.

Ballard-Rosa, Cameron, Layna Mosley, and Rachel L. Wellhausen. 2021. 'Contingent Advantage? Sovereign Borrowing, Democratic Institutions and Global Capital Cycles.' *British Journal of Political Science* 51: 353–373. https://doi.org/10.1017/S0007123418000455.

Ballard-Rosa, Cameron, Layna Mosley, and Rachel L. Wellhausen. 2022. 'Coming to Terms: The Politics of Sovereign Bond Denomination.' *International Organization* 76: 32–69. https://doi.org/10.1017/S0020818321000357.

Bank of Thailand, Communications and Relations Office, Management Assistance Department. 2002. 'The Fiscalization of Financial Institutions Development Fund's Losses.' 22. Bank of Thailand. https://www.bot.or.th/Thai/PressAndSpeeches/Press/News2545/n2245e.pdf.

Barnett, Michael N., and Martha Finnemore. 2004. *Rules for the World.* Ithaca, NY: Cornell University Press.

Barr, Robert R. 2003. 'The Persistence of Neopopulism in Peru? From Fujimori to Toledo.' *Third World Quarterly* 24 (6): 1161–1178.

Barta, Zsófia, and Alison Johnston. 2018. 'Rating Politics? Partisan Discrimination in Credit Ratings in Developed Economies.' *Comparative Political Studies* 51 (5): 587–620. https://doi.org/10.1177/0010414017710263.

Bassett, Carolyn, and Marlea Clarke. 2008. 'The Zuma Affair, Labour and the Future of Democracy in South Africa.' *Third World Quarterly* 29 (4): 787–803.

Bastida, Francisco, María-Dolores Guillamón, and Bernardino Benito. 2017. 'Fiscal Transparency and the Cost of Sovereign Debt.' *International Review of Administrative Sciences* 83 (1): 106–128. https://doi.org/10.1177/0020852315574999.

Bauerle Danzman, Sarah, W Kindred Winecoff, and Thomas Oatley. 2017. 'All Crises Are Global: Capital Cycles in an Imbalanced International Political Economy.' *International Studies Quarterly* 61 (4): 907–923. https://doi.org/10.1093/isq/sqx054.

Bearce, David H. 2003. 'Societal Preferences, Partisan Agents, and Monetary Policy Outcomes.' *International Organization* 57 (2): 373–410. https://doi.org/10.1017/S0020818303572058.

Beaulier, Scott A. 2003. 'Explaining Botswana's Success: The Critical Role of Post-Colonial Policy.' *The Cato Journal* 23 (2): 227–240.

Beaulier, Scott A., and J. Robert Subrick. 2006. 'The Political Foundations of Development: The Case of Botswana.' *Constitutional Political Economy* 17 (2): 103–115. https://doi.org/10.1007/s10602-006-0002-x.

Beaulieu, Emily, Gary W. Cox, and Sebastian Saiegh. 2012. 'Sovereign Debt and Regime Type: Reconsidering the Democratic Advantage.' *International Organization* 66 (04): 709–738.

Beazer, Quintin H., and Byungwon Woo. 2016. 'IMF Conditionality, Government Partisanship, and the Progress of Economic Reforms.' *American Journal of Political Science* 60 (2): 304–321. https://doi.org/10.1111/ajps.12200.

Bechtel, Michael M. 2009. 'The Political Sources of Systematic Investment Risk: Lessons from a Consensus Democracy.' *The Journal of Politics* 71 (2): 661–677.

Beck, Thorsten, George Clarke, Alberto Groff, Philip Keefer, and Patrick Walsh. 2001. 'New Tools in Comparative Political Economy: The Database of Political Institutions.' *World Bank Economic Review* 15 (1): 165–176.

Beeson, Mark, and Shaomin Xu. 2019. 'China's Evolving Role in Global Governance: The AIIB and the Limits of an Alternative International Order.' In *Handbook on the International Political Economy of China*, edited by Ka Zeng, 345–360. Cheltenham, UK; Northampton, MA, USA: Edward Elgar.

Behuria, Ashok K. 2018. 'How Sri Lanka Walked into a Debt Trap, and the Way Out.' *Strategic Analysis* 42 (2): 168–178.

Bermeo, Nancy. 2016. 'On Democratic Backsliding.' *Journal of Democracy* 27 (1): 5–19.

Bernhard, William, and David Leblang. 2002. 'Democratic Processes, Political Risk, and Foreign Exchange Markets.' *American Journal of Political Science* 46 (2): 316–333. https://doi.org/10.2307/3088379.

Bertelli, Anthony M., Mai Hassan, Dan Honig, Daniel Rogger, and Martin J. Williams. 2020. 'An Agenda for the Study of Public Administration in Developing Countries.' *Governance* 33 (4): 735–748. https://doi.org/10.1111/gove.12520.

Bertelsmann, Julia I. 2013. 'Independent Fiscal Institutions in the Face of Rising Public Indebtedness.' In *Restoring Public Debt Sustainability*, edited by George Kopits, 75–95. Oxford: Oxford University Press. https://doi.org/10.1093/acprof:oso/9780199644476.003.0005.

Besley, Timothy, and Torsten Persson. 2014. 'Why Do Developing Countries Tax So Little?' *Journal of Economic Perspectives* 28 (4): 99–120. https://doi.org/10.1257/jep.28.4.99.

Best, Jacqueline. 2014. *Governing Failure: Provisional Expertise and the Transformation of Global Development Finance*. Cambridge: Cambridge University Press.

Biglaiser, Glen, and Joseph L. Staats. 2012. 'Finding the "Democratic Advantage" in Sovereign Bond Ratings: The Importance of Strong Courts, Property Rights Protection, and the Rule of Law.' *International Organization* 66 (03): 515–535. https://doi.org/10.1017/S0020818312000185.

Blanton, Robert G., Shannon Lindsey Blanton, and Dursun Peksen. 2015. 'The Impact of IMF and World Bank Programs on Labor Rights.' *Political Research Quarterly* 68 (2): 324–336.

Bleich, Erik, and Erik Pekkanen. 2013. 'How to Report Interview Data.' In *Interview Research in Political Science*, edited by Layna Mosley, 84–105. Ithaca, NY: Cornell University Press.

Blommestein, Hans J., and Philip Turner. 2012. 'Interactions Between Sovereign Debt Management and Monetary Policy Under Fiscal Dominance and Financial Instability.' 3. OECD Working Papers on Sovereign Borrowing and Public Debt Management. OECD.

Bodea, Cristina, Tanya Bagashka, and Sung Min Han. 2019. 'Are Parties Punished for Breaking Electoral Promises? Market Oriented Reforms and the Left in Post-Communist Countries.' SSRN Scholarly Paper ID 3361134. Rochester, NY: Social Science Research Network. https://doi.org/10.2139/ssrn.3361134.

Bodea, Cristina, and Raymond Hicks. 2015a. 'International Finance and Central Bank Independence: Institutional Diffusion and the Flow and Cost of Capital.' *Journal of Politics* 77 (1): 268–284.

Bodea, Cristina, and Raymond Hicks. 2015b. 'Price Stability and Central Bank Independence: Discipline, Credibility, and Democratic Institutions.' *International Organization* 69 (1): 35–61. https://doi.org/10.1017/S0020818314000277.

Bordo, Michael D., Christopher M. Meissner, and David Stuckler. 2010. 'Foreign Currency Debt, Financial Crises and Economic Growth: A Long-Run View.' *Journal of International Money and Finance* 29 (4): 49.

Botlhale, Emmanuel. 2015. 'The Political Economy of Poverty Eradication in Botswana.' *Poverty & Public Policy* 7 (4): 406–419.

Bova, Eva, Nathalie Carcenac, and Martine Guergil. 2014. 'Fiscal Rules and the Procyclicality of Fiscal Policy in the Developing World.' IMF Working Paper WP/14/122. International Monetary Fund.

Bräutigam, Deborah. 2011. 'Aid "with Chinese Characteristics": Chinese Foreign Aid and Development Finance Meet the OECD-DAC Aid Regime.' *Journal of International Development* 23 (5): 752–764. https://doi.org/10.1002/jid.1798.

Bräutigam, Deborah, and Kevin P. Gallagher. 2014. 'Bartering Globalization: China's Commodity-Backed Finance in Africa and Latin America.' *Global Policy* 5 (3): 346–352. https://doi.org/10.1111/1758-5899.12138.

Breen, Michael, and Iain McMenamin. 2013. 'Political Institutions, Credible Commitment, and Sovereign Debt in Advanced Economies.' *International Studies Quarterly* 57 (4): 842–854.

Brender, Adi, and Allan Drazen. 2005. 'Political Budget Cycles in New versus Established Democracies.' *Journal of Monetary Economics* 52 (5): 1271–1295.

Brooks, Sarah M., Raphael Cunha, and Layna Mosley. 2015. 'Categories, Creditworthiness, and Contagion: How Investors' Shortcuts Affect Sovereign Debt Markets.' *International Studies Quarterly* 59 (3): 587–601. https://doi.org/10.1111/isqu.12173.

Brooks, Sarah M., Raphael Cunha, and Layna Mosley. 2022. 'Sovereign Risk and Government Change: Elections, Ideology and Experience.' *Comparative Political Studies* 55 (9): 1501–1538. https://doi.org/10.1177/00104140211047407.

Brooks, Sarah M., and Marcus J. Kurtz. 2012. 'Paths to Financial Policy Diffusion: Statist Legacies in Latin America's Globalization.' *International Organization* 66 (1): 95–128. https://doi.org/10.1017/S0020818311000385.

Brown, Andrew. 2007. 'Labour and Modes of Participation in Thailand.' *Democratization* 14 (5): 816–833. https://doi.org/10.1080/13510340701635670.

Bueno de Mesquita, Bruce, Alastair Smith, Randolph M. Siverson, and James D. Morrow. 2005. *The Logic of Political Survival*. Cambridge, MA: MIT Press.

Bulow, Jeremy, and Kenneth Rogoff. 1989. 'Sovereign Debt: Is to Forgive to Forget?' *The American Economic Review* 79 (1): 43–50.

Bunte, Jonas B. 2019. *Raise the Debt: How Developing Countries Choose Their Creditors*. New York: Oxford University Press.

Burke, Christopher, Sanusha Naidu, and Arno Nepgen. 2008. 'Scoping Study on China's Relations with South Africa.' AERC Scoping Studies on China-Africa Economic Relations, African Economic Research Consortium (AERC). Nairobi: Centre for Chinese Studies, University of Stellenbosch.

Cabral, Rodrigo. 2015. 'How Strategically Is Public Debt Being Managed around the Globe?' World Bank Report. World Bank.

Calitz, Estian, Krige Siebrits, and Ian Stuart. 2016. 'Enhancing the Accuracy of Fiscal Projections in South Africa.' *South African Journal of Economic Management Sciences* 19 (3): 330–343.

Calland, Richard. 2013. *The Zuma Years: South Africa's Changing Face of Power*. Cape Town: Zebra Press.

Campello, Daniela. 2015. *The Politics of Market Discipline in Latin America: Globalization and Democracy*. New York: Cambridge University Press.

Caraway, Teri L., Stephanie J. Rickard, and Mark S. Anner. 2012. 'International Negotiations and Domestic Politics: The Case of IMF Labor Market Conditionality.' *International Organization* 66 (4): 27–61.

Carré, Emmanuel, and Marie-Sophie Gauvin. 2018. 'Financial Crisis: The Capture of Central Banks by the Financial Sector?' *International Journal of Political Economy* 47 (2): 151–177. https://doi.org/10.1080/08911916.2018.1497576.

Centeno, Miguel A., Atul Kohli, and Deborah J. Yashar. 2017. 'Unpacking States in the Developing World: Capacity, Performance, and Politics.' In *States in the Developing World*, edited by Miguel A. Centeno, Atul Kohli, Deborah J. Yashar, and Dinsha Mistree, 1–32. Cambridge: Cambridge University Press. https://doi.org/10.1017/CBO9781316665657.002.

Cervellati, Matteo, Elena Esposito, Uwe Sunde, and Song Yuan. 2022. 'Malaria and Chinese Economic Activities in Africa.' *Journal of Development Economics* 154 (January): 102739. https://doi.org/10.1016/j.jdeveco.2021.102739.

Chapman, Terrence, Songying Fang, Xin Li, and Randall W Stone. 2015. 'Mixed Signals: IMF Lending and Capital Markets.' *British Journal of Political Science* 47: 329–349.

Cho, Hye Jee. 2014. 'Impact of IMF Programs on Perceived Creditworthiness of Emerging Market Countries: Is There a "Nixon-Goes-to-China" Effect?' *International Studies Quarterly* 58 (2): 308–321. https://doi.org/10.1111/isqu.12063.

Choi, Jungug. 2005. 'Economic Crisis, Poverty, and the Emergence of Populism in Thailand.' *Journal of International and Area Studies* 12 (1): 49–59.

Choi, Stephen J., Mitu Gulati, and Eric A Posner. 2011. 'Pricing Terms in Sovereign Debt Contracts: A Greek Case Study with Implications for the European Crisis Resolution Mechanism.' *Capital Markets Law Journal* 6: 163–187.

Choi, Stephen J., Mitu Gulati, and Eric A. Posner. 2012. 'The Evolution of Contractual Terms in Sovereign Bonds.' *Journal of Legal Analysis* 4 (1): 131–179. https://doi.org/10.1093/jla/las004.

Chwieroth, Jeffrey M. 2009. *Capital Ideas: The IMF and the Rise of Financial Liberalization.* Princeton, NJ: Princeton University Press.

Claessens, Stijn, Daniela Klingebiel, and Sergio L. Schmukler. 2007. 'Government Bonds in Domestic and Foreign Currency: The Role of Institutional and Macroeconomic Factors.' *Review of International Economics* 15 (2): 370–413. https://doi.org/10.1111/j.1467-9396.2007.00682.x.

Clark, Richard, and Lindsay R. Dolan. 2021. 'Pleasing the Principal: U.S. Influence in World Bank Policymaking.' *American Journal of Political Science* 65 (1): 36–51. https://doi.org/10.1111/ajps.12531.

Conaghan, Catherine M. 2005. *Fujimori's Peru: Deception in the Public Sphere.* Pittsburgh: University of Pittsburgh Press.

Connolly, Michael. 2007. 'Measuring the Effect of Corruption on Sovereign Bond Ratings.' *Journal of Economic Policy Reform* 10 (4): 309–323. https://doi.org/10.1080/17487870701552053.

Cook, Amelia, and Jeremy Sarkin. 2010. 'Is Botswana the Miracle of Africa-Democracy, the Rule of Law, and Human Rights versus Economic Development.' *Transnational Law & Contemporary Problems* 19: 453.

Coppedge, Michael, John Gerring, Staffan I. Lindberg, Svend-Erik Skaaning, Jan Teorell, David Altman, Michael Bernhard, et al. 2016. 'V-Dem Dataset v6.2.' *Varieties of Democracy (V-Dem) Project.*

Cordeiro, Anjali. 2011. 'S&P Lifts Peru to BBB on Prudent Fiscal Policy.' *Marketwatch*, August 30, 2011. https://www.marketwatch.com/story/sp-lifts-peru-to-bbb-on-prudent-fiscal-policy-2011-08-30.

Cormier, Ben. 2021. 'Interests over Institutions: Political-Economic Constraints on Public Debt Management in Developing Countries.' *Governance* 34 (4): 1167–1691. https://onlinelibrary.wiley.com/doi/10.1111/gove.12551.

Cormier, Ben. 2023a. 'Chinese or Western Finance? Transparency, Official Credit Flows, and the International Political Economy of Development.' *The Review of International Organizations* 18 (2): 2997–328. https://doi.org/10.1007/s11558-022-09469-x.

Cormier, Ben. 2023b. 'Democracy, Public Debt Transparency, and Sovereign Creditworthiness.' *Governance* 36 (1): 209–231. https://doi.org/10.1111/gove.12668.

Cormier, Ben. 2023c. 'Partisan External Borrowing in Middle-Income Countries.' *British Journal of Political Science* 53 (2): 717–727. https://doi.org/10.1017/S0007123421000697.

Cormier, Ben, and Mark Manger. 2022. 'Power, Ideas, and World Bank Conditionality.' *Review of International Organizations* 17 (3): 397–425. https://link.springer.com/article/10.1007/s11558-021-09427-z.

Cormier, Ben, Mirko Heinzel, and Bernhard Reinsberg. 2022. 'Informally Governing International Development: G7 Coordination and Orchestration in Aid.' In *IOs beyond [COW] IGOs Workshop*. Salzburg.

Cormier, Ben, and Natalya Naqvi. 2023. 'Delegating Discipline: How Indexes Restructured the Political Economy of Sovereign Bond Markets.' *Journal of Politics*. https://doi.org/10.1086/723997.

COSATU. 2012. 'International Policy: As Adopted by the 11th National Congress of COSATU.' http://www.cosatu.org.za/docs/policy/2012/internationalpolicy.pdf.

Cotoc, Ionut, Alok Johri, and César Sosa-Padilla. 2021. 'Sovereign Spreads and the Political Leaning of Nations.' Working Paper 29197. Working Paper Series. National Bureau of Economic Research. https://doi.org/10.3386/w29197.

Cotterill, Joseph. 2017. 'Fitch Cuts South Africa's Credit Rating to Junk.' *Financial Times*, April 7, 2017. https://www.ft.com/content/5b8e083c-1b91-11e7-bcac-6d03d067f81f.

Cotterill, Joseph. 2021. 'South Africa Counts the Cost of Its Worst Unrest since Apartheid.' *Financial Times*, July 25, 2021. https://www.ft.com/content/1b0badcd-2f81-42c8-ae09-796475540ccc.

Crabtree, John. 2001. 'The Collapse of Fujimorismo: Authoritarianism and Its Limits.' *Bulletin of Latin American Research* 20 (3): 287–303.

Crabtree, John, and Francisco Durand. 2017. *Peru: Elite Power and Political Capture*. London: Zed Books.

Cruz, Cesi, Philip Keefer, and Carlos Scartascini. 2018. 'Database of Political Institutions 2017 (DPI 2017).' Inter-American Development Bank. https://publications.iadb.org/handle/11319/7408.

Cukierman, Alex. 2008. 'Central Bank Independence and Monetary Policymaking Institutions— Past, Present and Future.' *European Journal of Political Economy* 24 (4): 722–736. https://doi.org/10.1016/j.ejpoleco.2008.07.007.

Currie, Elizabeth, Jean-Jacques Dethier, and Eriko Togo. 2003. 'Institutional Arrangements for Public Debt Management.' Policy Research Working Paper 3021. Washington, D.C.: World Bank.

Danevad, Andreas. 1995. 'Responsiveness in Botswana Politics: Do Elections Matter?' *The Journal of Modern African Studies* 33 (3): 381–402.

Das, Udaibir S., Michael G. Papaioannou, Guilherme Pedras, Jay Surti, and Faisal Ahmed. 2011. 'Managing Public Debt and Its Financial Stability Implications.' In *Sovereign Debt and the Financial Crisis: Will This Time Be Different?*, edited by Carlos A. Primo Braga and Gallina A. Vincelette, 357–381. Washington, D.C.: World Bank.

Dehn, Jan. 2020. 'The EM Fixed Income Universe Version 9.0.' The Emerging View. London: Ashmore Investment Management Limited.

Dempsey, John R. 2000. 'Thailand's Privatization of State Owned Enterprises During the Eocnomic Downturn.' *Law and Policy in International Business* 31 (2): 373–402.

Diamond, Mr Jack, and Mr Barry H. Potter. 1999. *Guidelines for Public Expenditure Management*. International Monetary Fund.

Doner, Richard F., and Ben Ross Schneider. 2016. 'The Middle-Income Trap.' *World Politics* 68 (04): 608–644. https://doi.org/10.1017/S0043887116000095.

Drazen, Allan. 2001. 'The Political Business Cycle after 25 Years.' In *NBER Macroeconomics Annual 2000*, edited by Ben S. Bernanke and Kenneth Rogoff, 15: 75–138. Cambridge, MA: MIT Press.

Dreher, Axel, Andreas Fuchs, Brad Parks, Austin M. Strange, and Michael J. Tierney. 2018. 'Apples and Dragon Fruits: The Determinants of Aid and Other Forms of State Financing from

China to Africa.' *International Studies Quarterly* 62 (1): 182–194. https://doi.org/10.1093/isq/sqx052.

Dreher, Axel, Andreas Fuchs, Bradley C. Parks, Austin M. Strange, and Michael J. Tierney. 2017. *Aid, China, and Growth: Evidence from a New Global Development Finance Datatset.* 1st ed. AidData Working Paper 46. Williamsburg, VA: AidData.

Dreher, Axel, Andreas Fuchs, Bradley C. Parks, Austin Strange, and Michael J. Tierney. 2022. *Banking on Beijing: The Aims and Impacts of China's Overseas Development Program.* Cambridge: Cambridge University Press.

Dreher, Axel, Peter Nunnenkamp, and Rainer Thiele. 2011. 'Are "New" Donors Different? Comparing the Allocation of Bilateral Aid Between NonDAC and DAC Donor Countries.' *World Development* 39 (11): 1950–1968.

Dreher, Axel, Jan-Egbert Sturm, and James R. Vreeland. 2015. 'Politics and IMF Conditionality.' *Journal of Conflict Resolution* 59 (1): 120–148. https://doi.org/10.1177/0022002713499723.

Eaton, Jonathan, and Mark Gersovitz. 1981. 'Debt with Potential Repudiation: Theoretical and Empirical Analysis.' *The Review of Economic Studies* 48 (2): 289–309. https://doi.org/10.2307/2296886.

Eaton, Jonathan, Mark Gersovitz, and Joseph E. Stiglitz. 1986. 'The Pure Theory of Country Risk.' *European Economic Review* 30: 481–513.

Eichengreen, Barry, and Ricardo Hausmann. 1999. 'Exchange Rates and Financial Fragility.' w7418. Cambridge, MA: National Bureau of Economic Research. https://doi.org/10.3386/w7418.

Eichengreen, Barry, Ricardo Hausmann, and Ugo Panizza. 2007. 'Currency Mismatches, Debt Intolerance, and Original Sin: Why They Are Not the Same and Why It Matters.' In *Capital Controls and Capital Flows in Emerging Economies: Policies, Practices, and Consequences*, edited by Sebastian Edwards, 121–169. Chicago: University of Chicago Press.

Eichengreen, Barry, Ricardo Hausmann, and Ugo Panizza. 2023. 'Yet It Endures: The Persistence of Original Sin.' *Open Economies Review* 34 (1): 1–42. https://doi.org/10.1007/s11079-022-09704-3.

el Comercio. 2011. 'Alejandro Toledo: "Implementamos Muy Tarde El Programa Juntos".' *El Comercio*, March 9, 2011, sec. Politica. http://archivo.elcomercio.pe/politica/gobierno/alejandro-toledo-implementamos-muy-tarde-programa-juntos-noticia-724914.

Eskom. 2017. 'Eskom Signs a US$1.5 Billion Loan Agreement with the China Development Bank.' http://www.eskom.co.za/news/Pages/Jull6B.aspx.

Eyraud, Luc, Xavier Debrun, Andrew Hodge, Victor Lledó, and Catherine Pattillo. 2018. 'Second-Generation Fiscal Rules: Balancing Simplicity, Flexibility, and Enforceability.' IMF Staff Discussion Note SDN/18/04. International Monetary Fund.

Fastenrath, Florian, Michael Schwan, and Christine Trampusch. 2017. 'Where States and Markets Meet: The Financialisation of Sovereign Debt Management.' *New Political Economy* 22 (3): 273–293. https://doi.org/10.1080/13563467.2017.1232708.

Fatás, Antonio, Mr Atish R. Ghosh, Ugo Panizza, and Mr Andrea F. Presbitero. 2019. 'The Motives to Borrow.' WP/19/101. International Monetary Fund.

Fernández-Albertos, José. 2015. 'The Politics of Central Bank Independence.' *Annual Review of Political Science* 18 (1): 217–237. https://doi.org/10.1146/annurev-polisci-071112-221121.

Fernandez-Arias, Eduardo. 1996. 'The New Wave of Private Capital Inflows: Push or Pull?' *Journal of Development Economics* 48 (2): 389–418. https://doi.org/10.1016/0304-3878(95)00041-0.

Findley, Michael G., Helen V. Milner, and Daniel L. Nielson. 2017. 'The Choice among Aid Donors: The Effects of Multilateral vs. Bilateral Aid on Recipient Behavioral Support.' *Review of International Organizations* 12: 307–334.

Fine, Ben. 2009. 'Development as Zombieconomics in the Age of Neoliberalism.' *Third World Quarterly* 30 (5): 885–904. https://doi.org/10.1080/01436590902959073.

Fleck, Robert K., and Christopher Kilby. 2006. 'World Bank Independence: A Model and Statistical Analysis of US Influence.' *Review of Development Economics* 10 (2): 224–240.

Franzese, Robert J. 2002. 'Electoral and Partisan Cycles in Economic Policies and Outcomes.' *Annual Review of Political Science* 5 (1): 369–421. https://doi.org/10.1146/annurev.polisci.5. 112801.080924.

Franzese, Robert J. 2019. 'The Comparative and International Political Economy of Anti-Globalization Populism.' *Oxford Research Encyclopedia of Politics*, April. https://doi.org/10. 1093/acrefore/9780190228637.013.638.

Franzese, Robert J., and Karen Long Jusko. 2009. 'Political-Economic Cycles.' In *The Oxford Handbook of Political Economy*, edited by Donald A. Wittman and Barry R. Weingast, 545–561. Oxford University Press.

Frieden, Jeffry. 1991. *Debt, Development, and Democracy*. Princeton, NJ: Princeton University Press.

Frot, Emmanuel, and Javier Santiso. 2013. 'Political Uncertainty and Portfolio Managers in Emerging Economies.' *Review of International Political Economy* 20 (1): 26–51. https://doi. org/10.1080/09692290.2011.625916.

Fuchs, Andreas, and Marina Rudyak. 2019. 'The Motives of China's Foreign Aid.' In *Handbook on the International Political Economy of China*, edited by Ka Zeng, 392–410. Cheltenham, UK; Northampton, MA, USA: Edward Elgar.

Gadanecz, Blaise, Ken Miyajima, and Chang Shu. 2014. 'Exchange Rate Risk and Local Currency Sovereign Bond Yields in Emerging Markets.' *BIS Monetary and Economic Department Working Paper No. 474*, December.

Galindo, Arturo J., and Ugo Panizza. 2018. 'The Cyclicality of International Public Sector Borrowing in Developing Countries: Does the Lender Matter?' *World Development* 112 (December): 119–135. https://doi.org/10.1016/j.worlddev.2018.08.007.

Gandhi, Jennifer, and Adam Przeworski. 2006. 'Cooperation, Cooptation, and Rebellion Under Dictatorships.' *Economics and Politics* 18 (1): 1–26. https://doi.org/10.1111/j.1468-0343.2006. 00160.x.

Garrett, Geoffrey. 1998. *Partisan Politics in the Global Economy*. New York: Cambridge University Press.

Gauss, Bertrand. 2014. 'After the Boom–Commodity Prices and Economic Growth in Latin America and the Caribbean.' IMF Working Paper WP/14/154. IMF.

Gelos, R. Gaston, Ratna Sahay, and Guido Sandleris. 2011. 'Sovereign Borrowing by Developing Countries: What Determines Market Access?' *Journal of International Economics* 83 (2): 243–254. https://doi.org/10.1016/j.jinteco.2010.11.007.

Gelpern, Anna, Sebastian Horn, Scott Morris, Brad Parks, and Christoph Trebesch. 2021. 'How China Lends: A Rare Look into 100 Debt Contracts with Foreign Governments.' AidData. https://docs.aiddata.org/reports/how-china-lends.html#section3-4.

George, Alexander L., and Andrew Bennett. 2004. *Case Studies and Theory Development in the Social Sciences*. Cambridge, MA: MIT Press.

Glennerster, Rachel, and Yongseok Shin. 2008. 'Does Transparency Pay?' *IMF Staff Papers* 55 (1): 183–209.

Gomomo, John. 1996. 'Address by COSATU President John Gomomo to the World Economic Forum.' Address to the World Economic Forum presented at the World Economic Forum, Cape Town, May 23. https://www.sahistory.org.za/archive/address-cosatu-president-john-gomomo-world-economic-forum.

Good, Kenneth. 2003. 'Bushmen and Diamonds: (Un)Civil Society in Botswana.' Discussion Paper 23. Uppsala: Nordiska Afrikainstitutet.

Good, Kenneth. 2005. 'Resource Dependency and Its Consequences: The Costs of Botswana's Shining Gems.' *Journal of Contemporary African Studies* 23 (1): 27–50. https://doi.org/10. 1080/0258900042000329448.

Government of Japan. 2006. 'Japan's Economic Cooperation Program for Thailand.' JICA. http://www.mofa.go.jp/policy/oda/region/e_asia/thailand.pdf.

Grabel, Ilene. 1996. 'Marketing the Third World: The Contradictions of Portfolio Investment in the Global Economy.' *World Development* 24 (11): 1761–1776. https://doi.org/10.1016/0305-750X(96)00068-X.

Gray, Julia. 2013. *The Company States Keep.* New York: Cambridge University Press.

Greene, William. 2004. 'Fixed Effects and Bias Due to the Incidental Parameters Problem in the Tobit Model.' *Econometric Reviews* 23 (2): 125–147. https://doi.org/10.1081/ETC-120039606.

Griffith-Jones, Stephany, David Griffith-Jones, and Dagmar Hertova. 2008. 'Enhancing the Role of Regional Development Banks.' 50. G-24 Discussion Paper Series. UN. http://stephanygj.net/papers/Enhancing-Role-RDBs.pdf.

Groenwald, Yolandi, and Matthew le Cordur. 2017. 'Eskom Banks Heavily on China, Inks R20bn Loan Deal.' *Fin24*, July 6, 2017.

Gulati, Mitu, and Mark Weidemaier. n.d. 'Clauses and Controversies: Ep. 48 Ft. Layna Mosley.' Clauses and Controversies. Accessed August 17, 2021.

Güven, Ali Burak. 2018. 'Whither the Post-Washington Consensus? International Financial Institutions and Development Policy before and after the Crisis.' *Review of International Political Economy* 25 (3): 392–417. https://doi.org/10.1080/09692290.2018.1459781.

Hagen, Jürgen von. 2009. *Political Economy of Fiscal Institutions.* Edited by Donald A. Wittman and Barry R. Weingast. Oxford University Press. https://doi.org/10.1093/oxfordhb/9780199548477.003.0026.

Hagen, Jürgen von. 2013. 'Scope and Limits of Independent Fiscal Institutions.' In *Restoring Public Debt Sustainability*, edited by George Kopits, 32–53. Oxford: Oxford University Press. https://doi.org/10.1093/acprof:oso/9780199644476.003.0003.

Hallerberg, Mark, Carlos Scartascini, and Ernesto Stein, eds. 2009. *Who Decides the Budget? A Political Economy Analysis of the Budget Process in Latin America.* Cambridge, MA: Inter-American Development Bank. https://publications.iadb.org/publications/english/document/Who-Decides-the-Budget-A-Political-Economy-Analysis-of-the-Budget-Process-in-Latin-America.pdf.

Hallerberg, Mark, and Sami Yläoutinen. 2010. 'Political Power, Fiscal Institutions and Budgetary Outcomes in Central and Eastern Europe.' *Journal of Public Policy* 30 (1): 45–62. https://doi.org/10.1017/S0143814X09990213.

Handley, Antoinette. 2008. *Business and the State in Africa: Economic Policy-Making in the Neo-Liberal Era.* Cambridge: Cambridge University Press.

Hardie, Iain. 2006. 'The Power of the Markets? The International Bond Markets and the 2002 Elections in Brazil.' *Review of International Political Economy* 13 (1): 53–77. https://doi.org/10.1080/09692290500396651.

Hardie, Iain, and Lena Rethel. 2019. 'Financial Structure and the Development of Domestic Bond Markets in Emerging Economies.' *Business and Politics* 21 (1): 86–112. https://doi.org/10.1017/bap.2018.11.

Harvey, William S. 2011. 'Strategies for Conducting Elite Interviews.' *Qualitative Research* 11 (4): 431–441. https://doi.org/10.1177/1468794111404329.

Hausmann, Ricardo, and Ugo Panizza. 2003. 'On the Determinants of Original Sin: An Empirical Investigation.' *Journal of International Money and Finance* 22 (7): 957–990. https://doi.org/10.1016/j.jimonfin.2003.09.006.

Hawkins, Darren G., David A. Lake, Daniel L. Nielson, and Michael J. Tierney, eds. 2006. *Delegation and Agency in International Organizations.* Cambridge: Cambridge University Press. http://ebooks.cambridge.org/ref/id/CBO9780511491368.

Heinzel, Mirko, Ben Cormier, and Bernhard Reinsberg. 2023. 'Earmarked Funding and the Control-Performance Trade-Off in International Development Organizations.' *International Organization* 77 (2): 475–495.

Heinzel, Mirko, Jonas Richter, Per-Olof Busch, Hauke Feil, Jana Herold, and Andrea Liese. 2021. 'Birds of a Feather? The Determinants of Impartiality Perceptions of the IMF and the World Bank.' *Review of International Political Economy* 28 (5): 1249–1273. https://doi.org/10.1080/09692290.2020.1749711.

Hernandez, Diego. 2017. 'Are "New" Donors Challenging World Bank Conditionality?' *World Development* 96 (August): 529–549. https://doi.org/10.1016/j.worlddev.2017.03.035.

Hernández, Leonardo, Pamela Mellado, and Rodrigo Valdés. 2001. 'Determinants of Private Capital Flows in the 1970's and 1990's: Is There Evidence of Contagion?' *IMF Working Papers* 2001 (064). https://doi.org/10.5089/9781451848564.001.A001.

Herskovitz, Jon. 2010. 'Scenarios—What Next in South Africa Public Sector Strike?' *Reuters*, August 29, 2010, sec. World News. https://www.reuters.com/article/uk-safrica-strike-scenarios-idUKTRE67S0SK20100829.

Hewison, Kevin. 2000. 'Thailand's Capitalism before and after the Economic Crisis.' In *Politics and Markets in the Wake of the Asian Crisis*, edited by Richard Robison, Mark Beeson, Kanishka Jayasuriya, and Hyuk-Rae Kim, 192–211. London: Routledge.

Hewison, Kevin. 2002. 'The World Bank and Thailand: Crisis and Social Safety Nets.' *Public Administration and Policy* 11 (1): 1–21.

Hewison, Kevin. 2004. 'Crafting Thailand's New Social Contract.' *The Pacific Review* 17 (4): 503–522. https://doi.org/10.1080/0951274042000326041.

Hewison, Kevin. 2005. 'Neo-Liberalism and Domestic Capital: The Political Outcomes of the Economic Crisis in Thailand.' *Journal of Development Studies* 41 (2): 310–330. https://doi.org/10.1080/0022038042000309269.

Hewison, Kevin. 2010. 'Thaksin Shinawatra and the Reshaping of Thai Politics.' *Contemporary Politics* 16 (2): 119–133. https://doi.org/10.1080/13569771003783810.

Hewison, Kevin. 2014. 'Considerations on Inequality and Politics in Thailand.' *Democratization* 21 (5): 846–866. https://doi.org/10.1080/13510347.2014.882910.

Hillbom, Ellen. 2008. 'Diamonds or Development? A Structural Assessment of Botswana's Forty Years of Success.' *The Journal of Modern African Studies* 46 (02). https://doi.org/10.1017/S0022278X08003194.

Hodula, Martin, and Aleš Melecký. 2020. 'Debt Management When Monetary and Fiscal Policies Clash: Some Empirical Evidence.' *Journal of Applied Economics* 23 (1): 253–280. https://doi.org/10.1080/15140326.2020.1750120.

Hostland, Doug. 2009. 'Low-Income Countries' Access to Private Debt Markets.' Policy Research Working Paper 4829. Washington, D.C.: World Bank. http://papers.ssrn.com/sol3/papers.cfm?abstract_id=1344714.

Huang, Meibo, Xiuli Xu, and Xiaojing Mao. 2018. *South-South Cooperation and Chinese Foreign Aid*. Singapore, SINGAPORE: Springer Singapore Pte. Limited. http://ebookcentral.proquest.com/lib/londonschoolecons/detail.action?docID=5611885.

Humphrey, Chris. 2014. 'The Politics of Loan Pricing in Multilateral Development Banks.' *Review of International Political Economy* 21 (3): 611–639. https://doi.org/10.1080/09692290.2013.858365.

Humphrey, Chris, and Katharina Michaelowa. 2013. 'Shopping for Development: Multilateral Lending, Shareholder Composition and Borrower Preferences.' *World Development* 44 (April): 142–155. https://doi.org/10.1016/j.worlddev.2012.12.007.

Humphrey, Chris, and Katharina Michaelowa. 2019. 'China in Africa: Competition for Traditional Development Finance Institutions?' *World Development* 120 (August): 15–28. https://doi.org/10.1016/j.worlddev.2019.03.014.

IMF. 2021a. '*Review of the Debt Sustainability Assessment Framework for Market Access Countries.*' Washington, D.C.: International Monetary Fund.

IMF. 2021b. '*Guidance Note for Developing Government Local Currency Bond Markets.*' Washington, D.C.: International Monetary Fund.

International Monetary Fund. 1997a. 'Thailand Letter of Intent, August 14, 1997.' International Monetary Fund. https://www.imf.org/external/np/loi/112597.htm.

International Monetary Fund. 1997b. 'Thailand Letter of Intent, November 25, 1997.' International Monetary Fund. https://www.imf.org/external/np/loi/112597.htm.

International Monetary Fund. 1998a. 'Thailand Letter of Intent, February 24, 1998.' International Monetary Fund. https://www.imf.org/external/np/loi/112597.htm.

International Monetary Fund. 1998b. 'Thailand Letter of Intent, May 26, 1998.' International Monetary Fund. https://www.imf.org/external/np/loi/112597.htm.

International Monetary Fund. 2002a. 'IMF Concludes Post-Program Monitoring Discussions with Thailand.' Public Information Notice 02/33. International Monetary Fund. https://www.imf.org/external/np/sec/pn/2002/pn0233.htm.

International Monetary Fund. 2002b. 'Botswana: Selected Issues and Statistical Appendix.' IMF Country Report 02/243. IMF Staff Country Reports. Washington, D.C.: International Monetary Fund.

International Monetary Fund. 2004. 'Thailand: Selected Issues.' IMF Country Report 04/1. Washington, D.C.: International Monetary Fund.

International Monetary Fund, and World Bank. 2018a. 'G20 Notes: Improving Public Debt Recording, Monitoring, and Reporting Capacity in Low and Lower Middle-Income Countries.' International monetary Fund and World Bank Group.

International Monetary Fund, and World Bank. 2018b. 'G20 Notes on Strengthening Public Debt Transparency.' International Monetary Fund and World Bank Group.

Isaksson, Ann-Sofie, and Andreas Kotsadam. 2018a. 'Chinese Aid and Local Corruption.' *Journal of Public Economics* 159 (March): 146–159. https://doi.org/10.1016/j.jpubeco.2018.01.002.

Isaksson, Ann-Sofie, and Andreas Kotsadam. 2018b. 'Racing to the Bottom? Chinese Development Projects and Trade Union Involvement in Africa.' *World Development* 106 (June): 284–298. https://doi.org/10.1016/j.worlddev.2018.02.003.

Jafarov, Etibar, Rodolfo Maino, and Marco Pani. 2020. 'Financial Repression Is Knocking at the Door, Again. Should We Be Concerned?' Working Paper WP/19/21. International Monetary Fund.

Jansen, Karel, and Khannabha Choedchai. 2009. 'The Fiscal Space of Thailand.' In *Fiscal Space: Policy Options for Financing Human Development*, edited by Rathin Roy and Antoine Heuty, 325–398. London: Earthscan.

Jayasuriya, Kanishka, and Kevin Hewison. 2004. 'The Antipolitics of Good Governance: From Global Social Policy to a Global Populism?' *Critical Asian Studies* 36 (4): 571–590. https://doi.org/10.1080/1467271042000273257.

Jeanne, Olivier, and Jeromin Zettelmeyer. 2001. 'International Bailouts, Moral Hazard, and Conditionality.' *Economic Policy* 16 (33): 407–432.

Jensen, Nathan M., and Scott Schmith. 2005. 'Market Responses to Politics: The Rise of Lula and the Decline of the Brazilian Stock Market.' *Comparative Political Studies* 38 (10): 1245–1270.

JICA. 2008. 'JBIC Signs Japanese ODA Loan Agreement for New Project in Thailand.' Overseas Economic Cooperation Operation NR/2007-94. https://www.jica.go.jp/english/news/jbic_archive/autocontents/english/news/2008/000021/index.html.

Kaplan, Stephen B. 2013. *Globalization and Austerity Politics in Latin America*. New York: Cambridge University Press.

Kaplan, Stephen B. 2021. *Globalizing Patient Capital: The Political Economy of Chinese Finance in the Americas*. Cambridge: Cambridge University Press. https://www.cambridge.org/core/books/globalizing-patient-capital/DDC9270164B59CCC78E0E107AA093B3A.

Kaplan, Stephen B., and Kaj Thomsson. 2017. 'The Political Economy of Sovereign Debt: Global Finance and Electoral Cycles.' *The Journal of Politics* 79 (2): 605–623. https://doi.org/10.1086/688441.

Kaya, Ayse, and Mike Reay. 2019. 'How Did the Washington Consensus Move within the IMF? Fragmented Change from the 1980s to the Aftermath of the 2008 Crisis.' *Review of International Political Economy* 26 (3): 384–409. https://doi.org/10.1080/09692290.2018.1511447.

Kazmin, Amy. 2002. 'Thai PM Pledges to Repay IMF Debt Earlier.' *Financial Times*, August 27, 2002.

Kazmin, Amy. 2006. 'Thailand's Thaksin Warns of Return to IMF Aid.' *Financial Times*, March 20, 2006.

Kentikelenis, A., T. Stubbs, and L. King. 2016. 'IMF Conditionality and Development Policy Space, 1985–2014.' *Review of International Political Economy* 23 (4): 543–582.

Kern, Andreas, and Bernhard Reinsberg. 2021. 'The Political Economy of Chinese Debt and IMF Conditionality.' SSRN Scholarly Paper ID 3951586. Rochester, NY: Social Science Research Network. https://doi.org/10.2139/ssrn.3951586.

Khama, Seretse. 1971. 'Trade Unions in Botswana.' *Africa Today* 19 (2): 9–16.

Kikeri, Sunita, and Aishetu Fatima Kolo. 2005. 'Privatization: Trends and Recent Developments.' Policy Research Working Paper 3765. Washington, D.C.: World Bank.

Kilby, Christopher. 2006. 'Donor Influence in Multilateral Development Banks: The Case of the Asian Development Bank.' *The Review of International Organizations* 1 (2): 173–195. https://doi.org/10.1007/s11558-006-8343-9.

Kilby, Christopher. 2009. 'The Political Economy of Conditionality: An Empirical Analysis of World Bank Loan Disbursements.' *Journal of Development Economics* 89 (1): 51–61. https://doi.org/10.1016/j.jdeveco.2008.06.014.

Kilby, Christopher. 2011. 'Informal Influence in the Asian Development Bank.' *The Review of International Organizations* 6 (3–4): 223–257. https://doi.org/10.1007/s11558-011-9110-0.

King, Daniel E. 1996. 'Thailand in 1995: Open Society, Dynamic Economy, Troubled Politics.' *Asian Survey* 36 (2): 135–141. https://doi.org/10.2307/2645810.

Kitirianglarp, Kengkij, and Kevin Hewison. 2009. 'Social Movements and Political Opposition in Contemporary Thailand.' *The Pacific Review* 22 (4): 451–477. https://doi.org/10.1080/09512740903127978.

Kitti, Prasirtsuk. 2015. 'Thailand in 2014.' *Asian Survey* 55 (1): 200–206.

Kitti, Prasirtsuk. 2016. 'Thailand in 2015.' *Asian Survey* 56 (1): 168–173.

King, Daniel E. 1996. 'Thailand in 1995: Open Society, Dynamic Economy, Troubled Politics.' *Asian Survey* 36 (2): 135–141. https://doi.org/10.2307/2645810.

Kitirianglarp, Kengkij, and Kevin Hewison. 2009. 'Social Movements and Political Opposition in Contemporary Thailand.' *The Pacific Review* 22 (4): 451–477. https://doi.org/10.1080/09512740903127978.

Kitti, Prasirtsuk. 2015. 'Thailand in 2014.' *Asian Survey* 55 (1): 200–206.

Kitti, Prasirtsuk. 2016. 'Thailand in 2015.' *Asian Survey* 56 (1): 168–173.

Knack, Stephen, Lixin Colin Xu, and Ben Zou. 2014. 'Interactions among Donors' Aid Allocations: Evidence from an Exogenous World Bank Income Threshold.' Policy Research Working Paper 7039. Washington, D.C.: World Bank. https://doi.org/10.1596/1813-9450-7039.

Knight, Malcolm D. 2003. 'Three Observations on Market Discipline.' Speech presented at the BIS-Federal Reserve Bank of Chicago Conference on Market Discipline, Chicago, October 30. https://www.bis.org/speeches/sp031030.htm.

Koepke, Robin. 2019. 'What Drives Capital Flows to Emerging Markets? A Survey of the Empirical Literature.' *Journal of Economic Surveys* 33 (2): 516–540.

Kohli, Atul. 2004. *State-Directed Development: Political Power and Industrialization in the Global Periphery.* Cambridge: Cambridge University Press.

Kopits, George. 2001. 'Fiscal Rules: Useful Policy Framework or Unnecessary Ornament.' IMF Working Paper WP/01/145. International Monetary Fund.

Kopits, George, ed. 2013. *Restoring Public Debt Sustainability: The Role of Independent Fiscal Institutions*. New York: Oxford University Press.

Kotchen, Matthew J, and Neeraj Kumar Negi. 2019. 'Cofinancing in Environment and Development: Evidence from the Global Environment Facility.' *The World Bank Economic Review* 33 (1): 41–62. https://doi.org/10.1093/wber/lhw048.

Kozak, Robert. 2014. 'Peru to Cut Taxes and Increase Spending to Boost Economy; Economists Predict Weaker 2014 Economic Growth.' *Wall Street Journal*, November 21, 2014.

Krasner, Stephen D. 1985. *Structural Conflict: The Third World against Global Liberalism*. Berkeley: University of California Press.

Kriangchai, Pungprawat. 2009. 'Budgeting System and Bureau of the Budget in Thailand.' *Chulalongkorn Journal of Economics* 21 (1): 49–71.

Laeven, Luc, and Fabián Valencia. 2012. 'Systemic Banking Crises Database: An Update.' IMF Working Paper WP/12/163. Washington, D.C.: International Monetary Fund.

Lefevre, Amy Sawitta. 2012. 'Thai Cabinet Reshuffle Sees Return of Thaksin Loyalists.' *Reuters*, October 29, 2012. https://www.reuters.com/article/us-thailand-thaksin/thai-cabinet-reshuffle-sees-return-of-thaksin-loyalists-idUSBRE89S0GH20121029.

Leith, J. Clark. 2005. *Why Botswana Prospered*. Quebec City: McGill-Queen's University Press.

Levitsky, Steven. 1999. 'Fujimori and Post-Party Politics in Peru.' *Journal of Democracy* 10 (3): 78–92.

Levitsky, Steven, and Lucan A. Way. 2010. *Competitive Authoritarianism: Hybrid Regimes After the Cold War*. Cambridge: Cambridge University Press.

Lewin, Michael. 2011. 'Botswana's Success: Good Governance, Good Policies, and Good Luck.' In *Yes Africa Can—Success Stories from a Dynamic Continent*, 81–90. Washington, D.C.: World Bank.

Liang, Wei. 2019. 'China and the BRI: Contested Multilateralism and Innovative Institution-Building.' In *Handbook on the International Political Economy of China*, edited by Ka Zeng, 361–376. Cheltenham, UK; Northampton, MA, USA: Edward Elgar.

Lim, Daniel Yew Mao, and James Raymond Vreeland. 2013. 'Regional Organizations and International Politics Japanese Influence over the Asian Development Bank and the UN Security Council.' *World Politics* 65 (1): 34–72.

Lledó, Victor, and Marcos Poplawski-Ribeiro. 2013. 'Fiscal Policy Implementation in Sub-Saharan Africa.' *World Development* 46 (June): 79–91. https://doi.org/10.1016/j.worlddev.2013.01.030.

Lledó, Victor, Sungwook Yoon, Xiangming Fang, Samba Mbaye, and Young Kim. 2017. 'Fiscal Rules at a Glance.' Washington D.C., IMF. https://www.imf.org/external/datamapper/fiscalrules/fiscal%20rules%20at%20a%20glance%20-%20background%20paper.pdf.

Loser, Claudio M. 2004. 'External Debt Sustainability: Guidelines for Low- and Middle- Income Countries.' 26. G-24 Discussion Paper Series. New York and Geneva: United Nations.

Lührmann, Anna, Nils Düpont, Masaaki Higashijima, Yaman Berker Kavasoglu, Kyle L. Marquardt, and Michael Bernhard. 2020. 'Varieties of Party Identity and Organization (V-Party) Dataset V1.' Varieties of Democracy (V-Dem) Project.

Lupu, Noam. 2016. *Party Brands in Crisis: Partisanship, Brand Dilution, and the Breakdown of Political Parties in Latin America*. New York: Cambridge University Press.

MacIntyre, Andrew. 2001. 'Institutions and Investors: The Politics of the Economic Crisis in Southeast Asia.' *International Organization* 55 (1): 81–122. https://doi.org/10.1162/002081801551423.

Mail & Guardian. 2020. 'A Chance to "Reimagine South Africa".' *Mail & Guardian*, April 21, 2020, sec. Business. https://mg.co.za/article/2020-04-21-a-chance-to-reimagine-south-africa/.

Makgala, Christian John, and Mokganedi Zara Botlhomilwe. 2017. 'Elite Interests and Political Participation in Botswana, 1966–2014.' *Journal of Contemporary African Studies* 35 (1): 54–72. https://doi.org/10.1080/02589001.2017.1285010.

Makinana, Andisiwe. 2020. 'ANC, Alliance Partners "Reject" Getting Funding from IMF or World Bank to Fight Covid-19.' *Sunday Times*, April 6, 2020, Online edition, sec. Politics. https://www.timeslive.co.za/politics/2020-04-06-anc-alliance-partners-reject-getting-funding-from-imf-or-world-bank-to-fight-covid-19/.

Mattlin, Mikael, and Matti Nojonen. 2015. 'Conditionality and Path Dependence in Chinese Lending.' *Journal of Contemporary China* 24 (94): 701–720.

Melecky, Martin. 2007. 'A Cross-Country Analysis of Public Debt Management Strategies.' Policy Research Working Paper 4287. Washington, D.C.: World Bank.

Milesi-Ferretti, Gian-Maria, and Cédric Tille. 2011. 'The Great Retrenchment: International Capital Flows during the Global Financial Crisis.' *Economic Policy* 26 (66): 289–346.

Ministry of Foreign Affairs of Japan. 2009. 'Working Toward the Development of the Mekong Region: Thailand.' http://www.mofa.go.jp/region/asia-paci/mekong/development/thailand.html.

Montgomery, Jacob M., Brendan Nyhan, and Michelle Torres. 2018. 'How Conditioning on Post-treatment Variables Can Ruin Your Experiment and What to Do about It.' *American Journal of Political Science* 62 (3): 760–775. https://doi.org/10.1111/ajps.12357.

Moody's. 2020. 'Rating Action: Moody's Downgrades South Africa's Ratings to Ba1, Maintains Negative Outlook.' Paris: Moody's Investors Service. https://www.moodys.com/research/Moodys-downgrades-South-Africas-ratings-to-Ba1-maintains-negative-outlook—PR_420630.

Morris, Scott, Brad Parks, and Alysha Gardner. 2020. 'Chinese and World Bank Lending Terms: A Systematic Comparison Across 157 Countries and 15 Years.' CGD Policy Paper. Washington, D.C.: Center for Global Development.

Mosley, Layna. 2003. *Global Capital and National Governments*. Cambridge Studies in Comparative Politics. New York: Cambridge University Press.

Mosley, Layna. 2010. 'Regulating Globally, Implementing Locally: The Financial Codes and Standards Effort.' *Review of International Political Economy* 17 (4): 724–761. https://doi.org/10.1080/09692290903529817.

Mosley, Layna. ed. 2013. *Interview Research in Political Science*. Ithaca, NY: Cornell University Press. https://www.jstor.org/stable/10.7591/j.ctt1xx5wg.

Mosley, Layna, Victoria Paniagua, and Erik Wibbels. 2020. 'Moving Markets? Government Bond Investors and Microeconomic Policy Changes.' *Economics & Politics* 32 (2): 197–249.

Mosley, Layna, and B. Peter Rosendorff. 2023. 'Government Choices of Debt Instruments.' *International Studies Quarterly* 67 (2): 1–13.

Murillo, M. Victoria. 2002. 'Political Bias in Policy Convergence: Privatization Choices in Latin America.' *World Politics* 54 (4): 462–493. https://doi.org/10.1353/wp.2002.0014.

Murillo, M. Victoria. 2005. 'Partisanship Amidst Convergence: The Politics of Labor Reform in Latin America.' *Comparative Politics* 37 (4): 441–458.

Murillo, M. Victoria, and Andrew Schrank. 2005. 'With a Little Help from My Friends: Partisan Politics, Transnational Alliances, and Labor Rights in Latin America.' *Comparative Political Studies* 38 (8): 971–999. https://doi.org/10.1177/0010414004274402.

Mustapha, Shakira, and Annalisa Prizzon. 2018. 'Africa's Rising Debt: How to Avoid a New Crisis.' Briefing Note. Overseas Development Institute. https://www.odi.org/sites/odi.org.uk/files/resource-documents/12491.pdf.

Nabi, Ijaz, and Jayasankar Shivakumar. 2001. *Back from the Brink*. Washington, D.C.: World Bank.

Naqvi, Natalya. 2019. 'Manias, Panics and Crashes in Emerging Markets: An Empirical Investigation of the Post-2008 Crisis Period.' *New Political Economy* 24 (6): 759–779. https://doi.org/10.1080/13563467.2018.1526263.

Navia, Patricio, and Andres Velasco. 2003. 'The Politics of Second-Generation Reforms.' In *After the Washington Consensus: Restarting Growth and Reform in Latin America*, edited by Pedro-Pablo Kuczynski and John Williamson, 265–303. Washington, D.C.: Institute for International Economics.

Nedbank. 2020. 'Moody's Downgrade Comment.' Nedbank Private Wealth. March 2020. https://www.nedbankprivatewealth.co.za/content/dam/npw/NPWRSA/Investments/Moody%27sRatingReview-Final.pdf.

Nelson, Stephen C. 2017. *The Currency of Confidence: How Economic Beliefs Shape the IMF's Relationship with Its Borrowers*. Ithaca, NY: Cornell University Press.

Nyathi, Kitsepile. 2021. 'Zimbabwe: China Clashes with Zimbabwean Unions over "Systematic Abuse".' *The East African*, July 9, 2021, sec. News. https://allafrica.com/stories/202107090366.html.

OECD. 2011. *Smart Rules for Fair Trade: 50 Years of Export Credits*. Paris: OECD Publishing.

Pacheco Pardo, Ramon, and Pradumna B. Rana. 2018. 'Co-Operation Not Competition: The New Multilateral Development Banks and the Old.' *Global Asia* 13 (1): 70–77. https://www.globalasia.org/v13no1/feature/co-operation-not-competition-the-new-multilateral-development-banks-and-the-old_ramon-pacheco-pardopradumna-b-rana.

Pandolfi, Lorenzo, and Tomas Williams. 2019. 'Capital Flows and Sovereign Debt Markets: Evidence from Index Rebalancings.' *Journal of Financial Economics* 132 (2): 384–403. https://doi.org/10.1016/j.jfineco.2018.10.008.

Panizza, Ugo. 2010. 'Is Domestic Debt the Answer to Debt Crises?' In *Overcoming Developing Country Debt Crises*, 91–108. Oxford: Oxford University Press. https://oxford-universitypressscholarship-com.gate3.library.lse.ac.uk/view/10.1093/acprof:oso/9780199578788.001.0001/acprof-9780199578788-chapter-4.

Panizza, Ugo, and Filippo Taddei. 2020. 'Local Currency Denominated Sovereign Loans.' *IHEID Working Paper* (Working Paper No. HEIDWP09-2020): 62.

Papke, Leslie E., and Jeffrey M. Wooldridge. 2008. 'Panel Data Methods for Fractional Response Variables with an Application to Test Pass Rates.' *Journal of Econometrics* 145 (1–2): 121–133. https://doi.org/10.1016/j.jeconom.2008.05.009.

Pasuk, Phongpaichit, and Chris Baker. 1999. 'The Political Economy of the Thai Crisis.' *Journal of the Asia Pacific Economy* 4 (1): 193–208.

Petry, Johannes, Jan Fichtner, and Eelke Heemskerk. 2019. 'Steering Capital: The Growing Private Authority of Index Providers in the Age of Passive Asset Management.' *Review of International Political Economy* (December): 1–25. https://doi.org/10.1080/09692290.2019.1699147.

Pinto, Pablo M. 2013. *Partisan Investment in the Global Economy: Why the Left Loves Foreign Direct Investment and FDI Loves the Left*. New York: Cambridge University Press.

Poteete, Amy R. 2012. 'Electoral Competition, Factionalism, and Persistent Party Dominance in Botswana.' *The Journal of Modern African Studies* 50 (1): 75–102.

Prizzon, Annalisa, Romilly Greenhill, and Shakira Mustapha. 2017. 'An "Age of Choice" for External Development Finance? Evidence from Country Case Studies.' *Development Policy Review* 35 (S1): O29–45. https://doi.org/10.1111/dpr.12268.

Putnam, Robert D. 1988. 'Diplomacy and Domestic Politics: The Logic of Two-Level Games.' *International Organization* 42 (3): 427–460.

Raman, K. Ravi. 2009. 'Asian Development Bank, Policy Conditionalities and the Social Democratic Governance: Kerala Model under Pressure?' *Review of International Political Economy* 16 (2): 284–308.

Ratha, Dilip, Prabal K. De, and Sanket Mohapatra. 2011. 'Shadow Sovereign Ratings for Unrated Developing Countries.' *World Development* 39 (3): 295–307. https://doi.org/10.1016/j.worlddev.2010.08.006.

Ray, Rebecca. 2021. 'Who Controls Multilateral Development Finance?' *Global Governance* 27 (1): 118–143.

Reinhart, Carmen M., and Kenneth S. Rogoff. 2009. *This Time Is Different: Eight Centuries of Financial Folly*. Princeton, NJ: Princeton University Press.

Reinsberg, Bernhard. 2017. 'Five Steps to Smarter Multi-Bi Aid.' London: Overseas Development Institute.

Reinsberg, Bernhard, Thomas Stubbs, Alexander Kentikelenis, and Lawrence King. 2019. 'The Political Economy of Labor Market Deregulation during IMF Interventions.' *International Interactions* 45 (3): 532–559. https://doi.org/10.1080/03050629.2019.1582531.

Reinsberg, Bernhard, Thomas Stubbs, Alexander Kentikelenis, and Lawrence King. 2020. 'Bad Governance: How Privatization Increases Corruption in the Developing World.' *Regulation & Governance* 14 (4): 698–717. https://doi.org/10.1111/rego.12265.

Republic of Botswana Ministry of Finance and Economic Development. 2016. 'Medium-Term Debt Management Strategy: 2016/17–2018/19.'

Republic of South Africa National Treasury. 2009a. 'Budget Review 2009.' Republic of South Africa National Treasury.

Republic of South Africa National Treasury. 2009b. 'The African Development Bank (AfDB) Approves 1.86 Billion Euro Loan for Eskom Medupi Power Project,' November. http://www.treasury.gov.za/comm_media/press/2009/2009112601.pdf.

Republic of South Africa National Treasury. 2010. 'Budget Review 2010.' Republic of South Africa National Treasury.

Republic of South Africa National Treasury. 2013. 'Debt Management Report 2013/14.' Republic of South Africa National Treasury.

Republic of South Africa National Treasury. 2014a. 'Debt Management Report 2014/15.' Republic of South Africa National Treasury.

Republic of South Africa National Treasury. 2014b. 'Budget Review 2014.' Republic of South Africa National Treasury. http://www.treasury.gov.za/documents/national%20budget/2014/review/FullReview.pdf.

Republic of South Africa National Treasury. 2015. 'Debt Management Report 2015/16.' Republic of South Africa National Treasury.

Republic of South Africa National Treasury. 2017a. '2017 Estimates of National Expenditure (Abridged Version).' Republic of South Africa National Treasury. http://www.treasury.gov.za/documents/national%20budget/2017/ene/FullENE.pdf.

Republic of South Africa National Treasury. 2017b. 'Budget Review 2017.' Republic of South Africa National Treasury. http://www.treasury.gov.za/documents/national%20budget/2014/review/FullReview.pdf.

Republic of South Africa Parliament. 2011. 'Budget Analysis Manual.' Parliament of South Africa. https://www.parliament.gov.za/storage/app/media/BusinessPubs/BudgetAnalysisManual.pdf.

Reuters. 2010. 'Jacob Zuma: Public Sector Strike Must End.' *The Guardian*. August 30, 2010. http://www.theguardian.com/world/2010/aug/30/jacob-zuma-public-sector-strike.

Reuters. 2011. 'Factbox: Peruvian Leader Humala's Policy Promises.' *Reuters*, October 13, 2011. http://mobile.reuters.com/article/amp/idUSTRE79C57A20111013.

Reuters. 2012. 'Peru's Doctors End Long Strike after Humala Grants Pay Hike.' *Reuters*, October 22, 2012. https://www.reuters.com/article/us-peru-strike-doctors/perus-doctors-end-long-strike-after-humala-grants-pay-hike-idUSBRE89L1AG20121022.

Reuters. 2018. 'ADB, China-Backed AIIB to Co-Finance More Projects This Year.' *Reuters*, January 12, 2018, Digital edition, sec. Financials. https://www.reuters.com/article/adb-asia-aiib-idUSL4N1P72UI.

Rey, Hélène. 2015. 'Dilemma Not Trilemma: The Global Financial Cycle and Monetary Policy Independence.' Working Paper 21162. National Bureau of Economic Research. https://www.nber.org/papers/w21162.

Robinson, James A., and Q. Neil Parsons. 2006. 'State Formation and Governance in Botswana.' *Journal of African Economies* 15 (Supplement 1): 100–140. https://doi.org/10.1093/jae/ejk007.

Rodrik, Dani. 2006. 'Goodbye Washington Consensus, Hello Washington Confusion? A Review of the World Bank's Economic Growth in the 1990s: Learning from a Decade of Reform.' *Journal of Economic Literature* 44: 973–987.

Rodrik, Dani. 2016. 'Premature Deindustrialization.' *Journal of Economic Growth* 21 (1): 1–33. https://doi.org/10.1007/s10887-015-9122-3.

Rodrik, Dani. 2017. 'Populism and the Economics of Globalization.' NBER Working Paper 23559. Cambridge, MA: National Bureau of Economic Research. https://www.nber.org/papers/w23559.pdf.

Rogoff, Kenneth. 1985. 'The Optimal Degree of Commitment to an Intermediate Monetary Target.' *The Quarterly Journal of Economics* 100 (4): 1169–1189.

Rogowski, Ronald. 2009. *Trade, Immigration, and Cross-Border Investment*. Edited by Donald A. Wittman and Barry R. Weingast. Vol. 1. Oxford University Press. https://doi.org/10.1093/oxfordhb/9780199548477.003.0045.

Rommerskirchen, Charlotte. 2020. 'Foreign Bond Investors and Market Discipline.' *Competition & Change* 24 (1): 3–25. https://doi.org/10.1177/1024529419872171.

Roos, Jerome. 2019. *Why Not Default?: The Political Economy of Sovereign Debt*. Princeton, NJ: Princeton University Press.

Root, Hilton L. 1998. 'Distinct Institutions in the Rise of Industrial Asia.' In *Behind East Asian Growth: The Political and Social Foundations of Prosperity*, edited by Henry S. Rowen, 60–77. London: Routledge.

Rossini, Renzo, and Alejandro Santos. 2015. 'Peru's Recent Economic History: From Stagnation, Disarray, and Mismanagement to Growth, Stability, and Quality Policies.' In *Peru: Staying the Course of Economic Success*, edited by Alejandro Santos and Alejandro Werner, 9–33. Washington, D.C.: International Monetary Fund.

Rossouw, Jannie. 2016. 'Civil Service Pay: South Africa Has Some Harsh Choices to Make.' *The Conversation*, January 29, 2016, sec. Business & Economy. http://theconversation.com/civil-service-pay-south-africa-has-some-harsh-choices-to-make-53389.

Rudra, Nita, and Jennifer Tobin. 2017. 'When Does Globalization Help the Poor?' *Annual Review of Political Science* 20 (1): 287–307. https://doi.org/10.1146/annurev-polisci-051215-022754.

Sadeh, Tal, and Yehuda Porath. 2020. 'Autonomous Agencies and Relational Contracts in Government Bond Issues.' *Regulation & Governance* 14: 741–763. https://doi.org/10.1111/rego.12257.

Sadeh, Tal, and Eyal Rubinson. 2018. 'Do the IMF and World Bank Promote Autonomous Sovereign Debt Management?' Working Paper presented at the 11th Annual Conference on Political Economy of International Organizations, Madison, WI, February 8.

Saiegh, Sebastian M. 2005. 'Do Countries Have a "Democratic Advantage"?: Political Institutions, Multilateral Agencies, and Sovereign Borrowing.' *Comparative Political Studies* 38 (4): 366–387. https://doi.org/10.1177/0010414004273204.

Samatar, Abdi Ismail. 1999. *An African Miracle: State and Class Leadership and Colonial Legacy in Botswana Development*. Portsmouth: Heinemann.

Sattler, Thomas. 2013. 'Do Markets Punish Left Governments?' *The Journal of Politics* 75 (2): 343–356. https://doi.org/10.1017/s0022381613000054.

Schady, Norbert R. 2000. 'The Political Economy of Expenditures by the Peruvian Social Fund (FONCODES), 1991–95.' *American Political Science Review* 94 (2): 189–304.

Schultz, Kenneth A., and Barry R. Weingast. 2003. 'The Democratic Advantage: Institutional Foundations of Financial Power in International Competition.' *International Organization* 57 (1): 3–42.

Schwan, Michael, Christine Trampusch, and Florian Fastenrath. 2021. 'Financialization of, Not by the State. Exploring Changes in the Management of Public Debt and Assets across Europe.' *Review of International Political Economy* 28 (4): 820–842. https://doi.org/10.1080/09692290. 2020.1823452.

Smith, David. 2012. 'Workers Claim Abuse as China Adds Zimbabwe to Its Scramble for Africa.' *The Guardian*, January 2, 2012, sec. World news. https://www.theguardian.com/world/2012/jan/02/china-zimbabwe-workers-abuse.

St. John, Ronald Bruce. 2010. *Toledo's Peru: Vision and Reality*. Gainesville: University of Florida Press.

Standard & Poor's. 2020. 'An Overview of Sovereign Rating Actions Related to COVID-19.' S&P Global Ratings. https://www.spglobal.com/ratings/en/research/articles/200511-an-overview-of-sovereign-rating-actions-related-to-covid-19-11484790.

Stasavage, David. 2003. *Public Debt and the Birth of the Democratic State: France and Great Britain, 1688–1789*. Cambridge: Cambridge University Press.

Stifel, Laurence D. 1976. 'Technocrats and Modernization in Thailand.' *Asian Survey* 16 (12): 1184–1196.

Stiglitz, Joseph E. 2002. *Globalization and Its Discontents*. New York: W.W. Norton & Co.

Stiglitz, Joseph E., and Andrew Weiss. 1981. 'Credit Rationing in Markets with Imperfect Information.' *The American Economic Review* 71 (3): 393–410.

Stokes, Susan C. 2004. *Mandates and Democracy: Neoliberalism by Surprise in Latin America*. Cambridge: Cambridge University Press.

Stone, Randall W. 2011. *Controlling Institutions: International Organizations and the Global Economy*. Cambridge: Cambridge University Press. http://ebooks.cambridge.org/ref/id/CBO9780511793943.

Suchitra, Punyaratabandhu. 1998. 'Thailand in 1997: Financial Crisis and Constitutional Reform.' *Asian Survey* 38 (2): 161–167. https://doi.org/10.2307/2645674.

Sun, Xiaolun, Luis Alvaro Sanchez, Carla Paecz, Shoghik Hovhannisyan, Xue Li, and Geeta Batra. 2015. 'Selectivity in Country Strategies: The Evidence.' Washington, D.C.: World Bank. https://openknowledge.worldbank.org/handle/10986/21707.

Taglioni, Daria, and Deborah Winkler. 2016. *Making Global Value Chains Work for Development*. Washington, D.C.: World Bank.

Taj, Mitra, and Terry Wade. 2012. 'Pressure Grows on Peru's Humala as Public Health Strike Widens.' *Reuters*, October 18, 2012. http://www.reuters.com/article/us-peru-politics-strikes/pressure-grows-on-perus-humala-as-public-health-strike-widens-idUSBRE89H1N220121018.

Tansey, Oisín. 2007. 'Process Tracing and Elite Interviewing: A Case for Non-Probability Sampling.' *PS: Political Science and Politics* 40 (4): 765–772.

Taylor, Ian. 2003. 'As Good as It Gets? Botswana's "Democratic Development".' *Journal of Contemporary African Studies* 21 (2): 215–231.

Taylor, Ian. 2004. 'The HIV/AIDS Pandemic in Botswana: Implications for the "African Miracle".' In *The Political Economy of AIDS in Africa*, edited by Nana K. Poku and Alan Whiteside, 151–164. Abingdon, Oxon: Routledge.

Thailand PDMO. 2018. 'Domestic and External Debt.' PDMO Public Debt Data. 2018. http://www.pdmo.go.th/en/debt_country.php?m=money&years=2015.

The Economist. 2006. 'Alan Garcia's Second Chance; Peru.' *The Economist*, June 10, 2006.

The Economist. 2014. 'Life after the Commodity Boom.' *The Economist*, March 29, 2014. https://www.economist.com/news/americas/21599782-instead-crises-past-mediocre-growth-big-riskunless-productivity-rises-life.

The Economist. 2017. 'Why Cambodia Has Cosied up to China.' *The Economist*, January 21, 2017. https://www.economist.com/asia/2017/01/21/why-cambodia-has-cosied-up-to-china.

The Economist. 2020. 'Covid-19 Has Throttled South Africa's Economy.' *The Economist*, July 18, 2020. https://www.economist.com/middle-east-and-africa/2020/07/18/covid-19-has-throttled-south-africas-economy.

The Economist. 2021. 'End of the Line for ANC Economics.' *The Economist*, July 24, 2021.

The Nation. 2003. 'Lending by Banks Too Risky.' *The Nation*, October 10, 2003.

Thirlwall, A. P. 2011. 'Balance of Payments Constrained Growth Models: History and Overview.' 1111. *Studies in Economics*. Studies in Economics. School of Economics, University of Kent. https://ideas.repec.org/p/ukc/ukcedp/1111.html.

Thompson, Helen, and David Runciman. 2006. 'Sovereign Debt and Private Creditors: New Legal Sanction or the Enduring Power of States?' *New Political Economy* 11 (4): 541–555.

Thompson, Leonard Monteath. 2001. *A History of South Africa*. 3rd ed. New Haven: Yale University Press.

Thornton, Susan A. 2020. 'China in Central Asia: Is China Winning the "New Great Game"?' *Brookings*, June. https://www.brookings.edu/articles/china-in-central-asia-is-china-winning-the-new-great-game/.

Tomz, Michael. 2007. *Reputation and International Cooperation: Sovereign Debt Across Three Centuries*. Princeton, NJ: Princeton University Press.

Trampusch, Christine. 2019. 'The Financialization of the State: Government Debt Management Reforms in New Zealand and Ireland.' *Competition & Change* 23 (1): 3–22. https://doi.org/10.1177/1024529418800778.

Trampusch, Christine, and Philip Gross. 2021. 'Do Parliaments Have Control over Sovereign Debt Management?' *West European Politics* 44 (2): 299–326. https://doi.org/10.1080/01402382.2019.1680513.

Ülgentürk, Hans J. 2017. 'The Role of Public Debt Managers in Contingent Liability Management.' 8. OECD Working Papers on Sovereign Borrowing and Public Debt Management. OECD.

Vaaler, Paul M., Burkhard N. Schrage, and Steven A. Block. 2006. 'Elections, Opportunism, Partisanship and Sovereign Ratings in Developing Countries.' *Review of Development Economics* 10 (1): 154–170.

Vadlamannati, Krishna Chaitanya. 2020. 'Can IMF Program Design Resurrect Investor Sentiment? An Empirical Investigation.' *Business and Politics* 22 (2): 339–382. https://doi.org/10.1017/bap.2019.16.

Von Soest, Christian. 2009. 'Stagnation of a "Miracle": Botswana's Governance Record Revisited.' Working Paper 99. Hamburg: German Institute for Global and Area Studies.

Vreeland, James Raymond. 2002. 'The Effect of IMF Programs on Labor.' *World Development* 30 (1): 121–139.

Vreeland, James Raymond. 2003. 'Why Do Governments and the IMF Enter into Agreements? Statistically Selected Cases.' *International Political Science Review* 24 (3): 321–343.

Wade, Robert. 2002. 'US Hegemony and the World Bank: The Fight over People and Ideas.' *Review of International Political Economy* 9 (2): 215–243. https://doi.org/10.1080/09692290110126092.

Walter, Andrew. 2008. *Governing Finance*. Ithaca, NY, and London: Cornell University Press.

Warr, Peter. 2005. 'Boom, Bust and Beyond.' In *Thailand Beyond the Crisis*, edited by Peter Warr, 3–65. London: Routledge Curzon.

Warr, Peter, and Nidhiprabha Bhanupong. 1996. *Thailand's Economic Miracle: Stable Adjustment and Sustained Growth*. Kuala Lumpur: World Bank and Oxford University Press.

Way, Christopher. 2000. 'Central Banks, Partisan Politics, and Macroeconomic Outcomes.' *Comparative Political Studies* 33 (2): 196–224. https://doi.org/10.1177/0010414000033002002.

Weaver, Catherine. 2008. *Hypocrisy Trap: The World Bank and the Poverty of Reform*. Princeton, NJ: Princeton University Press.

Wheeler, Graeme. 2004. *Sound Practice in Government Debt Management.* Washington, D.C.: The World Bank.

Wibbels, Erik. 2006. 'Dependency Revisited: International Markets, Business Cycles, and Social Spending in the Developing World.' *International Organization* 60 (02). https://doi.org/10.1017/S0020818306060139.

Wichit, Chaitrong. 2003. 'Debts Still a Threat, Critics Warn.' *The Nation*, December 30, 2003.

Wigglesworth, Robin, and Nicholas Megaw. 2017. 'S&P Downgrades South Africa Rating.' *Financial Times*, November 25, 2017. https://www.ft.com/content/c9328624-d194-11e7-b781-794ce08b24dc.

Williams, Martin J. 2020. 'Beyond State Capacity: Bureaucratic Performance, Policy Implementation and Reform.' *Journal of Institutional Economics*, 1–19. https://doi.org/10.1017/S1744137420000478.

Williams, Mike. 2013. 'Debt and Cash Management.' In *The International Handbook of Public Financial Management*, edited by Richard Allen, Richard Hemming, and Barry H. Potter, 661–684. London: Palgrave Macmillan.

Williamson, John. 1990. 'What Washington Means by Policy Reform.' In *Latin American Adjustment: How Much Has Happened?*, edited by John Williamson, 7–20. Washington, D.C.: Institute for International Economics.

Winter, Jacob, Ben Cormier, Teresa Kramarz, and Mark Manger. 2022. 'The Political Economy of World Bank Loan Stringency.' In *COMPTEXT*. Dublin.

Wise, Carol. 2003. *Reinventing the State: Economic Strategy and Institutional Change in Peru.* Ann Arbor: University of Michigan Press.

Woods, Ngaire. 2006. *The Globalizers.* Ithaca, NY: Cornell University Press.

World Bank. 1998. 'World Bank Guarantee for Thai Bond Issue.' *World Bank Business Partnership Center News*, December 1998.

World Bank. 2002. 'Implementation Completion Report (SCL-45150; TF-26106).' 23276. World Bank. http://documents.worldbank.org/curated/en/854341468303533087/pdf/multi0page.pdf.

World Bank. 2003. 'Thailand Country Assistance Strategy, FY 03-05.' 25077-TH. World Bank.

World Bank. 2006. 'Thailand Country Development Partnership: Financial and Corporate Sector Competitiveness Program Assessment and Completion Report.' 37281. World Bank.

World Bank. 2010a. 'Project Paper, Thailand: Additional Financing—Highways Management Project.' 52994-TH. World Bank. http://documents.worldbank.org/curated/en/278151468132599812/pdf/529940PJPR0P11101Official0Use0Only1.pdf.

World Bank. 2010b. 'Project Appraisal Document On A Proposed Loan In The Amount Of Us$3,750 Million To Eskom Holdings Limited Guaranteed By Republic Of South Africa For An Eskom Investment Support Project.' Project Appraisal Document 53425-ZA. World Bank. https://documents1.worldbank.org/curated/en/126361469672138599/pdf/534250R20101005914.pdf.

World Bank. 2010c. 'World Bank Approves $1 Billion Development Policy Loan for Thailand.' World Bank. http://www.worldbank.org/en/news/press-release/2010/11/18/world-bank-approves-1-billion-development-policy-loan-thailand.

World Bank. 2012. 'Review of IDA's Graduation Policy.' International Development Association. http://documents.worldbank.org/curated/en/833691468338981825/pdf/733630BR0IDA0R0Official0Use0Only090.pdf.

World Bank. 2015a. '2015 Development Policy Financing Retrospective: Results and Sustainability.' World Bank. http://pubdocs.worldbank.org/en/420441457100264616/DevelopmentPolicyRetrospective2015.pdf.

World Bank. 2015b. *Debt Management Performance Assessment (DeMPA) Methodology.*

World Bank. 2017. 'Loan Handbook for World Bank Borrowers.' http://siteresources.worldbank.org/LOANS/Resources/Disbursement09.pdf.

World Bank. 2020. 'Product Note: IBRD Local Currency Financing.' World Bank Treasury.   https://thedocs.worldbank.org/en/doc/204311507314967032-0340022017/original/productnoteibrdlocalcurrencyfinancingMay2020.pdf.

World Bank. 2021a. *Debt Transparency in Developing Economies*. Washington, D.C.: World Bank.

World Bank. 2021b. 'IBRD Flexible Loan with Variable Spread: Major Terms and Conditions.' World Bank. https://thedocs.worldbank.org/en/doc/f6bf43b93fd7b3fd1a30b4f3853fffe6-0340012021/original/IBRD-Flexible-Loan-IFL-Major-Terms-Product-Note-EN.pdf.

World Bank. 2021c. 'IBRD Flexible Loan with Variable Spread: Pricing Basics.' World Bank. https://thedocs.worldbank.org/en/doc/77844b3f4182f7519f58add85ecaff3f-0340012021/original/IBRD-Flexible-Loan-IFL-Pricing-Basics-Product-Note.pdf.

Wren-Lewis, Simon. 2013. 'Comparing the Delegation of Monetary and Fiscal Policy.' In *Restoring Public Debt Sustainability: The Role of Independent Fiscal Institutions*, edited by George Kopits, 28. Oxford: Oxford University Press.

Zeitz, Alexandra O. 2021. 'Emulate or Differentiate? Chinese Development Finance, Competition, and World Bank Infrastructure Funding.' *Review of International Organizations* 16: 265–292.

Zeitz, Alexandra O. 2022. 'Global Capital Cycles and Market Discipline: Perceptions of Developing-Country Borrowers.' *British Journal of Political Science* 52 (4): 1944–1953. https://doi.org/10.1017/S0007123421000405.

Index

For the benefit of digital users, indexed terms that span two pages (e.g., 52–53) may, on occasion, appear on only one of those pages.

Note: The following abbreviations have been used – f = figure; n = footnote; t = table

accountability 20
ADB/AfDB *see* African Development Bank
AFC *see* Asian Financial Crisis
Africa 62f
African Development Bank (ADB/AfDB) 1, 83, 87, 90
African National Congress (ANC) 51–52, 143
 emerging markets sovereign debt structure 7–8, 36–37
 partisanship and 80–81, 84–86, 91, 93, 95, 100
ALM *see* Asset and Liabilities Management (ALM) (South Africa)
Americas, The 63f
ANC *see* African National Congress
Apartheid (South Africa) 8, 29, 81–83, 85, 88
Asia 64f
Asian Development Bank (ADB) 133, 135
Asian Financial Crisis (AFC) 37, 52, 104, 112, 140
 Thai foreign borrowing 123–124, 126, 127t, 128
 Thai partisanship 119–122, 125–126, 132, 133, 136
Asian Infrastructure Investment Bank 17
Asset and Liabilities Management (ALM) (South Africa) 86
austerity 50, 104, 110, 129–130, 146
authoritarian regimes 46–47, 48–49 n.4, 147
autonomy 3–4
 borrowers and borrowing 4, 25, 27, 37–38, 109, 139
 Debt Management Offices (DMOs) 40, 51–55
 implications of external EM sovereign debt accumulation 31–33
 research/policy implications 137–138, 140, 145–146
 South Africa 7–8
 Thailand 120–121, 123–125, 130, 133

balance of payments 20, 43, 52–53
banks and banking 97–99, 132

emerging markets sovereign debt structure 10–11, 13, 29–30
BDP *see* Botswana Democratic Party
'big-tent' approach: deficits 84
bilaterals *see* multilaterals and bilaterals
Bloomberg 67, 82f, 110t, 127t
BOB *see* Bureau of the Budget (BOB) (Thailand)
bond markets 59
 annual external borrowing needs 36–38
 Botswana 88–89, 92, 97–100
 Debt Management Offices (DMOs) 50–52, 54
 emerging markets sovereign debt structure 1, 6–7, 23, 33
 Peru during Fujimori period 109–112
 Peru during Garcia period 114–115
 Peru during Humala period 117
 Peru during Toledo period 113–114
 Peru's external borrowings 102–104, 107–108
 research/policy implications 137–138, 142–146
 South Africa/Botswana 80–81, 85, 86 n.4, 86–88
 Thailand 119–120, 122, 123, 126, 127–130, 134–135
borrowers and borrowing 43, 65, 70, 105, 117–118
 annual foreign borrowing (all countries) 6, 23–25, 24f, 29, 81f, 82f, 120f
 annual foreign borrowings (South Africa) 80, 81f, 81, 84f, 84–89, 91f, 91, 100
 autonomy 23, 24f, 32
 average external borrowing mixture 11, 12f
 emerging markets sovereign debt structure 2–3, 5, 7–8, 19, 21, 31
 research/policy implications 137, 139, 140–142, 145, 146–147
 preferences and debt accumulation 33
 processes and choices in Botswana 80, 97
 sovereign debt accumulation and 44f
 strategies 45
 Thailand 121–125, 130, 133–135

Thailand's debt history (1990–2015) 126, 127t, 128f, 128–134
Botswana
  annual foreign borrowings 51–52, 79, 81f, 82f, 100, 107, 142–143
  emerging markets sovereign debt structure 23–25, 24f, 29, 36–37
  external borrowings 80, 91, 92f, 100
  partisanship and 92, 94f, 96–97
Botswana Democratic Party (BDP) 80–81, 92, 94f, 96, 99, 143
Botswana Power Corporation 97 n.15
Brady Bond program (Peru) 111, 114
budgets
  Peru 105, 113, 114–115
  South Africa/Botswana 84–86, 96–97
  sovereign debt accumulation 39, 42–43
  testing the partisan model 68–69
  Thailand 121, 123, 125–126, 135
Bunte, Jonas B. 33–34
Bureau of the Budget (BOB) (Thailand) 121
bureaucracy 23, 35, 40–41, 46–47, 81–83, 99, 127–128, 134

cabinet approval: borrowing 106
CAF see Development Bank of Latin American and the Caribbean
Cambodia 16
capital accumulation 9–10
capital allocation 2–3, 7, 139
capital flows 1–2, 11, 21, 52–53, 69
capital markets 10–11, 85, 90–91, 98
capital-oriented governments 33
central bank independence (CBI) 20, 35, 55
central banks 69, 98, 112–113
  sovereign debt accumulation 40–41, 47, 54–55
centrism 65–66, 75, 102, 113, 143
China
  Botswana and 68, 87, 90, 99–100, 133, 140, 143
  emerging markets sovereign debt structure 1, 8, 9, 13, 15–17
class-based politics 26, 34, 48–50, 84–85, 93
co-financing arrangements 16–17
commercial banks 1, 22, 50, 59, 97, 111, 127–128
commodity booms 114–117
comparative political economy: institutions 39, 54, 56
competition 14, 27, 95, 146
'competitive authoritarianism' 48–49
competitive-hybrid regimes 46–47
conditionality 46, 51–52, 123–124

emerging markets sovereign debt structure 13–14, 17–20, 22, 26–27, 32, 36–37
Peru 108, 110, 113–115, 117
project and program loans and conditions 14, 46, 49–50, 87, 135
research/policy implications 137, 139, 142–143, 146
South Africa 80–81, 83–84, 87–88
Thailand 123–124, 126–130, 135
Congress of South African Trade Unions (COSATU) 83–84
'conservative' borrowers see right-leaning politics
constituents and constituencies (political) 48–50, 54
Constitution (Thailand) 125
constrained institutions 139–140
  South Africa/Botswana 82–83, 85, 86–87, 94–97
  sovereign debt accumulation 43, 44f, 45, 48, 56
contract enforcement 2
corruption 8, 20, 84, 88, 112
COSATU see Congress of South African Trade Unions
countercyclical see economic cycles
country categorizations 21
Country Income Level Coding 60t
Covid-19 pandemic 6, 8, 47, 146
credit flows 11–12, 16, 25, 33, 132
creditors (market/official) 12–13, 87, 105–106
credit ratings
  Botswana 51–54, 91–92, 98, 100, 141
  emerging markets sovereign debt structure 6, 20, 21, 36–37
  partisan theory of emerging markets borrowing (model) 66–67, 69, 72–74, 69t
  Peru 109–110, 110t, 111–118
  South Africa/Botswana 80, 82f, 87–89
  Thailand 119–120, 127t, 126, 129, 132–135
creditworthiness 67, 129
  emerging markets sovereign debt structure 1–2, 19, 30–33
  Peru 111, 117–118
  research/policy implications 139, 141, 142
  South Africa/Botswana 88–89, 91
currency debt 9, 46, 54
currency swap mechanisms 9 n.6

Database of Political Institutions (DPI) 28–29, 36, 48–49 n.4, 51
  testing the partisan model 65–66, 69–70, 75–78

Debswana 95
debt accumulation 3–4, 56, 105, 117–119,
    131–132
  partisanship/constrained institutions 43, 44f,
    54, 56
  research/policy implications 137, 139, 142,
    145
debt composition 39–40, 85, 121–122
debt flows 2–3, 140
Debt Management Committee
    (Thailand) 122–123
Debt Management Offices (DMOs) 79
  emerging markets sovereign debt
    structure 10–11, 15, 34–38
  partisan borrowing and debt
    accumulation 28–31
  Peru 102, 105, 116–117
  political/economic constraints 43, 44f, 45, 48
  research/policy implications 137–140, 142,
    143–145
  South Africa/Botswana 80, 84–86, 97, 100
  sovereign debt accumulation in emerging
    markets (EMs) 39, 49–50, 52, 53–56
  sovereign financing landscape 4–5
  Thailand 120, 127–128
  see also sovereign debt
debt markets see public debt; sovereign debt
debt portfolios 67
debt reduction 27, 50, 146
debt restructuring 111
debts 44–45, 86
  Botswana 96, 99
  partisan borrowing 26–28
  South Africa 80–82, 88, 100
debt sustainability 9, 41–42, 44–45, 47, 51,
    142–143
default on borrowings 19–20, 25
deficits 121
  Peru 104–105, 111
  South Africa/Botswana 84f, 84
  testing the partisan model 67–69, 69t
demand side 52–53
  emerging markets sovereign debt
    structure 2–4, 22, 31, 37–38
  research/policy implications 137–138,
    140–142
democracy and democratic advantage thesis 67,
    74, 91–92, 141
  emerging markets sovereign debt structure 2,
    20, 29
  sovereign debt accumulation 46–49, 53–54
  Thailand 119–120, 127–128
'democratic backsliding' 147

Democrat Party (Thailand) 119–120, 124,
    134–135
  pre- and post-Asian Financial Crisis 126–128
  Thai Rak Thai and 131–133
developing/developed countries 67, 93
  Debt Management Offices (DMOs) 41,
    43–45, 52–54
  emerging markets sovereign debt
    structure 4–5, 10–11, 16, 17–21
  partisan external sovereign debt
    accumulation 26–28, 31–33, 35
  research/policy implications 137–138, 142,
    143–145
Development Bank of Latin American and the
    Caribbean (CAF) 107 n.3
diamond mining industries 91–95
discipline 19
diversification 6–7, 16, 37–38, 115
  research/policy implications 137–138, 142
  South Africa/Botswana 88–93
DMOs see Debt Management Offices
domestic debt 9, 97–98, 122, 123, 129 n.12, 143
  see also Debt Management Offices (DMOs);
    sovereign debt
DPI see Database of Political Institutions
DTI see General Directorate of Treasury and
    Indebtedness (Dirección General de
    Endeudamiento y Tesoro Público) (DTI)
    (Peru)

econometric hypothesis testing see partisan
    theory of emerging markets borrowing
economic cycles 21, 44, 130, 137–138, 140
  Peru 104–105, 108, 113–116
economic elites 48–50, 74, 92–93
economic growth and development 67
  South Africa/Botswana 80, 83–84, 91f, 88,
    91–92, 100
  Thailand 119–120, 126, 128–132
  Peru 108, 112, 114, 116–117
economic interest groups 55, 147
economic policies 48–49
  Botswana 93, 96, 100
  Peru 102, 109, 112–114, 117–118
  research/policy implications 137, 139–140,
    145, 147
  testing the partisan model 65–67
  Thailand 119–121, 126–127, 132
Ecuador 140
'elite kickback' schemes 15–16
elites (economic) 74–75, 75f, 76t
  Botswana 93–96, 99
El Niño events 104–105
EMBIG (sovereign bond index) 145–146

Emerging Markets (EM)
  borrower preferences and sovereign debt
    accumulation 33
  definition 57
  external borrowing 62f, 63f, 64f, 136
  international political economy of sovereign
    debt 19–23, 24f
  partisan external sovereign debt accumulation
    in emerging markets 31–35
  Peru's sovereign debt structure 23–25, 24f, 29,
    37
  research/policy implications 138–139, 142,
    145–146
  sovereign debt accumulation 43, 44f, 57, 68
  sovereign debt structure 1 n.1, 5, 16, 36–37,
    137
  sovereign financing landscape 9–10, 12f, 13,
    13f, 14f, 14–17
employment see labour markets
environmental standards 123–124, 135
Eskom 87, 90
estimation strategies 68
Europe 64f, 90
exchange rates 10, 20–21, 69, 88, 98–99
expenditure ceilings 85
explicit guarantees 89–90
external borrowing and debts 123
  emerging markets 40, 45–46, 49, 55, 62f, 63f,
    64f, 66, 69, 75f
  emerging markets sovereign debt structure 1,
    9, 10, 19, 22
  partisan external sovereign debt
    accumulation 26–27, 29, 31–33
  South Africa 80, 81f, 81, 82f, 84f, 84–89, 91f,
    91
  trade-offs 13, 13f, 14f, 145–147
external borrowing and debts 123
  Botswana 80, 91, 92f, 97–98, 100
  options 10, 12f
  Peru 102, 109, 117
  research/policy implications 137, 139, 142
external debt: emerging markets 49, 125
extra-concessional windows 10–11

FDI see foreign direct investment
finance ministry officials 29–30, 125
financial crisis countries 13, 67, 75–78
Financial Institutions Development Fund
    (Thailand) 129 n.12
financialization 35–36, 39–40, 53, 54
fiscal deficit 42, 84f
fiscal policies 20–21, 27, 29, 35, 68, 111f, 142
  Botswana 93–96

  partisan politics and constrained
    institutions 39, 44, 46, 48, 50, 55
  Peru 104–105, 109
  South Africa/Botswana 80–86, 100
  Thailand 124, 126–127, 128f, 129, 131, 134
Fiscal Prudence and Transparency Act (1999)
    (Peru) 104–105, 111, 117
Fitch 6, 67, 82f, 110t, 112, 115, 127t
foreign currency 40–42
foreign debt 8, 10, 47
  Peru 103f, 107–108, 110t, 111f, 112–115
foreign direct investment (FDI) 95, 100
foreign exchange reserves 129, 132
foreign firms 15–16, 50
foreign ownership 95, 131
fractional dependent variable 68–69
frontier markets 10–11, 57, 147
Fujimori, Alberto 104, 107–108, 112–114

Garcia, Alan 108, 114, 115–116
GDP see gross domestic product
General Assembly (United Nations) 68
General Directorate of Treasury and
    Indebtedness (Dirección General de
    Endeudamiento y Tesoro Público) (DTI)
    (Peru) 102, 104, 106–107, 114–115
Generalized Method of Moments
    (GMM) 68–70, 71t, 72t
global financial crisis 47, 80, 115–116, 135
globalization 26–27, 49, 66, 121, 131, 137–138
global liquidity 2, 52–53, 140–141
GMM see Generalized Method of Moments
Gordhan, Pravin 88–89
governance 17–18, 23, 25, 88, 95, 100, 147
government borrowing and spending 6, 8, 9, 27,
    48, 116
Government Finance Statistics (International
    Monetary Fund) 111f, 128f
government partisanship 48, 70–71, 79, 80–81
grants 10–11, 59, 132
gross domestic product (GDP) 20, 59
guarantees 45, 89, 107, 125–126

hard currency debt 9, 9 n.6
High Income Countries (HICs) 10–11, 22, 51,
    57, 59–61, 75–78, 143, 146–147
HIV/AIDS epidemic 91–92
Humala, Ollanta 115

IDA see International Development Association
IDB see Inter-American Development Bank
IFIs see International Financial Institutions
IMF see International Monetary Fund
implicit guarantees 89

incidental parameter problem 68–69
Indebtedness Law (*Ley de Indeudamiento*)
    (1999) (Peru) 105
independent central banks (ICBs) *see* central
    bank independence (CBI)
index investment practices 22
inflation 47, 88, 108
    emerging markets debt structure 10, 20–21,
    35
    testing the partisan model 67, 69*t*, 69, 74
informational shortcuts 2
institutional capacity 25
institutional independence 21, 35–36
    sovereign debt accumulation 39–40, 53–55
institutions 4, 144
    constraints on 39, 53–54, 56, 96–97
integrative macroeconomic policies 126–127
Inter-American Development Bank (IDB) 107
    n.3, 115
interest-based political economy models 55
interest rates 51–52, 66, 145
    emerging markets sovereign debt
    structure 13, 21, 25, 36–37
    new external debts in emerging markets 13*f*
    Peru 116–117
    South Africa/Botswana 80, 90, 98–100
International Development Association
    (IDA) 59, 75–78, 78*t*
International Financial Institutions
    (IFIs) 108–109
International Monetary Fund (IMF) 142
    emerging markets sovereign debt structure 8,
    12, 23, 25, 30, 33
    Peru 107–110, 111*f*, 113–114
    South Africa/Botswana 83, 84*f*, 94*f*, 95
    Thailand 119–120, 128*f*, 129–133
International Political Economy (IPE) 2, 25,
    31–33, 37–38, 137–138, 141
interventionist protections 14
interview-based research 30–31
investment banks 114
investment grade credit ratings 36–37, 51–52,
    117–118
investment policies 14, 17–18
investment programs 96
investor irrationality 140–141
investors 51–52, 140–141, 145–146
    emerging markets sovereign debt structure 1,
    7, 10, 19–22, 28, 33, 36–37
    Peru 102–103, 111, 112
    South Africa/Botswana 88–89, 98, 100
    Thailand 122–123, 134–135
IPE *see* International Political Economy

Japan 90, 108–109, 127–128, 135
Japan International Cooperation Agency
    (JICA) 125
JICA *see* Japan International Cooperation
    Agency
J.P.Morgan 145–146
junk credit ratings 36–37, 51–52, 88–90, 100,
    129

Khama, Seretse 93, 95

labour markets 65, 123–124
    Botswana 95
    emerging markets sovereign debt
    structure 14–17, 25, 27, 34
    government partisanship 48, 50, 52–53
    Peru 108–109, 113
    research/policy implications 146–147
    South Africa 81–83, 93
left-leaning politics
    Botswana 94–95
    class-based politics 48, 48–49 n.4, 49–52
    emerging markets sovereign debt
    structure 3–4, 7–8, 18, 21, 137–138
    fiscal policymaking processes 36–38
    partisan external sovereign debt
    accumulation 25–29, 32, 33 n.9, 34
    partisan theory of emerging markets
    borrowing (model) 57, 65–66, 69*t*, 70–71,
    72*t*, 73*f*, 75, 79
    Peru during Fujimori period 108–109
    Peru during Toledo period 112–114
    Peru during Garcia period 115–118
    Peru's external borrowings 102–104, 106,
    107–108
    research/policy implications 138–140,
    142–143
    South Africa 7–8, 36–37, 51–52, 80, 81–83,
    84–85
    Thailand 119–121, 131, 132–133
legislation 81, 84–85, 146
lender-of-last-resort credit 108–110, 140
Letter of Intent (International Monetary Fund)
    (1997) 129
LIBOR *see* London Inter-Bank Offered Rate
line ministries 123
    Peru 102–103, 106
    South Africa/Botswana 89, 96–97
liquidity 40, 41 n.1, 67, 88–89, 135, 140–141,
    145
local currency debt 9
local-denominated government debt 120, 143
logit model 68–70, 71*t*, 72*t*, 76*t*, 77*t*

London Inter-Bank Offered Rate (LIBOR)
  rates 6–7 n.4, 13, 87
long-term domestic debt 98
long-term maturities 41–42, 46, 49–52
Low Income Countries (LICs) 11, 12*f*, 26–27,
  49, 57, 59, 146–147

macroeconomic institutions 31, 34, 35
Mandela, Nelson 83–84
market-based finance
  emerging markets sovereign debt
    structure 3–4, 10–11, 15–16, 21, 32
  flows 11–13
  partisan theory of emerging markets
    borrowing (model) 57, 67, 70, 79
  Peru 104, 107, 112–114, 117
  research/policy implications 137–140–142,
    144, 145
  South Africa/Botswana 81, 97–99
  sovereign debt accumulation 48, 51, 54
  Thailand 128–130, 132, 136
'market discipline' principle 2, 7, 20, 31,
  139–140
maturity rates 5, 13, 22, 54, 139
  new external debt in emerging markets 14*f*
Mbeki, Thabo 83–84
MEF *see* Ministry of Finance and Economics
  (*Ministerio de Economi´a y Finanzas*)
  (MEF) (Peru)
MFED *see* Ministry of Finance and Economic
  Development (MFED) (Botswana)
middle classes 65, 75
Middle East 62*f*
Middle Income Countries (MICs) 1 n.1, 57–61,
  66, 75–78
'Middle Income Trap' 26–27
military coups 119–121, 125, 126–128, 134–135
military expenditure 94
ministerial institutions 5, 41, 47, 53, 137–138
Ministry of Finance (Thailand) 122
Ministry of Finance and Economic
  Development (MFED) (Botswana) 91–92
  n.10, 93–94, 96, 98, 100
Ministry of Finance and Economics (*Ministerio
  de Economi´a y Finanzas*) (MEF)
  (Peru) 102–104
  borrowing process and politics 106–107
  budgets and politics 104–105
  foreign borrowing 107–109, 111, 112–118
modelling strategies 68
monetary policies *see* fiscal policies
Moody's 6, 67, 82*f*, 91–92 n.10, 110*t*, 127*t*
multilaterals and bilaterals 1, 45, 50, 147

emerging markets sovereign debt
  structure 1–2, 9 n.6, 19, 23, 29–30, 32–33
  external borrowing 10–11, 13, 14, 16–17
  Peru 107, 107 n.3, 107, 109, 112–115, 117
  South Africa 81–82, 87
  Thailand 122–125, 129, 131, 133, 135
national accounts/balance sheets 11, 34, 42,
  81–82, 105, 139
National Development Plan (NDP)
  (Botswana) 96
National Revenue Fund (South Africa) 87
National Treasury (South Africa) 85–86, 89, 90
natural disasters 104–105
neoliberalism 37, 52, 82–83, 102, 108–109, 112
nondemocracies 48–49 n.4, 75–78
nonguaranteed loans 89–90

Office of Budget Analysis and Debt Management
  (Botswana) 97
official creditors and credit flows 1, 8, 16–17, 25,
  50, 80, 139
  annual external borrowing needs 36–38
  borrower autonomy in markets and 32
  Botswana 80, 96, 97–100
  Debt Management Offices (DMOs) 40, 45,
    46, 49–52, 54
  emerging markets and 22, 57, 59, 66, 67, 70,
    74–79
  Peru during Fujimori period 108–112
  Peru during Garcia period 114–115
  Peru during Humala period 116–118
  Peru during Toledo period 112–114
  Peru's external borrowings 102–104, 107–108
  Peru's external borrowings 102–104, 106, 107
  research/policy implications 137–143, 145,
    146–147
  South Africa and financing
    requirements 84–85, 87–92
  South Africa and partisanship 81–84
  Thailand and foreign borrowing 126–136
  Thailand's borrowing processes 119–121,
    123–126
oil industries 107
one-party democracies *see* Botswana; South
  Africa
Ordinary Least Squares (OLS) 68–70, 71*t*, 72*t*,
  76*t*

partisan politics 117–118
  Botswana 80–81, 92, 94*f*, 96–97
  constrained institutions 46, 48, 56, 117–118
  research/policy implications 140–142
  South Africa 80–81, 84*f*, 84–85
  Thailand 119, 126

partisan theory of emerging markets borrowing (model) 51, 57, 79
  control variables 57, 66–67
  dataset 57, 58t
  debt accumulation 9, 26–28
  dependent variable 59, 60t, 61t, 62f, 63f, 64f
  emerging markets sovereign debt structure 1, 3, 4–5, 8, 14, 21, 28, 36
  empirical strategy 68–69, 69t
  external borrowings 49
  external sovereign debt accumulation in emerging markets 31–35
  independent variables 65
  results 70, 71t, 72t, 73f, 74, 75f, 76t, 77t, 78t
PDMO see Public Debt Management Office (PDMO) (Thailand)
Peru 52, 79, 80–81, 100, 142–143
  borrowing process and politics 106–107, 107 n.3
  budgets and politics 104–105
  emerging markets sovereign debt structure 23–25, 24f, 29, 37
  foreign borrowing (1990–2015) 103f, 107–108, 110t, 111f, 112–115
  partisan effect on external borrowing 102, 117
PeruPetro (oil company) 107
Pheu Thai party (Thailand) 135
policy making and conditions 2, 5, 17, 46–47, 121
political accountability 45
political business cycles (PolCycle) 67–68, 61t, 74–78
political economy studies 4–5, 52, 55
political science research 30–31
politics and political policies 45, 66, 67
  emerging markets sovereign debt structure 1–2, 5, 20–21, 35
  Peru's borrowing process and 106–107
  Peru's budget and 104–105
  research/policy implications 137, 139, 144–145
poor countries see Low Income Countries (LICs)
populism 112–113, 115–116, 120–121, 131, 132, 136
portfolio management 1, 40, 41
post-treatment bias 57, 69, 69t
poverty and the poor 65, 73f, 107–108
price-based cost–benefit calculations 139–140
pricing approach 13–14, 22, 90, 132, 139, 141
primary dealers 30
principal–agent theory 55

private creditors 1, 12, 33, 81–82, 102–103, 126, 129
privatization policies 20–21, 27, 48, 50, 95, 132, 146
  Peru 104, 107, 109, 113–114
probit model 68–70, 71t, 72t, 76t, 77t, 78t
procyclical see economic cycles
production costs 14, 90
profit motives 13–14
'Programa Juntos' spending plan (2005) (Peru) 113
project and program loans and conditions 14, 46, 49–50, 87, 135
property rights 67, 74
public administration research 36
public debt
  Debt Management Offices (DMOs) 34–36
  emerging markets sovereign debt structure 4–6, 10, 20, 28–29
  government partisanship 40, 42, 45, 52, 53–56
  research/policy implications 142, 144, 146
Public Debt Management Act (2005) (Thailand) 122
Public Debt Management Office (PDMO) (Thailand) 122–123
  borrowing options 123–124
  foreign borrowing 128–136
  state-owned enterprises (SOEs) 125–126
Public Finance Management Act (South Africa) 85
push and pull factors 19–21, 36, 66

quantitative hypothesis testing 28–29

Raise the Debt: How Developing Countries Choose Their Creditors (Bunte) 33–34
ratification power 46
regimes 25, 67, 119
regional development banks 13, 23, 30
repayments 41–42, 46, 67, 98–100, 108, 123, 144
  emerging markets debt structure 2, 10, 11, 19–20, 25, 34
reserves 67, 74, 114, 129
  South Africa/Botswana 93–94, 97–98
revenue generation 69
  Botswana 88, 97, 98–99
  Peru 105, 111, 114–116
right-leaning politics 65–66
  Botswana 80–81, 92, 94f, 96
  emerging markets sovereign debt structure 25, 27, 28, 32, 36–37
  fiscal rules in Botswana 96

government partisanship 48, 48–49 n.24,
    49–52
Peru 102, 107–110
Thailand 119–121, 126–127, 132, 136
risk management 2, 13–14, 67, 96, 139–140, 146
robustness 57, 59, 65–67, 74, 75f, 76t, 77t, 78t
rule of law 67, 74, 95

SACP *see* South African Communist Party
savings-oriented fiscal policy 94–95
selection bias 57, 59–61
short-term borrowing 34, 54
short-term treasury bills 86
'silent' borrowing 27, 51
social spending 132
SOEs *see* state-owned enterprises
South Africa 51–52, 107, 142–143
    annual foreign borrowing 6, 23–25, 24f, 29,
        81f, 82f
    Apartheid 8, 29, 81–83, 85, 88
    emerging markets sovereign debt structure 5,
        16, 36–37
    external borrowing strategies 80, 81f, 81, 84f,
        84–89, 91f, 91, 92f, 100
    partisanship 93, 95, 96–97
South African Communist Party (SACP) 83
sovereign debt 66
    accumulation in emerging markets (EMs) 39,
        52–53, 56, 57, 68, 80, 117–118, 127–128,
        147
    borrower preferences and debt
        accumulation 33
    financing landscape 9–10, 12f, 13, 13f, 14f,
        14–17
    institutions in 53
    international political economy 19–23, 24f,
        141
    partisan debt accumulation in emerging
        markets 31–35
    political economy and 52
    research/policy implications 138, 141, 142,
        145–146
    structure 1, 7–8, 45, 137, 139
    Thailand 23–25, 24f, 29, 37, 125, 131–132
    see also Debt Management Offices (DMOs);
        domestic debt
Standard & Poors (S&P) 6, 67, 82f, 91–92 n.10,
    110t, 111–112, 115, 127t
state intervention 27, 48, 132
state-owned enterprises (SOEs) 81, 85, 89,
    96–97, 97 n.15, 100, 107, 125, 129–130
statistical tests 36
status-quo protections and production 14
structural adjustment 87, 123–124

supply-side
    Debt Management Offices (DMOs) 45, 51,
        52–53
    emerging markets sovereign debt
        structure 1–4, 8, 19–20, 23, 25, 31–32, 36
    research/policy implications 141, 145, 146
surpluses 93–94, 100

taxation 9, 17–18, 50, 69, 88, 109, 112–113, 116
technical assistance 99–100, 102–103, 123, 135
technocratic governance 121, 124, 127–128,
    131–132, 136, 140
Thai Airways 126
Thailand 52, 79, 80–81, 100, 119, 120f, 136, 140,
    147
    borrowing processes 122–125
    emerging markets sovereign debt
        structure 23–25, 24f, 29, 37
    fiscal and debt laws 121
    foreign borrowing (1990–2015) 126, 127t,
        128f, 128–134
Thai Rak Thai (TRT) (Thailand) 119–120,
    122–126, 131–134, 136
Thaksin Shinawatra 124–125, 132, 133–134
Toledo, Alejandro 107–108, 112, 114
Tomz, Michael 25
trade-offs 13, 13f, 14f, 46–47, 145, 146–147
trade and trade policies 14, 17–18, 26–27, 95
trade unions 8, 14, 15–16, 27, 48, 50, 65, 83, 95
transparency 95, 137–138, 142
    emerging markets sovereign debt structure 2,
        17, 20, 25, 35, 37–38
    Thailand 123–125, 135
'tripartite alliance': South Africa 83
TRT *see* Thai Rak Thai (TRT) (Thailand)

United Nations 68
United States (US) 22–23, 68, 90, 108–109,
    127–128, 145
utility companies 87, 90

value chains 50
variable-rate debt 47
Varieties of Party Identity and Organization
    (dataset) (V-Party) 28–29, 36, 51, 65,
    66–67, 61t, 69–70, 74–75
volatility: financial markets 88
V-Party *see* Varieties of Party Identity and
    Organization (dataset)

wages 14, 27, 83–84
    Peru 109, 113, 116
Washington Consensus 17–18, 104, 108–109,
    114, 123–124

within-unit change 52
working classes 119–120, 146, 147
  emerging markets sovereign debt structure 3,
    6, 8, 36
  external borrowing trade-off 14–15, 17–18
  government partisanship and 48–51
  partisan borrowing and debt
    accumulation 26–29
  partisan theory of emerging markets
    borrowing (model) 57, 65, 66, 69, 69t, 70,
    73f, 74–75, 71t, 79
  Peru 102, 107–108

World Bank 92f, 142
  emerging markets sovereign debt structure 1
    n.1, 6–8, 16–17, 23, 25, 30
  Peru 107 n.3, 114–115
  South Africa/Botswana 80, 83, 87, 90 n.8–9,
    90, 95, 99
  testing the partisan model 57, 59, 75–78
  Thailand 121, 127–130, 133, 135
World Development Indicators 12f, 13f, 14f, 24f,
  67, 81f, 92f, 103f, 120f

Zimbabwe 16
Zuma, Jacob 84–86, 88–89